Another
Forgotten Child

Also by Cathy Glass

Damaged
Hidden
Cut
The Saddest Girl in the World
Happy Kids
The Girl in the Mirror
I Miss Mummy
Mummy Told Me Not to Tell
My Dad's a Policeman (a Quick Reads novel)
Run, Mummy, Run
The Night the Angels Came
Happy Adults
A Baby's Cry
Happy Mealtimes For Kids

Another Forgotten Child
Cathy Glass

THE MILLION COPY BESTSELLING AUTHOR

Too late to help?
A shocking true
story of abuse and
neglect

Certain details in this story, including names, places and dates,
have been changed to protect the family's privacy.

HarperElement
An imprint of HarperCollins*Publishers*
77–85 Fulham Palace Road,
Hammersmith, London W6 8JB

www.harpercollins.co.uk

and HarperElement are trademarks of
HarperCollins*Publishers* Ltd

First published by HarperElement 2012

3

A catalogue record of this book
is available from the British Library

ISBN 978-0-00-748677-9

Printed and bound in Great Britain by
Clays Ltd, St Ives plc

MIX
Paper from
responsible sources
FSC™ C007454

Acknowledgements

A big thank you to Vicky, Carole, Laura and all the team at HarperCollins; my literary agent Andrew and my editor Anne.

Another Forgotten Child

Chapter One
The Child from Hell

Aimee is aggressive. She kicks, bites, screams in her mother's face, and pulls out her mother's hair. Her mother states she is afraid of Aimee and has to lock herself in the bathroom or run to neighbours for protection when Aimee attacks her. Her mother states that Aimee killed the kittens their cat had by strangling them.

'What!' I gasped, glancing up from reading the referral.

Jill nodded sombrely. 'Read on. It doesn't get any better.' Jill was my support social worker (also known as a link worker) from Homefinders, the agency I fostered for. We were in my sitting room and Jill was watching me carefully as I read the details of the eight-year-old girl the social services were bringing into care and looking for a foster home for.

I continued to read:

Aimee's parents live apart and Aimee lives mainly with her mother. The flat is always dirty and freezing cold, and there is never any food in the cupboards. Aimee and her mother sleep on a stained mattress on the floor in the living room, as the one bedroom is too damp to use. Aimee is often unkempt, grubby, and has head lice. She refuses to go to school. Her mother is unable to cope with Aimee and often leaves her with other

1

*adults, many of them men and registered drug users. Susan
(Aimee's mother) is unable to set boundaries or routines for
Aimee and states that Aimee becomes violent if she is not
allowed to do what she wants. A family support worker was put
in to try and help, but Susan was unable to stand up to her
daughter. Aimee's mother and father have been intravenous
drug users. It is likely they still use. Both parents have served
prison sentences for drug dealing.*

I turned the page and under the heading 'Family members and
other related persons' I read that Aimee had five older half-
brothers and -sisters, all of whom had different fathers and all of
whom had been taken into care as young children. The eldest of
the siblings was now twenty-seven and the family had been
known to the social services since he was born – twenty-seven
years ago!

'So why didn't the social services bring Aimee into care
sooner?' I asked, looking up at Jill. 'With the mother's history of
drug abuse and being unable to care for her children, why leave
Aimee at home for eight years?'

'It looks as if Aimee fell through the net,' Jill said. 'She was
on the child protection register at birth.'

'At birth! All that time – eight years – and no one
intervened?'

'I know,' Jill sighed.

I leant back in my chair and stared at the referral in my
hand. In the twenty-five years I'd been fostering I'd looked
after children before who'd 'fallen through the net', which
meant they had been overlooked or simply forgotten by the
social services and society generally. How many more children
were going to be left unprotected before sweeping changes
were made to our social services system? A child is placed on
the child protection (CP) register, also known as the 'at risk'

register, when there are serious concerns for his or her safety. Such a measure is supposed to be a short-term one to allow help to be put into the family, resulting in either the child being removed from the register when the concerns have gone or, if no improvements are made, the child being brought into care. Clearly in Aimee's case neither had happened; and while what I'd read about Aimee's background was bad, it wasn't enough to explain the disturbed and aggressive behaviour Aimee was exhibiting.

Jill seemed to think so too. 'The social services are applying for a care order based on severe neglect,' she said, 'but there's a good chance Aimee has been abused as well. She's very angry.' I nodded. 'A new social worker took over the case two months ago and couldn't understand why Aimee hadn't been brought into care sooner. Questions are now being asked in the department.'

'I should think so!' I said. 'I dread to think what has gone on at home to make Aimee behave as she does.'

Jill nodded. 'The case is in court on Thursday, and in view of Aimee's reported cruelty to children and animals the social worker is looking for a foster family with no young children and preferably no pets.'

'And I fit the bill,' I said with a knowing smile.' For my children – Adrian, Lucy and Paula – were twenty-one, nineteen and seventeen respectively, and our cat, Toscha, had died from old age a few years previously.

'Obviously it has to be your decision as to whether you offer to take Aimee,' Jill said. 'She's a very damaged child.'

'Very,' I said, and we both fell silent. Jill looked at me as I sat deep in thought. I knew I had to make a decision now. It was Tuesday and Jill had said the case was in court on Thursday, when the social services would have to show the judge that they had a suitable foster carer ready to take Aimee if the judge granted a care order. At present Aimee was still living at home.

'The mother's flat is on the other side of town,' Jill offered, after a moment. 'So you are unlikely to bump into her. I understand Susan can be aggressive and has threatened the foster carers of the older siblings – so much so that all the children have been moved to foster homes out of the county.'

'I'm not so much worried about bumping into Aimee's mother,' I said. 'It's happened before with other children I've fostered. But I am concerned about the impact looking after Aimee will have on Paula. As you know, Adrian is away at university, and Lucy has finished studying and is often out with her friends after work in the evening. But Paula is at home and has her A-level exams in six months' time.'

'I am sure you will be able to settle Aimee quickly,' Jill said with far more confidence than I felt.

'I have big reservations. I have a nasty feeling something dreadful has happened to Aimee to make her behave so cruelly.'

'Agreed,' Jill said. 'Do you know who Aimee reminded me of when I first read the referral?'

'No. Who?'

'Jodie.'

I held Jill's gaze and my heart sank. Jodie (the girl whose story I told in *Damaged*) was the most disturbed child I'd ever looked after. I'd fostered her for a year, three years previously, before a psychiatrist recommended that she should live in a therapeutic residential home. Jodie's highly disturbed behaviour was the result of years of abuse, including being passed around a paedophile ring. Jodie had been eight when she'd arrived – the same age as Aimee.

'What makes you say that?' I asked after a moment, as a cold shiver ran down my back. 'There's no suggestion in the referral that Aimee has suffered the level of abuse Jodie did, and there's no mention of sexual abuse.'

'No, but I think there's a lot the social services don't know in this case, and Aimee's violent behaviour is very similar to Jodie's. There's a reason why she's behaving as she is.'

I had to agree. My thoughts returned to Jodie. Her behaviour had been so violent that in the four months she'd been in care before coming to me, she'd had five foster carers, all of whom had been unable to cope with her aggressive behaviour, and my family and I had struggled to cope as well.

'At least Aimee won't have been moved around,' I said, thinking out loud. 'She'll be coming from home straight to me.'

'So you'll take her?' Jill asked eagerly.

I nodded. 'I just hope my children are as understanding with Aimee as they were with Jodie.'

'I'm sure they will be,' Jill said.

Chapter Two
Awaiting Aimee

'You've done what!' Paula cried, staring at me in disbelief. 'You've never agreed to take her? I don't believe it! You haven't thought about me at all! What about my feelings? I won't be able to have any of my friends round and I won't be able to study. How could you, Mum? There's nothing else for it, you're forcing me to move out.' Paula turned and flounced out of the room and upstairs.

Well done, Cathy, I thought. You handled that well. Full marks for tact and diplomacy. 'Paula!' I called after her, but she'd disappeared into her bedroom and had shut the door. I knew better than to follow her; to try to talk to her now would do more harm than good. She needed some cooling-off time – as I did, too.

I was in the sitting room and I went over to the patio windows and looked out. It was the beginning of November and the garden was bare. The trees had lost their leaves and the sky was grey and overcast. Another English winter had begun and this year I would be spending it with a highly disturbed child, I acknowledged despondently. Perhaps Paula was right and I had made the wrong decision. For while I thought Paula had over-reacted – understandably, as she was seventeen and anxious about her forthcoming exams – I knew fostering Aimee would have a huge impact on us all. Supposing she didn't settle as quickly as Jill had hoped; supposing the damage done to her was so great that I couldn't help her. What then? Would Aimee follow the same downward spiral into mental illness as Jodie had, resulting in her going to live in a residential therapeutic unit? I didn't think I could face all that again. It had been a nightmare for us all – to watch Jodie's decline and not be able to do anything to help her.

Then, as if to darken my thoughts further, the phone rang and when I answered it was Aimee's social worker, Kristen, with more horrors to share.

'I thought I'd introduce myself,' she began brightly, clearly relieved that she'd found a foster carer daft enough to take Aimee. 'I'll give you some more background information and also explain the arrangements for bringing Aimee to you on Thursday if we are granted the court order.'

'If?' I repeated. 'Surely with Aimee's history there's no doubt you'll be given the care order.'

'We were in court two weeks ago but the case was adjourned,' Kristen said. 'Susan, Aimee's mother, has a good barrister, but fingers crossed we'll be granted the order this time.'

I sighed but didn't say anything. Adjourning a case in care proceedings is not uncommon, and essentially means that the child stays at home to suffer more neglect and abuse, for longer.

'Aimee's parents won't be told your contact details,' Kristen continued. 'Susan is opposed to her daughter coming into care and is angry. She's also been working on Aimee and poisoning her mind against the move, and now Aimee is determined she won't be taken away from her mother. Removing Aimee on Thursday is going to be fraught and I've notified the police. Aimee is likely to arrive at your place very upset and angry. She'll need a bath – she's filthy – and she has a bad infestation of head lice, which will need treating straightaway. She wouldn't let her mother treat her hair and kicked her if she tried to comb it. But you're a very experienced foster carer, so I'm sure you'll find a way round this.' Kristen stopped, expecting confirmation.

'I expect I will,' I said. 'But why is Aimee so angry with her mother and behaving so badly? There's always a reason why children behave as they do.'

'I agree,' Kristen said. 'There's a lot we don't know in this case. I only took it over two months ago and I couldn't understand why Aimee had been left at home for so long.' Hearing a social worker admit that a case should have been handled differently – better – wasn't unique; neither was shifting culpability. But Kristen wasn't wholly to blame for Aimee not being brought into care sooner, as she'd only taken over the case recently. Doubtless, prior to her there had been many other social workers, all of whom had done their best and then, for any number of reasons, moved on. Frequent changes of social worker is not unusual but can be one of many reasons why children fall through the safety net of care.

'Aimee has been spending time at both her parents' flats,' Kristen continued. 'We believe that both flats have been used for drug dealing. The last time the police raided her mother's flat they found used syringes close to where Aimee was sleeping on a mattress on the floor, but no drugs. Both flats are dirty and poorly furnished. When Susan can't cope with Aimee she leaves her with anyone who will have her. Aimee can't wash or dress herself, she wets the bed, and will only eat biscuits – she demands them. She can't read or write – unsurprisingly, as she hardly ever goes to school. And a word of warning.'

'Yes?' I asked, wondering what else there could possibly be.

'Aimee's mother makes allegations against foster carers and she's good at it, so practise your safer caring.'

'I will,' I said, as I realized this was going to be something else I'd have to contend with on top of looking after Aimee and trying to change her appalling behaviour.

'Now, on Thursday,' Kristen continued, 'assuming we are granted the care order, we'll take Aimee from school and bring her straight to you. She'll just have the clothes she's wearing. I'll try to get her things another day when her mother is less angry, but don't count on it. Her clothes are in shreds anyway. I assume you'll have some emergency clothes to put her in?'

'I should think so,' I said. 'What size is she?'

'I don't know. I don't have kids.'

'Is she of average build and height for an eight-year-old?'

'I guess so, although she's a bit overweight.'

'OK. I'll find something for her to wear, and then I'll take her shopping on Friday for new clothes.'

'We want her in school on Friday,' Kristen said, 'to keep some continuity going. Aimee hasn't been at school much but she says she likes her teacher. It will be reassuring for Aimee to see her on Friday after all the trauma of Thursday.'

'Which school does she attend?'

'Hayward Primary School. It's on the opposite side of the town to you. Do you know it?'

'No, but I'll find it.'

'Well, I think that's all for now,' Kristen said. 'I'm sure your support worker told you that you will need to set firm boundaries and a routine for Aimee. She's had neither.'

'I understand.'

'Roll on next Thursday,' Kristen sighed, as we wound up the conversation. 'I'll be pleased to get rid of this case. The mother is impossible to work with.'

'You're leaving, then?' I asked, surprised.

'No, but once Aimee is in care, the case will go from the children in need team to the children in care team.' Which, although I knew to be current practice, would mean another change of social worker. It used to be that the social worker who had worked with the family stayed as the child's social worker after the child was brought into care, but that changed some years ago with restructuring, resulting in further discontinuity.

With my thoughts even darker now after hearing more about Aimee's neglect and her parents' drug-fuelled background, Kristen and I said goodbye and I replaced the handset. I went upstairs. Paula should have had enough time to cool off now, and I tentatively knocked on her bedroom door. There was no reply, so I knocked again, and then slowly opened the door.

'Can I come in?' I asked, poking my head round the door. Paula was sitting on her bed, facing away from me and towards the window.

'Don't mind,' she said with a small shrug, which I knew meant yes.

I continued into her room and sat on the edge of the bed next to her. She was looking down at her lap and fiddling with her hands, looking very glum.

'I love you,' I said, which I find is always a good icebreaker and can't be said too often.

'Love you too,' she said quietly but without looking at me.

Now I knew she was receptive and willing to hear what I had to say, I was ready with my explanation as to why I'd agreed to look after Aimee. I would also reassure Paula that I'd do all I could to minimize the disruption that Aimee staying with us would cause. I took a breath, ready to speak, but before I had a chance Paula said quietly: 'It's OK, Mum. I understand about Aimee coming.'

'Do you? I'm not sure I do,' I said with a small nervous laugh. 'I think I'm too impulsive sometimes and I make decisions before I've properly thought them through.'

'Only when it comes to fostering,' Paula said. 'You let your heart rule your head. The rest of the time you're quite sane.'

I gave another small laugh and Paula managed to raise a smile too. 'Look, love,' I said, taking her hand in mine. 'I know you have an important six months coming up with your A-level exams and I promise you I'll keep things as calm as I can here. Also I want you to feel comfortable bringing your friends home, and I'll make sure Aimee doesn't interfere. You work hard and need to relax sometimes. I'll keep Aimee amused.' It sounded as though I was ostracizing Aimee, but we'd looked after children before with complex needs and I knew, as Paula did, just how demanding such children can be.

'There's no need to worry,' Paula said, with another small shrug. 'I'll be fine.'

'Good.' I patted her hand. 'Your feelings are very important to me,' I said. 'I hope you know I would never knowingly do anything I thought would upset you. I wouldn't have agreed to look after Aimee if I thought you, Adrian or Lucy were really opposed to it.' Fostering is always a balancing act between the needs of the foster child and those of the carer's own children.

'I'm not opposed to it,' Paula said. Then she slipped her arms around my waist and laid her head on my shoulder, ready for a cuddle and to make up. I put my arms around her and we held each other for some time before she said, 'You know, Mum, Aimee sounds a bit like Jodie.'

I looked at her, surprised that she too had made the connection. 'I hope not,' I said. 'But if she is, then at least I'll be better prepared to deal with her problems this time. I learnt a lot from looking after Jodie and I won't make the same mistakes again.' Although in truth I doubted I could have done much more to help Jodie, so deep was the damage that had been done to her. She needed specialist help.

Paula and I hugged each other for a while longer and once I was satisfied she'd recovered I left her to relax and listen to her music before she began her homework, while I went downstairs to make the dinner. I was grateful my children were so understanding and I was pleased that although we had disagreements – like any family – no one sulked and the air soon cleared.

At 5.30 p.m. Lucy, my adopted daughter, arrived home from her work as a nursery assistant.

'Hi!' I called from the kitchen as she let herself in the front door.

'Hi, what's for dinner?' she returned from the hall.

'Chicken and pasta bake.'

'Great.'

I smiled to myself, for when Lucy had first arrived as a foster child seven years previously, she'd been borderline anorectic: she had been very thin and had hardly eaten anything. Now she was a healthy weight and enjoyed her food, as we all did. I'd adopted Lucy five years ago, so she was a permanent and much-loved member of my family.

Having taken off her coat in the hall Lucy came into the kitchen and as usual greeted me with a big kiss on the cheek.

'Have you had a good day?' I asked, as I always did when my children came home.

'Yes, although the four-year-olds were over-excited after their visit to the fire station. So was my manager – by the firemen.'

I laughed, and decided I'd better tell Lucy straightaway about Aimee. 'It's possible we might be having an eight-year-old girl coming to stay on Thursday,' I said.

'Cool,' Lucy said, helping herself to a biscuit.

'She's been badly neglected and has behavioural problems,' I clarified.

'OK. What's her name?'

'Aimee.'

'That's nice. Have I got time for a shower before dinner? I'm going to the cinema later.'

'Yes, a quick one. Dinner will be fifteen minutes.'

'Cool,' Lucy said again, and planting another kiss on my cheek hurried off for a shower. Older than Paula, with a more robust constitution from her own experiences before coming into care, and with a life outside our home, Lucy had taken Aimee's proposed arrival in her stride.

We ate at six o'clock and Aimee wasn't mentioned again, and the evening progressed as usual, with Lucy out socializing and Paula doing her homework in between MSNing and texting her friends.

I didn't hear anything further from either Jill or Kristen until Thursday morning, by which time Aimee's room was prepared, even if I wasn't. I'd already given the bedroom a good clean after Reece (the little boy whose story I told in *Mummy Told Me Not to Tell*) had left the month before. Now I changed the Batman duvet cover for one with pictures of butterflies, which I hoped would appeal to Aimee, and I arranged some cuddly toys on the bed. As well as the bedroom furniture there was a toy box in the room with some games and puzzles; the rest of the toys were kept in cupboards downstairs. I'd sort out some clothes for Aimee once she arrived, when I'd have a better idea of her size. I kept an emergency supply of clothes (for both sexes and in most sizes) in the ottoman in my bedroom.

At lunchtime Jill telephoned and asked if I'd heard anything from Kristen. I hadn't, so we assumed the case was still in court. An hour later Kristen phoned and said she'd just come out of court and the judge had granted the care order, which was clearly a relief. Kristen said she and her colleague, Laura, were on their way to Hayward school to collect Aimee. 'Susan, Aimee's mother, was very upset in court,' Kristen said. 'And her barrister was good, so I had to agree to let Susan see Aimee for half an hour at the end of school to say goodbye.'

'All right,' I said. 'See you later.' I put down the phone and thought of Susan going to school to say goodbye to her daughter.

I felt sorry for her, as I did for many of the parents whose children I fostered, for none of them started life bad with the intention of failing and then losing their children. I guessed life had been cruel to Susan, just as it had to Aimee.

Chapter Three

A Challenge

Despite all the years I'd been fostering I still felt nervous when anticipating the arrival of a new child. Will the child like me? Will I be able to help the child come to terms with their suffering and separation from home? Will I be able to cope with the child's needs? Or will this be the one child I can't help? Once the child arrives there is so much to do that there isn't time for worrying, and I simply get on with it. But on that Thursday afternoon while I waited for Aimee to arrive, which I calculated would be between 4.30 and 5.00 p.m., my stomach churned, and all manner of thoughts plagued me so that I couldn't settle to anything. Jill had phoned to say she'd been called to an emergency so wouldn't be able to be with me for moral support when Aimee was placed. I'd reassured her I'd be all right.

Paula arrived home from school at four o'clock and, having had a drink and a snack, went to her room to unwind before starting her homework; Lucy wouldn't be home until about 5.30. My anxieties increased until at 4.40 the doorbell rang. With a mixture of trepidation and relief that Aimee had finally arrived, I went to answer it.

'Hello,' I said brightly, with a big smile that belied my nerves. 'Good to see you.' There were two social workers, whom I took to be Kristen and her colleague Laura, and they stood either side of Aimee, who carried a plastic carrier bag. 'I'm Cathy. Do come in.' I smiled.

It was clear who thought she was in charge, for, elbowing the social workers out of the way, Aimee stepped confidently into the hall and then stood looking at me expectantly.

The social workers followed. 'Hello, Cathy,' they said and introduced themselves.

'Shall we leave our shoes here?' Kristen said thoughtfully, slipping off her shoes, having seen ours paired in the hall.

'Thank you,' I said. 'And I'll hang your coats on the hall stand.'

As Kristen and Laura took off their shoes and coats I looked at Aimee, who was doing neither. 'Shall we leave your shoes and coat here?' I said encouragingly.

'No. Not taking 'em off,' Aimee said, jutting out her chin in defiance. 'And you can't make me.' My fault, I thought, for giving her a choice. What I should have said was: 'Would you like to take off your coat first or your shoes?' It's a technique called 'the closed choice' and would have resulted in action rather than refusal.

'No problem,' I said easily. 'You can do it later.'

'Not taking 'em off at all,' Aimee said challengingly. The two social workers looked at me and then raised their eyes.

'You can keep your shoes and coat on for now,' I said, aware I needed to be seen to be in charge. 'And we'll take them off later. Come on through.' Before Aimee could give me another refusal I turned and led the way down the hall and into the sitting room. My thoughts went again to Jodie. Although Aimee was the same age as Jodie, with similar blonde hair and grey-blue eyes, she wasn't so badly overweight and also seemed more astute. I knew I would need my wits about me in order to gain her cooperation.

In the sitting room Aimee plonked herself in the middle of the sofa, which left the two social workers to squeeze themselves in either side of her. 'This is nice,' Aimee said, running her eyes around the room. 'It ain't like this at my house. My 'ouse is a pigsty.' I smiled sadly at her heartfelt and innocent comparison – she was simply stating it as she saw it.

'No,' Kristen agreed, seizing the chance to demonstrate what an improvement coming into care was. 'Cathy's house is clean and warm and has lots of nice furniture. You'll have your own room here – we'll see it soon. And there'll always be plenty of food and hot water.' All of which I assumed had been missing from Aimee's house.

'It's nice, but it ain't me home,' Aimee said.

'It will be for now,' Laura put in.

'No it won't,' Aimee said, louder, turning to Laura and jutting out her chin. 'Me home's with me mother and neither you nor your bleeding lawyers can change that.'

Kristen and Laura both looked at me. 'I can guess where that's come from,' Kristen said. I nodded. It was a phrase an adult would have used, not an eight-year-old child, so I assumed Aimee was repeating something her mother had said.

'Cathy will be taking you to school and collecting you,' Kristen continued, unperturbed. 'And tomorrow you'll be able to see your mother after school.' Then, looking at me, Kristen said: 'I'll speak to you later about contact arrangements.'

'OK,' I said. Then I offered them a drink, as I hadn't done so before.

'No, I'm fine, thanks,' Kristen said. 'We'll settle Aimee and then get back to the office.' Laura agreed.

'What about you, Aimee?' I said. 'Would you like a drink?'

She shook her head, more interested in the objects in the room, which she was gazing at in awe, like a child in a toyshop. My sitting room was nothing special, but it clearly was to Aimee, who seemed mesmerized by the framed photographs on the walls, the potted plants, ornaments, etc. like those that adorn most sitting rooms.

'Aimee has one bag with her,' Kristen said. 'It's in the hall.' I nodded. 'We'll try to get some more of her things when Mum has calmed down, but I'm not sure how much use they'll be.' I nodded again, as I understood what she meant. If the clothes Aimee wore now were representative of the rest of her clothes, the others were likely to be suitable for the ragbag. The jacket she'd refused to take off was far too small, dirty and badly worn; the faded black jogging bottoms were too short and badly stained; and her plastic trainers had split at both toes, so that her socks poked through. I couldn't remember the last time I'd seen a child so poorly dressed.

'Is she in her school uniform?' I asked, mindful that Aimee had come to me straight from school.

'What there is of it,' Kristen said. 'You'll need to buy her a whole new uniform. I'll arrange for you to have the initial clothing allowance.' This allowance – approximately £80 – is a payment made to foster carers when a child arrives with nothing and needs a whole new wardrobe. It is often weeks before the money is paid and it only goes some way towards the clothes a child needs, but at least it is something.

'Thank you,' I said.

'Is there somewhere private where we can go to talk?' Kristen said to me. 'Laura could stay here with Aimee.'

'Of course,' I said, standing. 'We can go in the front room. There are some games over there,' I said to Aimee and Laura, pointing to the boxes of games I'd brought in.

Laura stood and went over to select a game while Aimee remained on the sofa, studying its fabric as though she'd never seen anything like it before. Then she began struggling out of her jacket. 'It's bleeding hot in 'ere,' she said. 'I'm gonna take me coat off.'

A Challenge

'Good choice,' I said, throwing her a smile.

Kristen took some papers from her briefcase and as we left the room we heard Laura suggest to Aimee they do a jigsaw together and Aimee ask what a jigsaw was.

'Aimee is eight,' I said quietly to Kristen in the hall. 'And she doesn't know what a jigsaw is?'

'It doesn't surprise me,' Kristen said. 'She's been so neglected. There were never any toys at her mother's flat, so Aimee watched television all day and night. Susan said the toys were at Aimee's father's flat but he wouldn't let me in, so I could never substantiate that. I doubt there were toys there, though. All their money went on drugs.'

Once we were in the front room with the door closed Kristen confided that Aimee's was one of the worse cases of neglect she'd ever come across, and repeated that she couldn't understand why she hadn't been removed from home sooner. Then she said again that Aimee had very bad head lice, so my family and I should be careful not to catch them.

'I'll treat her hair tonight,' I said. 'I have a bottle of lotion.'

'Good,' Kristen said. 'She needs a bath as well. She smells something awful.'

I nodded, for I had noticed as she'd walked in. 'I'll do that as well before she goes to bed.'

'You know Aimee used to kick and bite her mother when she tried to wash her?' Kristen reminded me.

'Yes, I know. I read it in the referral.'

'There's a high level of contact with her mother,' Kristen said, moving on. 'Face-to-face contact will be supervised at the family centre and it will take place after school on Monday, Wednesday and Friday. There will be telephone contact every night they don't see each other, including weekends. Can you monitor the phone contact, please, on speakerphone?'

'Yes,' I said. This was something I was often asked to do. 'So is the care plan eventually to return Aimee home?' I asked. That was the most likely explanation for the very high level of contact – so that the bond between Aimee and her mother would be maintained for when Aimee was eventually rehabilitated at home.

'Good grief! No!' Kristen exclaimed, shocked. 'There's no chance of Aimee being returned home. Her mother has been given enough chances to sort herself out in the past. The care plan is to try to find Aimee an adoptive home or, failing that, a long-term foster placement.'

'So why is there so much contact?' I asked, puzzled. 'It seems cruel if there's no chance of her going home.'

'Susan's barrister pushed for it in court and there was a good chance that if we hadn't agreed the judge wouldn't have granted us the care order.'

'What?' I asked, amazed. 'With this level of neglect?'

'I know, it's ludicrous.' Kristen sighed. 'But the threshold for granting care orders is so high now that children are being left at home for longer than they should.'

Not for the first time I thought how badly the whole child protection and care system needed reviewing and revising. While no one wants to see a family split, early intervention can give a child another chance at life. By the age of eight most of the damage is done and it is very difficult to undo.

'As mentioned in the referral,' Kristen continued, checking the essential information forms she'd taken from her briefcase, 'Aimee wets the bed.'

'I've put a protective cover on the mattress,' I said. 'It's not a problem.'

'Good. It was at home. The mattress Aimee and her mother slept on in the lounge stank of urine. It was disgusting and you could smell it as soon as you walked into the flat. Now, as you

know, Aimee needs firm boundaries and routine,' Kristen
continued. 'There were none at home. And as I mentioned
on the phone Susan is very good at making allegations and
complaints against foster carers, so be careful. She seems to
think that if she gets her children moved enough times they will
eventually be returned to her, but of course it doesn't work like
that.'

'Susan has contact with her other children?' I asked.

'Some. A lot of it is informal. Once kids become teenagers
you can't stop them getting on a bus and going to see their natural parents, and many of them seem to gravitate home.' Kristen
sighed again, and then, turning to the back page of the set of
forms, said: 'Can you sign this, please, and then we'll show
Aimee her room and I'll be off.'

We both signed the relevant form which gave me the
legal right to look after Aimee, and then we returned to the
sitting room. Laura and Aimee were on the floor poring over
a large-piece jigsaw. It was obvious Aimee hadn't got a clue
what to do and had been relying on Laura to do the puzzle
for her – a puzzle for pre-school children aged two to four
years.

'Aimee,' Kristen said brightly, 'Cathy is going to show us
your room now. Won't that be nice?'

Aimee seemed to agree that it would be nice and hauled
herself to her feet. I noticed she hadn't got Jodie's hyperactivity;
if anything Aimee's movements were very slow, lumbering
almost. Laura stood and I led the way out of the sitting room,
down the hall and upstairs. As we passed the bedrooms I said,
'This is my daughter Paula's bedroom. She's seventeen. You'll
meet her later. And this is Lucy's. She's at work now.'

'That'll be nice, won't it, Aimee?' Lauren enthused. 'Two
grown-up girls to play with.' I wondered if Paula had overhead
this comment and what she thought of it!

Aimee didn't say anything until we got to her room, when her face lit up. 'Cor, this is nice. Is it all for me?' she said with touching sincerity.

'Yes. This is your room. Just for you,' I said.

'Can me mum come and stay with me? She'd like it 'ere,' Aimee said, running her hands over the duvet on the bed.

'No,' Kristen said. 'You'll see your mum at the family centre. She won't be able to come here.'

'I know that,' Aimee snapped. 'You told me already. I ain't thick.'

Kristen let it go but I could see how easily Aimee could change from being polite and engaging to confrontational and aggressive.

'This is where you keep your clothes,' I said, opening the wardrobe door, and then the drawers, to show her.

'I won't be needing all that,' Aimee said. 'I ain't got many clothes.'

'I'll be buying you some,' I said positively, with a smile.

'No you won't,' Aimee said sharply. 'That's me mother's job.'

'Aimee,' Laura said evenly, 'while you are living here with Cathy she will buy your clothes and cook your meals, like your mother did at your house.'

'But she didn't,' Aimee said, quick as a flash. 'That why I'm in bleeding foster care. She didn't buy me clothes. They were given to us. She didn't take me to school, and she didn't give me any boundaries, whatever they are. And she gave me too many biscuits, so me teeth got bad. That's why I'm in foster care and not wiv me mum. You know that!'

I turned to stifle a smile as Aimee finished her lecture. Clearly Aimee didn't miss much and she had such a quaint way of putting things – a mixture of child-like honesty and middle-aged weariness. I didn't know if Aimee's explanation of why she was in care was something that had been said to her, possibly by a social worker, or if it was a deduction Aimee had made, but it was accurate. Laura and Kristen were smiling too.

'Is that telly mine?' Aimee said, pointing to the small portable television on top of the chest of drawers.

'Yes, it's yours to use while you're here,' I confirmed. 'But I limit its use. If you've had a good day you can watch it for a little while in bed before you go to sleep, but it's a treat.'

'And what if I ain't had a good day?' Aimee asked, turning to meet my gaze.

'Then you won't be watching it,' I said clearly.

'How you gonna stop me?' Aimee challenged. Her eyes flashed in defiance and I saw the social workers looking at me, waiting for my reaction.

'Very simple,' I said. 'I don't turn on the television, or I remove it from the room.'

'You can't do that,' Aimee said, her voice rising. 'It ain't allowed. I'll tell me mum and she'll have me moved from 'ere.'

Kristen and Laura exchanged another meaningful glance, for very likely Susan, employing tactics she'd used to disrupt the foster placements of her older children, had put this idea into her daughter's head. I relied on my usual strategy of trying to defuse confrontation by focusing on the positive. 'But I'm sure you won't be losing your television time, Aimee,' I said brightly. 'I've heard you're a good girl.'

I half expected her to say 'No, I ain't,' but she didn't. Indeed she looked quite taken aback that I'd suggested she could be good.

'Thanks,' she said. 'That's kind of ya.'

'You're welcome,' I said.

I was warming to Aimee. I liked her spunky repartee when she stated her thoughts simply and directly. I liked the fact that she could look me in the eyes. So my first impression was that all was not lost and I hoped I could work with her and eventually make a difference. I was relieved and grateful that Aimee didn't appear to have Jodie's problems, which had resulted from horrendous sexual abuse. Yet while I now thought Aimee had little in common with Jodie, beyond hair and eye colouring, I still felt there was something that reminded me of Jodie, something I couldn't quite put my finger on. That was until I stopped outside my bedroom and pushed open the door, so Aimee could see where I slept if she needed me in the night.

'Do you have a man?' she asked, peering in.

'No, I'm divorced,' I said.

'So who gives you one?' she asked with a knowing grin. It was then I knew that Aimee, like Jodie, had a sexual awareness well beyond her years: a knowledge she should not have had, and which could only have come from watching adult films or sexual abuse.

Chapter Four
'I Want Biscuits'

I ignored Aimee's remark, as did Kristen and Laura, and we made our way downstairs, but Aimee's words worried me deeply, as I knew they would the social workers. Kristen and Laura returned briefly to the sitting room for their bags, and then unhooked their coats from the hall stand and slipped on their shoes. Aimee was by my side, watching them. I knew it would be difficult for her as the social workers said goodbye and left. Then reality would hit her: that she was now in foster care and living with me, not with her mother or father. For no matter how bad things are at home children usually do not want to be parted from their parents, whom they have known all their lives and love despite everything that has happened.

'Well, goodbye then,' Kristen said to us both.

'Goodbye,' Laura said, then added 'Thank you' to me.

'I'll be in touch,' Kristen said.

'Where you going?' Aimee asked.

'To our office,' Kristen said. 'Then home.'

'Am I seeing me mum tonight?'

'No, you saw her after school,' Kristen said. 'It's evening now. You'll see your mum again tomorrow after school.'

'What's tomorrow?' Aimee asked, confused.

'After one sleep,' Laura said, using an explanation one would normally use with a much younger child.

Aimee looked blank.

'You'll sleep here for one night,' Laura explained. 'That is tonight. Then in the morning you'll go to school and after school you will see your mum.'

Aimee nodded, although I wasn't sure she understood. I'd explain again later. Clearly she had a poor grasp of time, well behind the understanding an average eight-year-old should have.

As the social workers left I reached for Aimee's hand to offer comfort but she snatched it away. I noticed the social workers hadn't tried to hug her as they'd said goodbye, as social workers often did, and I could understand why. Aimee wasn't a child who seemed to want to be hugged, held or even touched. There was a sense of 'keep away' in her body language, as though an imaginary line had been drawn around her, over which you wouldn't dare step.

As the social workers left, Lucy appeared.

'Hi,' I called as she came down the front garden path. 'This is Aimee.' Then to Aimee: 'This is my eldest daughter, Lucy.'

'Hello, how are you?' Lucy asked Aimee as she came in and kissed my cheek.

Aimee shrugged. 'Dunno.'

'Welcome to the world of foster care,' Lucy said brightly. 'Your life just got so much better.'

I smiled, grateful for Lucy's positive approach. Having come to me as a foster child herself, she knew what it felt like to be in care. But Lucy's welcome didn't touch Aimee and she just stared blankly at Lucy.

'We'll be eating a bit later tonight,' I said to Lucy. 'I need to get the lotion on Aimee's hair first.'

Lucy knew what I was referring to, as she too had been plagued by head lice before coming into care, as had many of the children we'd fostered. There seems to be an ongoing epidemic of head lice in England, with many school-age children affected. And while not life-threatening they're very unpleasant.

'You'll feel much better once they're all gone,' Lucy said to Aimee. 'All that nasty itching will stop.' For even in the few minutes since Lucy had come in Aimee had been scratching her head, as she had been doing on and off since arriving.

'Me mum didn't do it properly,' Aimee said to Lucy. 'The social worker gave her the bottle but it didn't work.'

'Don't worry, mine always works,' I said positively, aware that the most likely reason for the lotion not working was that its application had been interrupted by Aimee kicking her mother, as had been stated in the referral.

'See you later, Aimee,' Lucy said, disappearing up to her room to relax after her day at work.

'Come on,' I said to Aimee. 'Let's get rid of those nasty lice. The lotion smells but it won't hurt you.'

As I led the way upstairs I wondered what plan B would be if Aimee refused to have the lotion applied or if she got angry, as she had done with her mother, and kicked me. Clearly I couldn't forcibly apply the lotion, but nor could I not apply it. A bad infestation of head lice requires more than combing or brushing to get rid of it – not that she'd allowed her mother to do that either. Adopting my usual approach of being so positive that there was no room for refusal I went into the bathroom, took down the bottle of lotion, unscrewed the cap and then turned to Aimee, ready to apply the lotion.

'Good girl, lean over the sink so it doesn't run in your eyes,' I said. 'We'll soon have you feeling better.'

There was a moment's hesitation when Aimee looked at me, clearly deciding if she was going to do as I'd asked or not. 'Come on, be quick,' I encouraged. 'Then we can have our dinner.'

There was another hesitation before Aimee took the couple of steps to the basin and bent her head over. 'Good girl,' I said. 'Now stay as still as you can while I put on the lotion.' I began separating out the hair at the back of her head and on her crown and liberally applying the lotion.

Quite often the only indication a child has head lice is the minute white eggs that are glued by the adult head lice to the root of the hair, close to the scalp, where they incubate and hatch; very rarely does one actually see head lice, as they fix themselves to the hair and camouflage themselves. But now as I massaged the lotion into Aimee's hair and scalp head lice began appearing, drawn out by the toxic lotion. There were dozens and dozens, grouped in clusters, large adult lice that had been allowed to breed untouched for months. It was disgusting and my stomach churned. There were so many that they were crawling over each other in the thickest parts of her hair. It was one of the worst cases of head lice I'd ever seen and must have caused her untold misery. There were sores and scabs on Aimee's scalp where she'd been scratching and had broken the skin. I thought the lotion would sting the open sores but she didn't complain; she just stood with her head bent over the sink, quiet and still. 'Good girl,' I said repeatedly as I continued to apply the lotion. 'This will feel much better.'

'It does already,' Aimee said, which I could appreciate. Although it would take two hours for the lotion to kill all the lice, and the lotion would need to stay on overnight to kill the eggs, many lice were already coming out and dying and therefore not biting her scalp, which must have given her considerable relief.

Once I was sure all areas of her hair and scalp had been saturated in the lotion I praised her again and said she could stand up straight now, and I washed my hands in the sink.

'We need to leave the lotion on overnight,' I said. 'It will have dried by bedtime and I'll comb your hair with a special fine-tooth comb before you go to bed. Then in the morning we'll wash your hair before we go to school.'

Aimee nodded and I smiled. 'You were a very good girl standing there all that time,' I said pleased (and surprised) by her cooperation.

'That's OK,' she said amicably. 'I wish me mum had done it. Can I play in me bedroom now?'

'Yes, of course, if that's what you'd like to do. I'll call you when dinner is ready.'

I saw Aimee into her room and made sure she was all right. She wanted to play with the box of games I'd put in there. 'It's a nice room,' she said, squatting down on the floor by the toy box. 'I like me bed. I'll be comfortable in here.'

'Yes, you will, love,' I said, touched. I would have liked to put my arms around her and given her a hug, but I knew I would have to wait until she was ready and came to me for a cuddle.

I went downstairs, pleased that things were going smoothly so far. As I neared the foot of the stairs the phone began ringing and I picked up the extension in the hall. It was Jill, my support social worker, calling from her mobile.

'Has Aimee arrived?' she asked.

'Yes, and I've treated her head lice without a problem. But Jill, I've never seen so many. It must have been months since she was last treated, if at all. There are sores and scabs on her scalp from where she's been scratching. It's a wonder they weren't infected.'

'Poor kid,' Jill said. 'Make a note in your log and obviously tell Kristen when she phones. That's shocking neglect. What's Aimee doing now?'

'Playing in her room.'

'Good. I'll phone tomorrow to arrange a visit. I hope you have a good evening.'

'And you.'

Another Forgotten Child

Having said goodbye to Jill, I went into the kitchen to continue with the evening meal. I was feeling pretty confident and buoyed up that things were going well, given Aimee's history of violence towards her mother. I knew that Paula, shyer, quieter and more introverted than Lucy, and also concentrating on her exam work, would say hello to Aimee in her own time. When I called the girls down for dinner I heard Paula's bedroom door open first and her footsteps go round the landing and into Aimee's room. I heard Paula introduce herself and then they came downstairs together, with Lucy following a few steps behind.

I was aware just how grubby and smelly Aimee was and had she arrived earlier I would have given her a bath before dinner, but now I felt she should eat first, as it was getting late. I therefore suggested she just gave her hands a wash before we ate.

'Why?' Aimee asked.

'It's hygienic to wash your hands before a meal,' I said. 'It gets rid of all the germs and stops you from getting sick.'

'I ain't never sick,' Aimee said. 'So I don't need to wash me hands.'

Ignoring this questionable logic I led the way to the kitchen sink, where I turned on the taps and told Aimee to give her hands a quick wash. She looked at the running water and then at me and I saw the same hesitation loaded with determination as I'd seen before in the bathroom. 'Come on, be quick, good girl,' I said. More hesitation and then she pushed her hands under the running water just long enough to wet them. It was better than nothing and I held out the towel for her to dry her hands on, but she ran them down the sides of her (filthy) joggers instead.

'This is your place,' I said to Aimee, showing her to the dining table, where Lucy and Paula were already sitting.

'I Want Biscuits'

Aimee stared at the table and her chair but made no attempt to pull out the chair and sit. 'Sit down, good girl,' I said. 'Then I can bring in the hot dinner.'

'I can't!' Aimee said, slightly annoyed and glaring at me.

'Why not?'

'There ain't enough room.'

I looked at the dining table with its six chairs, only four of which were being used. Of course there was plenty of room. I saw Lucy and Paula looking questioningly at Aimee too.

'I can't fit in there,' Aimee said, pointing to the small gap where the chair was up against the table. 'I ain't that thin.'

Unable to believe that Aimee hadn't realized that the chair needed to be pulled out from the table in order to allow enough room for her to sit down, I gently eased it away.

'The chairs move!' Aimee said, surprised. 'They ain't like that in McDonald's. They're glued to the floor.'

Lucy and Paula knew better than to say anything but stared at Aimee in disbelief. Could her only experience of eating at a table be at McDonald's? It was possible. Aimee finally sat in her chair but made no attempt to draw it in close enough to the table so that she could eat. I slid the chair to the table.

'I guess your mum and dad didn't have a table at their flats?' I asked Aimee.

'No. We sit on the mattress on the floor.'

Children with parents who didn't own a dining table certainly wasn't unique; I'd looked after many children who'd come from homes where meals were eaten on the sofa in front of the television. But what did surprise me, indeed it took my breath away, was Aimee's reply to my next question.

'But surely when you're at school, you eat your school dinner at a table with everyone else?' I asked.

'I never get to school in time for dinner,' Aimee said matter-of-factly.

'What, never?' I asked, feeling I must have misunderstood. Aimee was in her fourth year of schooling, so it was inconceivable she had never done a full day in school which included lunch. 'I know you were often late for school but you must have got there on time some mornings, surely?'

'No, never,' Aimee said adamantly, shaking her head. 'Mum never woke up until it was too late. I tried shaking her but it weren't no good. She was out of it.'

Probably from drugs, I thought. But I still wasn't convinced Aimee had never been in school for a full day. Surely the school's head teacher, the social services or the education welfare officer would have acted? In the UK it is illegal not to send a child to school or provide an acceptable alternative education, which clearly Aimee's parents hadn't done. I would be taking Aimee to school the following day, when I would, I hoped, find out more. Now I went into the kitchen and returned with a cottage pie, which is a favourite of ours as well as all the children I'd fostered; I'd never come across a meat-eating child who didn't like cottage pie. Until now.

'Yuck! What's that?' Aimee asked rudely as I placed the dish on the table.

'Cottage pie. Mum's special,' Lucy said. 'It's yummy.'

'Ain't having it. I don't like cottage,' Aimee said, clearly having no idea what a cottage pie was. 'I have biscuits for me tea.'

'This is dinner,' Paula said. 'We have a cooked meal at dinner.'

'It's potato and minced meat,' I said.

'I want me biscuits,' Aimee said. 'Me mum packed 'em.'

Aimee slid off her chair quicker than I'd seen her move before, and going into the hall returned with the dirty plastic supermarket carrier bag she'd arrived with. She dumped it on the table where we were about to eat and began taking out its filthy contents, all of which were grey and stank of stale smoke: a dirty threadbare pyjama top; a chewed and filthy teddy bear; a pair of torn faded knickers; one filthy sock; and a half-eaten packet of chocolate biscuits. I moved the cottage pie to one side, away from the disgusting pile of rubbish that was Aimee's belongings. Aimee quickly peeled off the top biscuit from the packet and began stuffing it in her mouth.

'No more,' I said. 'You can have another biscuit after your dinner.' I quickly gathered up her belongings and returned them to the plastic carrier bag, which I put on the floor.

'Biscuits *are* me dinner,' Aimee said, her mouth full.

She was about to take another biscuit from the packet when, to her utter amazement and my surprise, Lucy leant across the table and whisked the packet out of Aimee's hand. 'Cathy said no more,' Lucy said with a sweet placatory smile.

'Give 'em back!' Aimee demanded aggressively.

'Later,' Lucy said. 'Things are different in foster care. They are much better. I used to have biscuits for my dinner before I came into care. Now I eat all the nice meals Cathy cooks, just as you will.'

'No, I ain't,' Aimee said.

'You can have another biscuit after your dinner,' I said.

'I don't like dinner,' Aimee said, swallowing the last of the biscuit with a loud gulp.

'Try some and you may,' I said, throwing Lucy and Paula a reassuring smile, for they were both looking concerned.

I served the dinner on to the plates, giving Aimee a small portion, which I placed in front of her. I sat down and Lucy, Paula and I started eating while Aimee sat with her arms folded across her chest and her face set in defiance, scowling and angry. Then after some moments she picked up her knife and fork and plunged them into her dinner, clearly with no idea how to use them. She certainly wasn't the first child I'd looked after who

33

didn't know how to use cutlery because they'd only ever eaten finger food at home.

'Like this,' I said, showing her how I was holding my knife and fork. 'Or you can use your spoon if it's easier.'

I saw Aimee glance at Lucy and Paula and perhaps she wanted to be like them for, to her credit, she picked up her knife and fork and made a good attempt to use them. She managed to get some food into her mouth and, finding the taste acceptable, scooped up some more, so that gradually as Lucy, Paula and I continued eating so too did she.

'Well done,' I said as she cleared her plate. Then to all three girls: 'Would you like pudding now or later?'

'Later,' Paula and Lucy said.

'I want me biscuits now,' Aimee said.

I nodded to Lucy, who'd tucked the packet of biscuits on to the chair next to her, and she passed the packet to Aimee, who set upon them ravenously. After four biscuits I said, 'That's enough for now. You'll make yourself ill.'

Aimee ignored me and took another biscuit from the packet and began stuffing it into her mouth. I knew I had to start as I meant to carry on and it wasn't in Aimee's best interest to gorge on biscuits. I quickly popped into the kitchen and returned with an attractive brightly coloured empty tin on which I'd already printed Aimee's name.

'This is your special tin,' I said with exaggerated enthusiasm. 'This is where you will keep your biscuits and your sweets, and you can have a few each day. They'll be safe in here and no one else will eat them.' Experience had taught me that children from homes where food has been in short supply often hoard and then gorge food once it is freely available in foster care. Having a tin of their own often helps. But although Aimee was looking at the tin with interest, she was also peeling off yet another biscuit. I gently took the packet from her hand and put it in the tin.

'I Want Biscuits'

''Ere! Give 'em to me!' Aimee demanded. 'They're my biscuits.'

'I know they are, love, and they'll be quite safe in your tin. You can have another one tomorrow.'

'I'm gonna tell me mum you took my biscuits and she'll make a complaint against you!' Aimee threatened, jutting out her chin.

I saw Lucy and Paula were about to say something in my defence but I motioned to them not to. Aimee was only repeating something she'd heard her mother say, probably in respect of her older half-siblings, all of whom were in care. I now concentrated on my next task, which was to get Aimee clean. 'Would you like a bath or a shower?' I asked, remembering to use the closed choice.

'None!' Aimee said. 'I don't like water.'

Chapter Five
Severe Neglect

'You'll like the water here,' Lucy said, continuing with her philosophy that things were different and better in foster care.

'No, I won't,' Aimee said, folding her arms and sulking.

'I'm going to do my homework,' Paula said, and escaped to her bedroom.

'Come on, I'll show you the new tiles I put in our bathroom,' I said to Aimee with excitement out of all proportion to my first attempt at tiling.

Sufficiently intrigued, she finally slid from her chair at the dining table and followed me upstairs and to the bathroom, where I pointed out the blue and white tiles around the bath. 'They're nice,' she said, with genuine admiration.

'Thank you,' I said.

'We have tiles in my bathroom,' Aimee said, 'but they're dirty and have green stuff growing on them,' which I assumed to be mould.

'Well, as you can see ours are all new,' I said. 'No nasty green stuff here. Now, would you like a bath or a shower? What did you have at home?'

'Nothing,' Aimee said, her face setting again. 'I don't have anything.'

I thought she must have had some sort of wash sometimes, so relying on the closed choice I said again: 'Bath or shower? You choose.'

She didn't answer but refolded her arms more tightly across her chest like a grumpy old woman. 'OK, I'll decide for you, then,' I said. 'I'll run you a nice warm bath.'

Aimee said: 'I want a shower.'

'Fine. You can have a shower,' I said. 'Undress while I set the shower to the right temperature.' Aimee was not old enough to be left alone to adjust a shower she'd never used before, so, turning my back on her to give her some privacy, I switched on the shower to a medium temperature.

As soon as the water began spurting from the showerhead Aimee squealed from behind me. 'I ain't having that on me!'

I switched off the shower and turned to face her. So far she'd only taken off her navy jumper, which was filthy, to reveal an equally filthy T-shirt. 'Aimee,' I said carefully, 'you need to have a shower or a bath tonight. Then once you're clean you'll be able to watch some television. It would be a great pity if you lost television time on your first night, wouldn't it?' This may have seemed harsh but Aimee was used to having her own way and I could see how determined she could be. For hygiene's sake alone she needed to have a bath or shower; her skin and clothes were filthy and she smelt. Also if I didn't start to put in place a routine and boundaries now it would become more difficult the longer I left it.

'Can I watch me telly in bed?' Aimee asked.

'Once you've had your bath, yes,' I said. Not blackmail but positive reward.

'I'll have your bath, then,' Aimee said, scowling.

'Good girl.' I turned to the bath and switched on the taps, adjusting the temperature as the water ran. But by the time the bath was ready Aimee still hadn't undressed and seemed to be waiting for me to do it for her. 'Take off your T-shirt,' I encouraged.

'Can't,' Aimee said, not attempting the task. 'You do it.'

'Aimee, you are eight years old, love. I'm sure a big girl like you can undress herself.' Children are usually taught self-care skills by the time they're five and go to school, but Aimee shook her head.

'I'll help you,' I said. 'But I would like you to learn how to dress and undress yourself. How did you manage to change for PE and swimming at school?' For I knew the teachers wouldn't have undressed her.

'Didn't do them,' Aimee said.

'What, you never did PE or swimming?'

'No.'

I was sure Aimee must be wrong – physical exercise is an essential part of every school curriculum – but I'd mention it the following day when I took Aimee to school. Now I began easing up her T-shirt and showing her how to undress. 'Like this,' I said. Aimee raised her arms cooperatively but had no idea what to do next.

'Who dressed you at home?' I asked.

'Mum.'

Underneath the T-shirt was an equally dirty and torn vest. 'You like your layers,' I smiled. 'Aren't you hot with all this on?' The rest of us wore one layer in our centrally heated house.

'It's cold at home,' Aimee said. 'What makes your house hot?'

I didn't answer, for having taken off Aimee's vest I was now staring at the small bruises dotted all over her chest. I stepped around her so I could see her back and that too was covered in the same small bruises, as were her arms and neck. The bruises were all roughly the same size, small and round, about the size of a small coin. They were in various stages of healing: some were old and faded while others looked new.

'How did you get all these bruises?' I asked carefully, point-ing to the ones she could see on her arms and chest.

'I fell,' Aimee said. 'I keep tripping over things.'

It was possible the bruises were a result of falling, I supposed. Some children are accident prone, and it's often the overweight children who aren't used to physical activity and have never developed good coordination and balance as more active chil-dren do. It was possible, yet there was something about the size and shape of the bruises that I couldn't identify and unsettled me. The bruises didn't require medical attention, but I'd obvi-ously make a note of what I'd found in my fostering log and then tell Jill and Kristen the following day.

'Sit on the floor and take off your socks now, good girl,' I said to Aimee, sure she could do this simple task without help. She did as I asked and sat down, and then very clumsily managed to pull off both her filthy and holed socks. 'Now step out of your joggers,' I said, testing the bath water with my hand. 'They're easy to take off. You just pull them down.'

Aimee yanked down her joggers and stepped out of them, to reveal more bruises running down both legs, from her thighs to her ankles – there were even some bruises on her feet. Most of the bruises were the same size and shape as those on her body and arms – round and small – although there were some larger ones on her knees and shins, consistent with falling over.

'How did you get all these?' I asked.

'I fell over.'

She stepped out of her pants to reveal more small round bruises on her buttocks. 'And the ones on your bottom?' I asked. 'How did you get those?'

'Same,' Aimee said, tossing her pants on top of the pile of smelly rags that were her clothes. She stood at the side of the bath, making no attempt to get in.

'Get into the bath while the water is nice and warm,' I said.

She reached out to my hand for me to help her and I steadied her while she climbed into the bath. Then she stood looking at me.

'Sit down,' I said.

'What, in the water?' Aimee asked.

'Yes.'

'Why?'

'So you can have a bath and wash all over.'

Very gingerly and slowly Aimee began to lower herself into the bath, and as the warm water lapped against her skin she gave a little sigh of pleasure. 'This is nice,' she said.

'Good,' I said, relieved. I passed her a new sponge and fresh bar of soap. 'Now rub the soap on to the sponge and then all over your body.'

But she just sat there with a smile on her face, enjoying the feel of the warm water without actually washing, despite my further encouragement.

'This is nice,' she said again. 'I like the warm water.'

'Aimee,' I said suspiciously, 'have you ever had a bath before?'

'No.' She grinned sheepishly.

'So did you usually have a shower at home?'

'No. All the water was cold and I don't like cold water.'

'Wasn't there any hot water in your flat at all?' I asked, aware that this was not as uncommon in poor homes as one might think.

'No,' Aimee said, shaking her head.

'So you never had a hot shower or bath?'

'Never. I stood in the kitchen and Mum used one of those.' Aimee pointed to the face flannel draped on the rail at the side of the bath. 'But the water was cold, so I didn't like it.' From which I deduced that Aimee had been given a stand-up wash in cold water and had never had a bath or shower in her life.

'Did your social worker, Kristen, know there was no hot water in your flat?' I now asked.

40

'Of course not!' Aimee said, surprised at my ignorance. 'Me and Mum told her the meter had just run out and we were going to get some more tokens, but we never had the money.' She giggled at the deceit she and her mother had perpetrated on the social worker, and not for the first time since I'd begun fostering I was shocked by the ease with which a social worker had been duped.

'Why didn't you tell Kristen there was no money for hot water?' I asked. 'She could have helped you.'

Aimee looked at me, confused, and I guessed it was because she wasn't used to hearing that a social worker could help. So often parents view social workers as the enemy.

'Mum said if we told Kristen I would be taken away and put in care like my brothers and sisters,' Aimee said. 'Mum said I wasn't to tell her about the water. There were lots of things I couldn't tell Kristen.' She suddenly stopped.

'Like what?' I asked gently, lathering the soap on to the sponge for her.

'Nothing,' Aimee said. 'They're secrets and I'll get shouted at if I tell.'

'Who will shout at you?' I asked.

'No one,' Aimee said, clamming up.

'All right. But sometimes it helps to tell a secret. Bad secrets can be very worrying, not like the surprises we have on our birthdays. When you feel ready to tell me I will listen carefully and try to help,' I said, although I knew it could be months, possibly years, before Aimee trusted me enough to tell me. I also knew that 'secrets' when the child had been threatened into not telling always involved abuse.

The bath water turned grey as Aimee washed; indeed the water was so dirty that I drained the bath and refilled it with fresh water. I explained to Aimee that I would just comb her hair before bed and then wash it in the morning after the lotion had done its job properly. I helped her out of the bath, wrapped her in a towel and left her to dry herself while I went to the otto- man in my bedroom for some clean pyjamas that would fit her. When I returned she was still standing with the towel around her, having made no attempt to dry herself.

'Come on, dry yourself,' I encouraged.

'No, you do it,' she said.

'I'll help you. But you need to learn to dry yourself at your age.' I showed her what to do – how to pat and rub the towel over her skin – but I didn't do it for her. I guessed that the reason Aimee didn't know how to towel dry herself was that, never having had a shower or bath, she'd never had to do it. This level of neglect – of even the most basic requirements – is a form of child abuse.

After about ten minutes, and with a lot of encouragement, Aimee had dried herself. 'These should fit,' I said, and held out the nearly new clean pyjamas I kept as spares for such an emergency.

'Not wearing them!' Aimee sneered, pulling a face and shrinking from the pyjamas I held. 'They're not mine.'

'They're yours for now,' I said. 'Then we'll buy you some new ones after school tomorrow.'

'Ain't wearing them,' Aimee said again, her face setting. 'I want me own.'

'You haven't brought any with you,' I reminded her gently.

'Yes I have!' Aimee snapped, jutting out her chin. 'They're in me bag downstairs.' I now remembered the threadbare and filthy pyjama top Aimee had tipped on to the dining table when she'd been looking for her biscuits.

'There was only the top, love, no bottoms, and it needs washing.'

'I want me top,' Aimee demanded rudely. 'I'll wear me knickers with it, like I do at home.' She made a move to retrieve her knickers from the pile of filthy clothes she'd taken off before her bath.

'No,' I said firmly. 'You can't wear those pants. You are nice and clean now. If you put on those you'll be dirty again. Wear these pyjamas for now and I'll wash your clothes tonight, and then you can have them in the morning.' I knew children were often attached to their own clothes and felt secure wearing them when they first came into care, and I always tried to use them whenever possible. But I was also aware that dirty clothes can harbour and transmit parasitic diseases such as scabies and ringworm; not only to Aimee but to the bed linen and anyone else who came in contact with the infected clothes. 'Put on these,' I said firmly, placing the pyjamas into her arms. 'You dress while I put your things in the washing machine.'

Before she had a chance to refuse I'd scooped up the ragged clothes and was hurrying downstairs and into the kitchen, where I threw the clothes in the washing machine. I took the pyjama top and knickers from the plastic carrier bag and put those in too. Then I added a generous measure of detergent and set the machine on a hot wash. I would have liked to have washed Aimee's teddy bear, which was in the plastic carrier bag, but I knew Aimee would need that tonight for security. I thoroughly washed my hands and then returned to the bathroom, where Aimee had made a good attempt to dress herself. The pyjama top was on back to front but that didn't matter.

'Well done. Good girl.' I smiled, and instinctively went to hug her, but she drew back.

'Don't you like hugs?' I asked.

'Not from you,' she said defiantly. 'You ain't me mum.'

'I understand. Let me know when you'd like a hug.'

'Never!' Aimee scowled.

Mindful that the evening was quickly passing and I would need to get Aimee up early for school the following morning, I continued with the bedtime routine. Now she was clean and in her pyjamas I gave her a new toothbrush and tube of toothpaste and told her to squeeze a little paste on to her brush and clean her teeth well. It soon became obvious that Aimee didn't know how to take the top off the toothpaste, let alone squirt some paste on to the brush, so I did it, showing her what to do so that she'd know for next time. 'Now give your teeth a very good clean,' I said, handing her the toothbrush.

She put the toothbrush into her mouth, sucked off the paste and swallowed it. 'Ahhh!' she cried, spitting the rest into the bowl. 'You're trying to kill me!'

'Aimee, love,' I said stifling a smile, 'you're not supposed to eat it. Just brush it over your teeth and then spit it out. Didn't you have toothpaste at home?'

Aimee shook her head.

'Didn't your mum and dad brush their teeth?'

'Mum ain't got many teeth,' Aimee said. 'And Dad takes his out and puts them in a jar.' From which I gathered that both her parents had lost most of their teeth and her father had false teeth. Her parents were only in their mid-forties but one of the side effects of years of drug abuse is gum disease and tooth loss.

'Do you know how to brush your teeth?' I asked Aimee. 'Did you brush them at home?'

Aimee shook her head.

Horrified that a child could reach the age of eight without regularly brushing their teeth, I took the toothbrush and said, 'Open your mouth, good girl, and I'll show you what to do.'

There was a moment's hesitation when Aimee kept her mouth firmly and defiantly closed; then, thinking better of it – perhaps remembering her parents' lack of teeth – she opened her mouth wide. 'Good girl,' I said, and I began gently brushing. Many of her back teeth were in advanced states of decay or missing. As I gently brushed Aimee's remaining teeth, showing her how to brush, her gums bled – a sign of gum disease.

'Did you ever see a dentist?' I asked as I finished brushing and Aimee rinsed and then spat out.

'Yeah. And I ain't going back. He put a needle in me mouth so he could pull me teeth out. I'll end up like me mum if he keeps that up.' So that I thought at least some of Aimee's missing teeth had been extracted by the dentist because of advanced tooth decay. The poor kid had really suffered and my anger flared at parents who could so badly neglect their daughter; but then drug-addicted parents would be more concerned with obtaining their next fix than making sure their daughter brushed her teeth.

Before we left the bathroom I told Aimee I wanted to fine-tooth comb her hair and I asked her to lean over the sink while I did it. She didn't object and ten minutes later the white porcelain basin was covered with hundreds of dead head lice. The lotion would stay on overnight so that it could complete its job and I would wash it off in the morning. When we'd finished I praised Aimee for keeping still.

'Will I have friends at school now?' Aimee asked.

'I'm sure you will. Why? Has there been a problem with your friends?'

'I ain't got none,' Aimee said bluntly. 'The other kids call me "nit head" and "smelly pants". When I try and play with them they run away.'

'Well, not any more,' I said, my heart going out to her. 'Now you're in foster care you will always be clean and have lots of friends.'

'Promise?'

'Yes.'

'And you never break a promise?'

'Never.'

'Cor, I'm looking forward to going to school.'

Chapter Six

'I'll Tell Me Mum!'

Aimee settled easily that first night. She was so pleased to be sleeping in a bed and in a room of her own that she forgot her anger at being in care. She sighed as she snuggled beneath the duvet and felt the caress of the soft clean pillow against her head.

'This is nice,' she said. 'I like me bed.'

'Good. I'm pleased. You'll be fine in care, here with me until everything is sorted out,' I said, and she didn't disagree.

I had read her a bedtime story downstairs and I now tucked her into bed and reminded her I would need to wake her early in the morning so that I could wash her hair before school. I asked her if she'd like a goodnight kiss but she said she wouldn't, so I told her to call me if she woke in the night and needed anything. Then I said goodnight and came out, closing her bedroom door as she'd asked.

When I checked on her ten minutes later she was sound asleep, lying flat on her back with her mouth slightly open and holding her teddy bear close to her chest. With her features relaxed in sleep and her blonde hair fanned out on the pillow she looked angelic, and I dearly wished I could have waved a magic wand and taken away all the bad that had happened to her and make everything all right. But realistically I knew, from what I'd seen of Aimee so far and from the referral, that it was going to be a long uphill climb to undo the harm that had been done to her before she could come close to leading a happy and fulfilling life.

Once Aimee was asleep I went downstairs, tidied the kitchen, wrote up my log notes and then watched a bit of television with Paula, while Lucy was on the computer MSNing her friends. When I asked the girls how they felt the evening had gone they agreed with me that Aimee's behaviour hadn't been as bad as we'd anticipated, although of course it was only the first night. Paula and I were in bed at ten o'clock and Lucy followed a little while afterwards.

I was expecting Aimee to wake in the night – her first night in a strange room – but she slept soundly and was still asleep when I went into her room to wake her for school the following morning. I'd also been expecting her to wet the bed, as the referral had stated and the social worker had confirmed she did, but she was dry.

'Good girl, well done,' I praised her as she climbed out of bed, yawning and stretching. 'We'll wash your hair before you get dressed, so go into the bathroom.'

'Ain't wearing those,' Aimee said, now fully awake and pointing to the skirt and jumper I'd taken from my emergency supply and laid ready at the foot of her bed. 'They ain't mine!'

'I know,' I said, 'but I thought you could wear those while we go to school. I'm going to buy you a new uniform from the school but you need to wear something to get there.'

'I want me own clothes,' Aimee demanded, her face setting defiantly.

'No problem,' I said lightly. 'There they are.' I pointed to the clothes she'd arrived in, which I'd also laid on the end of her bed, half anticipating they might be needed.

'Me clothes are clean!' Aimee exclaimed, astonished, as though some trickery had been done. 'How did you do that?'

'I washed and dried them in the machine last night,' I said. 'You know the washer/dryer in the kitchen?' I added as Aimee looked blank. 'Perhaps your mother used a launderette?'

'What's a laundry-net?' Aimee asked.

'A launderette is where you take your clothes for washing and drying if you don't have a machine at home.'

'We don't go there,' Aimee said, still eyeing the clean clothes suspiciously.'

'Perhaps there is a washing machine at your flat.'

'No. Me mum didn't wash clothes.'

I thought their clothes must have been washed sometimes by someone, but it clearly wasn't a regular occurrence, which didn't surprise me, given the filthy state of Aimee's clothes when she'd arrived.

'So I'm wearing me own clothes, then?' Aimee clarified.

'Yes, if you wish. Then you can change when I buy your uniform at school.'

Although I would have preferred Aimee to wear the clothes I'd provided rather than the threadbare and far too small clothes she'd arrived in, I knew I could surrender this smaller point for bigger issues. Looking after a child with behavioural problems is a balancing act between what I can reasonably let go and what I have to insist on, as Aimee was about to prove.

'Don't want me hair washed,' Aimee now said. 'It's stopped itching, so it don't need washing.'

'It does need washing,' I said. 'We have to wash out the lotion and the dead lice and eggs.'

'No, we don't!' Aimee said, making a move towards her clothes.

'You can't go to school with your hair smelling of nit lotion,' I said. 'And although the lice are dead your hair is still dirty.'

'No it ain't!' Aimee said again.

'I'll Tell Me Mum!'

I wasn't going to enter into a 'yes it is, no it ain't' argument, for in this matter she needed to do as she was told. Visions of us arriving late for school on our first morning, or Aimee arriving with unwashed hair, if she didn't cooperate, flashed through my mind. Not only would it create a bad first impression of my fostering, but it would also set a precedent that would allow Aimee to continue to do exactly what she wanted, as she had been doing at home.

'Aimee, I need to wash your hair, love,' I said evenly but firmly one last time.

'No!' Aimee said, plonking herself on the bed and folding her arms tightly across her chest.

'Then I'm afraid you won't be watching your television this evening, or tomorrow evening, or for the rest of the week, until I wash your hair. Now, get dressed and come down for breakfast.' I turned and began towards the bedroom door.

Loss of television time was a sanction I'd found very effective in the past, for nearly all children like to watch some television, and Aimee was no exception. As I placed my hand on the door and was about to leave the room I heard Aimee's voice from behind.

'All right! You win!' she shouted. Grabbing her clothes, she stomped past me and into the bathroom.

'Good girl,' I said, taking every opportunity to praise her. 'Sensible decision.'

'No it aint! I'm telling me mum what you did.' Which I ignored.

Washing Aimee's hair was no small achievement. Whereas the evening before when I'd applied the lotion I'd had Aimee's cooperation, now she worked against me. Part of her agitation was because she wasn't used to having her hair washed and part of it was sheer bloody mindedness – she was having to do something she didn't want to do, although it was for her own good.

She refused to lean over the bath properly, so that when I turned on the shower it was difficult to wet her hair without it running down her back; she wouldn't keep the flannel over her face to stop the water going into her eyes; she continually moved when I asked her to stand still; and when I applied the shampoo she yelled it was cold. In fact Aimee yelled so much that eventually Lucy and Paula were driven from their bedrooms and came to see what was the matter.

'I'm only washing her hair,' I said defensively.

Lucy smiled and raised her eyebrows. 'Aimee, you sound like you're being murdered. Be quiet.'

'Shut up,' Aimee said rudely, raising her head and flicking soapy water everywhere. Paula groaned and the girls returned to their rooms.

'Lucy and Paula wash their hair regularly,' I said, hoping Aimee might see this as a good example to follow.

'Don't care!' she snapped. 'That stuff's getting in me eyes!'

'Well, keep your eyes closed and the flannel over your face, like I've told you,' I said again.

'And it's in me mouth!' Aimee shouted.

'Keep that closed too.' But Aimee couldn't because she was too busy shouting and cursing at me, although she didn't try to kick me, as the referral had stated she had her mother.

Trying to pacify Aimee as best I could, I continued with what was probably the most stressful but most necessary hair wash I'd ever given a child. As I lathered the shampoo, rinsed and lathered again, the dirty water slowly began to run clean and dead head lice finally stopped dropping into the bath.

'All done!' I said at last. I wasn't sure who was more relieved. 'Next time we'll try washing your hair in the bath,' I added. 'It might be easier for you.'

'You ain't doing it again!' Aimee scowled, snatching the towel from my hand and rubbing her hair.

'Hair needs washing at least twice a week,' I said, planting the idea so that she had time to come to terms with it.

'No, it don't!' Aimee said.

I ignored this and told Aimee to go into her bedroom and I'd fetch the hairdryer and dry her hair. Throwing the towel on the bathroom floor she stomped off round the landing and into the bedroom, causing Lucy to call, 'Be quiet, Aimee!'

'No!' Aimee shouted. 'Shut up!'

I returned to Aimee's bedroom with the hairdryer and before I switched it on I explained to Aimee that it would make a loud noise and blow hot air, for I doubted her mother owned a hair-dryer. I was wrong.

'I ain't thick,' Aimee said. 'Me mum uses the hairdryer for killing me bugs.'

'You mean she washed your hair and then dried it?' I asked, slightly surprised, for certainly Aimee's hair hadn't looked as though it had been washed for weeks.

'No,' Aimee said. 'Mum never washed me hair. She blew the bugs away with the dryer so they were dead.' Which I could believe, although it was nonsense: you can't blow away head lice, as they fasten themselves on to the hair and glue their eggs to the root shaft. But I let the point go.

Aimee moaned some more as I brushed and dried her hair, but when I'd finished, her hair shone and was quite a few shades lighter. 'Fantastic!' I said.

'No it ain't!' Aimee said. 'I'm telling me mum.'

'I'm sure your mother will be very pleased,' I said, turning her threat into a positive.

'No she won't,' Aimee said. 'She'll report you.' Which I ignored.

I now explained to Aimee that I wanted her to get dressed as quickly as she could and then come down for breakfast. 'I need you downstairs by seven fifteen,' I said, nodding at the clock on the wall. Aimee stared blankly at the clock. 'When the big hand is here,' I said, pointing to the three. 'It's five past seven now, so you have ten minutes to get dressed, which is plenty of time. What would you like for your breakfast?'

'Biscuits.'

'Biscuits are bad for your teeth. Toast or cereal?'

'What's cereal?'

'We have cornflakes, wheat flakes, Rice Krispies or porridge.'

'Toast.'

'What would you like on your toast? Marmite, jam, honey or marmalade?'

'Nothing.'

'Sure?'

Aimee nodded.

Leaving Aimee to dress, I went downstairs and into the kitchen, where I made coffee for myself, and toast for Aimee and me. Paula and Lucy would make their own breakfasts when they came down. I lightly buttered the toast and added marmalade to mine; then I cut Aimee's toast in half and half again so that it was easier for her to eat. Setting the plates on the table, I called upstairs to Aimee that breakfast was ready. To her credit a minute later she appeared, dressed in her old but now clean clothes. The joggers were far too small, as was her jumper, and her toes poked out of the holes in her socks, but all that would change once we'd bought her new clothes.

'Well done,' I said with a smile. 'You dressed yourself very well.' I showed Aimee to her place at the table, where her toast was waiting. 'What would you like to drink?' I asked. 'Milk, juice or water?'

'Water,' Aimee said, sitting on the chair but too far from the table. I made a move to help her ease the chair under the table but she roughly pushed my hand away. 'I can do it,' she snapped.

'All right, love, but don't be rude. There are nice ways of saying things without being aggressive.'

'I talk to me mum and dad like that,' Aimee said, as though that justified her disrespect.

'I don't doubt it, love, but you shouldn't. And you certainly won't be talking to me like that.' I said it kindly but firmly so that Aimee could see that I meant it. Teaching a child to show respect to others is crucial in putting them on the road to achieving socially acceptable and good behaviour. 'Also, love, if you want to make friends you will need to speak to the children at school nicely too.' Obvious to children who have been correctly brought up but not to a child from a dysfunctional background.

Aimee looked at me but didn't say anything and I smiled again. Jumping her chair under the table until she was close enough, she took a bite of her toast and spat it out. 'That's disgusting,' she cried.

'It's toast, as you asked,' I said.

'It's got slimy stuff on it,' Aimee said, wiping her mouth on the sleeve of her clean jumper.

'I put a little butter on it,' I said. 'That's all.'

'What's butter?' Aimee asked.

I now took the butter from the fridge and showed her. She shrugged, indicating she'd never seen butter before. 'Perhaps you had spread at home?' I suggested.

Returning the butter to the fridge, I took out the tub of butter substitute and showed her, but Aimee shook her head. 'We didn't have that. I want me toast like I make it at home.'

'All right. Tell me how you made it and I'll do the same.'

Aimee turned to look at me and then, using her hand to gesticulate, explained: 'I get the bread from the packet and I scratch off the green bits. That's mould. Then I put the bread in the toaster and later it goes pop! It's ready then. It's hot, but it don't have slimy stuff on it. Our toaster don't do that. The man next door gave us the toaster. So I take me toast to the living room and I switch on the telly, only I have to have the sound on low because Mum is asleep on the mattress, and she gets angry if I wake her. Then I sit on the floor and eat me toast. I get toast and biscuits whenever I want.'

What a morning routine, I thought! I could picture Aimee waking in the morning beside her mother on the filthy mattress on the floor, then slipping out so she didn't wake her mother, and making toast from rotting bread, which she ate dry because there was nothing to put on it. Compare Aimee, I thought, with a child from a good home. A chasm of neglect lay between them.

I made Aimee another slice of toast and gave it to her dry with the glass of water she'd asked for, but I knew I should start introducing new foods into her diet as soon as possible. She was pale, her skin was dull and her movements were lethargic, which made me suspect she might be mineral and vitamin deficient. All children who come into foster care have a medical and I would raise my concerns with the paediatrician when we saw her, and while I couldn't give Aimee a vitamin supplement without the doctor's or her parents' consent, I could improve her diet.

Paula and Lucy came down to breakfast as Aimee finished eating hers.

'Feeling better?' Lucy asked, taking a bowl for her cereal from the cupboard.

'No,' Aimee scowled.

'What's the matter?' Paula asked, joining Aimee at the table.

Aimee looked at the girls for a moment, then at me, and her face crumpled. 'I want me mum,' she cried, and burst into tears.

'Oh, love,' I said, immediately going to her. 'Please don't upset yourself. You'll see her soon.' I went to put my arms around her, wanting to hold and comfort her, but she drew back, so I settled for laying my hand on her arm and standing close to her.

I saw Paula's eyes mist as Aimee sat at the table with her head in her hands and cried. 'I want me mum. Please take me to my mum.' For like most children, no matter how bad it has been at home, Aimee missed her mother, with whom she'd been all her life.

'You'll see her tonight,' I reassured her, 'straight after school.'

'Don't cry,' Paula said, her voice faltering. 'We'll look after you.'

'Better than your mother did,' Lucy added under her breath. I frowned at her, warning her not to say any more.

'Why can't I see me mum now?' Aimee asked, raising her tear-stained face. She looked so sad.

'Because your social worker has arranged for you to see your mum tonight,' I said. 'And we have to do what your social worker says.'

'Me mum didn't do what the social worker said,' Aimee said, oblivious to the fact that had she it would have probably helped them both.

'I know it's difficult to begin with,' Lucy said, going round to stand at the other side of Aimee. 'But it will get easier, I promise you. And doesn't your hair feel better already? No more itchy-coos.' Lucy lightly tickled the back of Aimee's neck, which made Aimee laugh.

'Good girl, let's wipe your eyes,' I said. I fetched a tissue from the box and went to wipe Aimee's eyes, but she snatched the tissue from my hand and wiped them herself. Children who have been badly neglected are often very self-sufficient; they've had to be in order to survive.

Chapter Seven
Should Have Done More

I called goodbye to Paula and Lucy, and Aimee and I left for school at 8.00 a.m. as planned. This would allow half an hour to drive through the traffic so that we arrived at school – on the opposite side of the town – well before the start of the school day at 8.50. This morning I wanted to go into school before the other children so that I could introduce myself at reception and, I hoped, meet Aimee's teacher or the member of staff responsible for looked-after children. All schools in England now have a designated teacher (DT) who is responsible in school for any child in care. The child is taught as normal in class but the designated teacher keeps an eye on the child, attends meetings connected with the child, and is the first point of contact for the social services, foster carer, child's natural parents and professionals connected with the case.

As I helped Aimee into the child seat in the rear of my car she asked why she had to sit in this seat and I explained it was so that the seatbelt could be fastened securely across her to keep her safe. She had no idea how to put on the seatbelt and I showed her what to do, how to fasten it, and then I checked it was secure. I closed the car door, which was child-locked and therefore couldn't be opened from the inside, and climbed into the driver's seat. I started the engine and reversed off the drive.

As I drove, Aimee asked many questions about the car and how I drove it, as though being in a car was a new experience for her, so that eventually I asked: 'Aimee, have you ever been in car before?'

'Only with the social workers yesterday,' she said. 'But it was dark and I couldn't see what was happening. Mum and Dad use buses.' Which was another indication of just how disadvantaged Aimee's background had been. For a child in a developed country to have reached the age of eight without regularly riding in a car was incredible; I'd never come across it before. Even if a child's parents didn't own a car (not uncommon for children in care) the child had usually been a passenger in the car of a relative or friend's parents; usually someone the child knew owned a car. But I believed Aimee when she said her first experience of riding in a car had been the day before, for her curiosity and questions about my car and driving it seemed to confirm this and were unstoppable: 'What's that blue light for?' 'Why's that number moving?' 'Why you holding that stick?' 'I can hear a clicking!' 'There's an orange light flashing!' And so on and so on.

Although I was happy to answer Aimee's questions, I soon began finding her constant dialogue very distracting while I was trying to drive through the traffic. A few minutes later I asked her to sit quietly and save her questions for when I'd stopped, as I needed to concentrate on driving. She did briefly and then began a running commentary on what was happening outside her window: 'There's a man with a big dog.' 'That girl's going to school.' 'I saw a bird, Cathy!' 'Look at that lady's hair! Cathy! Look! Look!'

'I can't look, love,' I said more firmly. 'I'm driving. I have to concentrate on driving or we'll have an accident. Let's listen to some music.' I switched on the CD player, which still contained a CD of popular children's songs and nursery rhymes from the last child I'd looked after. Aimee listened and then I said, 'I expect you know most of these nursery rhymes?'

'No,' Aimee replied.

So I guessed Aimee's parents hadn't recited, sung or read nursery rhymes to her as a child, although I thought she would have seen them in children's programmes on television.

'Your mum and dad had a television, didn't they?' I said, glancing in the rear-view mirror.

'Yeah, a great big telly,' Aimee said. 'A lot bigger than yours.'

'Didn't you watch children's programmes like *CBeebies*?'

'Na, they're silly,' Aimee sneered.

'What did you watch, then?' I asked, half anticipating her reply would include a list of adult programmes.

'Me and me mum watched *EastEnders* and horror films,' Aimee said. 'There was one about a woman who got chopped up with a big axe. First the man chopped off her arms and all blood spurted out of her shoulders, but she kept on walking 'cos she was a zombie. Then the man stabbed her in the face so her eyes came out, then he chopped off her head and it rolled on the floor and there was all blood spurting out of her neck and you could see her brain on the floor and –'

'All right, Aimee, that's enough, thank you. I understand,' I said, my stomach churning. Many parents don't realize the damage that can be done in allowing young impressionable minds to watch such horrific images.

'*EastEnders* is on tonight,' Aimee added, as I pulled up outside the school.

'So I believe,' I said. 'But we won't be watching it.'

'I will!' Aimee said.

'Not while you're living with me. That programme is for adults. You will be able to watch children's programmes.'

Aimee pulled a face. 'What about *Texas Chainsaw Massacre* or *Friday the 13th*? You got those DVDs?' she asked.

'No. But I have got *Mary Poppins*, *Toy Story*, *The Jungle Book*, *The Lion King* and many others that are nice.'

'Never heard of them,' Aimee scoffed.

'You will, love, I promise.'

The path that led to the school's main reception took us past the school playground.

Aimee pointed to children who'd arrived at school early and were playing. 'What are those kids doing?' she asked.

'Playing,' I said, feeling I was stating the obvious.

'They should be in their classrooms,' Aimee said.

'Not at this time. There's ten minutes before the bell goes for the start of school.'

Aimee frowned, puzzled, and we continued to the main door, where I pressed the security buzzer. The door was opened a minute later by a very pleasant lady, who smiled a warm hello. 'Good to see you, Aimee,' she said. 'Your hair looks nice.' Then to me: 'I'm the school secretary. Do come in.'

'I'm Cathy Glass, Aimee's foster carer,' I said. 'I expect you know she came to me yesterday evening?'

'Yes. How is she?'

'Doing very well,' I said, glancing at Aimee. 'I thought I'd come into school this morning to make sure you had my contact details, and also if possible to meet Aimee's teacher or the designated teacher.'

'Lynn Burrows is the designated teacher,' the school secretary said. 'She asked me to let her know when you came in. Take a seat and I'll fetch her.'

I thanked her and she disappeared through the double doors that led into the main body of the school while Aimee and I sat on the chairs in reception.

'She said my hair was nice,' Aimee said, running her fingers through her hair.

'It was worth all the pain and suffering, then?' I said lightly, with a smile.

'No it wasn't,' Aimee retorted. 'And you ain't doing it again!'

We'll see about that, I thought, but didn't say. I'd already discovered that Aimee automatically rejected or contradicted most of what I said – presumably as a result of there being no boundaries at home – so I let it go, although Aimee would be doing as she was told while she was with me.

'Look at you! Don't you look nice!' A lady said, coming through the double doors a few minutes later. 'I wouldn't have recognized you, Aimee.'

I thought she might, as Aimee was still wearing the clothes she'd arrived in, but Aimee smiled, pleased by the second compliment within a few minutes of arriving.

'Lynn Burrows, designated teacher,' the woman said as I stood. We shook hands. 'Pleased to meet you, Cathy.'

'And you.'

'Let's go to my office for a chat. I'm also the school's SENCO, so they give me an office of my own,' she added with a small laugh. The SENCO (Special Educational Needs Coordinator) helps children with special needs and also often assumes the role of designated teacher.

'Did you sleep well?' Lynn now asked Aimee as we made our way down the corridor.

Aimee didn't answer; she was more interested in the playground, which we could see through the windows on the right of the corridor. 'Mrs Burrows, can I go in the playground with the other kids?' she said, pausing at one of the windows. 'Please, I haven't been there before.'

'I don't see why not,' Lynn said as we drew to a halt. Then to me: 'It'll give us a chance to talk in private. I'll just ask the play-ground supervisor to keep an eye on Aimee.'

Aimee and Lynn went out of one of the doors that led into the playground while I waited in the corridor. The building was old, I guessed built in the 1950s, but my first impression was that it was a friendly and caring school. I liked Lynn, she was a warm and bubbly person, but I thought Aimee must have been mistaken when she'd said she hadn't been in the playground before, because, even allowing for her poor school attendance, she would have gone into the playground at break and lunch-time.

Lynn returned with a smile. 'She's happy enough and she looks so much better already. Amazing what a good wash can do.'

I smiled. 'I need to buy her a new school uniform,' I said, as I followed Lynn up a short flight of stairs and into her office.

'Aimee will love that. She's never had a school uniform before. We'll sort one out when we've finished talking. You know why Aimee was so keen to go in the playground just now?' Lynn said, as we settled in her small but comfortable office on the first floor.'

'No.'

'It's the first time she has had the opportunity of playing in the playground before the start of school, because she's never arrived on time before.'

I looked at Lynn amazed. 'Are you saying that in four years of schooling she never once arrived on time?'

'That's right. Aimee's attendance averaged about twenty per cent each year, and on the days she was in school she never arrived until the afternoon.'

'Good grief!' I said. 'That's probably the worst school attendance I've ever heard of for a young child. And it explains why Aimee was puzzled that the children were in the playground first thing. As we came in she remarked that the kids should be in their classrooms, not the playground.'

'That's because they were always in school doing their lessons when she arrived before.'

'But how did Aimee's parents get away with not sending her to school and always arriving late?' I asked.

'I wish I knew,' Lynn said with a sigh. 'We kept reporting it to the social services, together with all our other concerns: Aimee's poor hygiene and head lice, the rags she wore for clothes, the bruises we saw and also her bad behaviour, but nothing seemed to happen. A social worker must have visited the mother's flat, for we had some meetings here. But we never saw the same social worker twice and Aimee's mother, Susan, is very manipulative. She's had plenty of practice with all her older children being in care. She always had lots of excuses as to why Aimee wasn't in school, was always filthy dirty and didn't have a school uniform. Have you met Susan yet?'

'No. But I will tonight when I take Aimee to contact.'

'Be warned: she can be very aggressive. I guess it's all the drink and drugs. I've had her escorted off the school premises many times. Whenever I phoned the social services and raised my concerns she came in here looking for trouble. I have the feeling the social workers are frightened of her. She often has that nasty Rottweiler with her. God knows how much that dog must cost to feed!'

'I don't understand why Aimee wasn't brought into care sooner,' I said. 'The current social worker can't understand why she was left so long at home either.'

Lynn nodded. 'I blame myself for not doing more, although I'm not sure what else I could have done. When Aimee first came to the school and was in the nursery we tried to help Susan. We put in a lot of support – much of it with school funding – but it achieved nothing. She's followed the same path in the neglect of Aimee as she did with the other children. I've sat in case conferences and it's history repeating itself. It's so sad.'

'I'm sure you did all you could,' I said. 'At least Aimee is in care now.'

'Thank goodness.' Lynn sighed. 'Now, let me write down your contact details before I forget.'

Taking a pen and paper from her desk she wrote my name and then I gave her my address, telephone numbers – landline and mobile – and email address, all of which the social services should give the school but hardly ever do. 'You appreciate my details are confidential,' I said. 'Susan doesn't know where Aimee is staying.'

'Good. Less chance of her causing trouble,' Lynn said.

When she'd finished writing I said: 'Last night when I helped Aimee with her bath I noticed she had a lot of small bruises all over her, some of them quite new.'

Lynn nodded. 'We often saw bruises on Aimee and always reported them to the social services. Her mother said she was accident prone. Aimee was in school so little we couldn't monitor her properly, and she was never in school on the days she had PE – a classic sign a child may have something to hide and doesn't want to undress. When I asked Aimee how she got the bruises she said she fell over. I doubt it; they didn't appear to be in the right places for falling over.'

'No,' I agreed. 'I intend reporting what I've seen to the social worker when I speak to her later. I guess with so little schooling Aimee is a long way behind with her learning? Yesterday evening she struggled to do a simple puzzle that was suitable for a pre-school child.'

'Aimee is a long, long way behind in all her learning,' Lynn confirmed, shaking her head sadly. 'She can just about write her first name but that's the only word she can write; she can only count to ten, doesn't know her alphabet and has a sight vocabulary of three words.'

I gasped. 'She can only read three words at the age of eight?'

'Her mother says Aimee has learning difficulties but I don't think so. I'm sure it's a combination of virtually no schooling and not being able to concentrate when she has been in school. I've found before when children have difficult home lives that they spend all their time worrying about what's going on at home rather than concentrating on their lessons: if Mum is staying off the drink or drugs, if she's getting a beating from Dad, if they are going to receive another beating when they get home or if there's any food in the house. I'm sure now Aimee's in care she'll achieve great things.'

I nodded, although I hoped Lynn wasn't expecting too much too soon. Lynn had clearly had experience of children who'd been abused or neglected, but while I agreed with what she said about Aimee catching up I knew it would take time. Aimee would start to learn now she was safe and being looked after but she had eight years of neglect and goodness knew what else to overcome first, and they would leave emotional scars, many of them deep.

Lynn and I discussed Aimee's learning a while longer and I said I would do all I could to help her at home. Then Lynn's phone rang. 'Excuse me,' she said, picking up the handset. I couldn't hear what the person on the other end was saying, but it soon became clear it was bad news. Lynn's previous warm and positive expression vanished, and was replaced by concern and anxiety. 'I'll come straight down,' she said, standing. Then, replacing the receiver, she said to me: 'Stay here. Susan is in the school and is very angry. She's looking for trouble.'

Chapter Eight

Meeting Susan

As a foster carer I am used to meeting the parents of the child or children I am looking after and often it is very difficult. Parents are usually upset and angry that their child has been taken into care and it can be the foster carer who bears the brunt of their anger. Social workers and other professionals connected with the case can hide behind their offices and telephones, but the foster carer is an easy target; working by themselves they are on the front line, and they meet the parents regularly at contact as well as at any impromptu unsupervised meetings that may arise, as was happening now.

I sat alone in Lynn's office with the door firmly closed and listened for any sound of approaching footsteps. The bell signalling the start of school had sounded while Lynn and I had been talking, and after the initial clamour of children coming into the school, the building had fallen silent as lessons had begun. I wondered where Susan was in the building and hoped she'd been stopped before she got to Aimee, which would have been very upsetting for Aimee and probably for the rest of her class. The social services' policy of keeping foster children at the same school has its positive side as well as a downside. While the child is familiar with the school and feels secure there (it has often been the one safe place in a child's otherwise tumultuous life) the downside, as every foster carer knows, is that the school is usually known to the parents, so they know where and when they can find their child – and the foster carer, at the start and end of school.

I spent a very anxious fifteen minutes and then I heard footsteps coming down the corridor and towards the office. My heart beat louder as the door opened.

To my relief Lynn appeared. 'Dealt with,' she said matter-of-factly, and apparently unfazed. 'Susan has been escorted from the premises by our friendly neighbourhood police officer. She lost all control. Threatened a member of staff and threatened to snatch Aimee, so I had no choice but to call the police. Now, let's go downstairs so you can meet Aimee's TA (teaching assistant) and sort out Aimee's school uniform. They're in the quiet room – that's where we usually hide Aimee when her mother comes into school causing trouble.'

Marvelling at Lynn's composure, I stood and followed her out of her office, down the stairs and along the lower corridor. We passed the playground, which was empty now that all the children were in their classes. We turned left and stopped outside a door that was decorated with brightly coloured flowers and butterflies. Lynn knocked.

'Heather, it's Lynn with Cathy, Aimee's carer.'

The door opened from the inside and Aimee came out, clearly unaware that her mother had been in the building and causing trouble.

'Are you going to buy me a uniform now?' she asked, excited at the prospect.

'I am,' I said.

'Heather, this is Cathy.' Lynn said, introducing me to the lady who'd followed Aimee out of the quiet room. 'Cathy, meet Heather, Aimee's TA.'

'Pleased to meet you,' I said.

'And you.'

Meeting Susan

Heather was in her mid-forties and smartly dressed in a navy skirt and white blouse. I would be working closely with Aimee's teaching assistant as I consolidated at home what Aimee had learnt in school.

'When you've finished, Aimee can join her class,' Lynn said to Heather. Then to me: 'See you soon. Phone me if there's anything you're not sure of.' I thanked her and with a smile Lynn took her leave.

'Well! A whole new school uniform!' Heather said to Aimee. 'Aren't you a lucky girl!'

'No,' Aimee said bluntly. 'Me mum should have bought me a uniform ages ago. So I was like the other children.' Heather threw me a meaningful glance and I smiled. I liked Aimee for stating it how it was; she was, of course, right.

I followed Aimee and Heather along the lower corridor to a large walk-in cupboard situated behind the main office, which contained shelves stacked high with every size of school uniform. Reaching up, Heather selected packets of uniform she thought would fit Aimee. Aimee tried on a blouse, jumper and skirt and they fitted. We both told Aimee how smart she looked and Aimee grinned and looked really happy. I told Heather I wanted three complete sets of uniform, a PE kit and a book bag, which all the children had for taking their books to and from school. Heather took these from the shelves, and Aimee grinned again and stroked her uniform as though checking it was real.

I stooped and began gathering up Aimee's discarded ragged clothes from the floor.

'I'll get rid of those,' Heather offered.

'I have to keep them,' I explained. 'They belong to Aimee's mother and they will be offered back to her.' This is true for all possessions a child has when they come into care, including their worn-out clothes and broken toys, as legally they are the parents'.

Another Forgotten Child

I stuffed Aimee's old clothes into one of the plastic bags that the uniform had come out of and tucked it under my arm. 'I'll write your name in your uniform this evening,' I said to Aimee. 'So don't lose it during the day.'

'I won't,' Aimee said adamantly. And I knew she wouldn't, for I could see how precious her first school uniform was to her. It was a pity she still had to wear the worn-out trainers, but it would only be for one day.

'We'll buy your school shoes when we go shopping tomorrow,' I said.

Aimee nodded, again running her hands over her school uniform as though checking it was still there.

I confirmed with Heather that I would be in the school playground at the end of school; then I said goodbye. 'Have a good day,' I said to Aimee. I would have liked to give her a hug, but she was already going with Heather to join her class. I waited until they turned the corner and were out of sight, perhaps expecting Aimee to give a little wave, but she didn't. I then went to the office and paid for the school uniform.

I was vigilant when I left the school – on the lookout for Aimee's mother. Although I didn't know what Susan looked like, I felt sure that if she was still in the vicinity she'd make herself known to me, but I arrived at the car unaccosted and drove home.

The house was empty; Lucy was at work, Paula was at college and Adrian was away at university. He usually emailed a couple of times a week and I'd check my inbox later when I switched on the computer.

Ten minutes after I'd arrived home Jill phoned and wanted to know how Aimee's first night with us had gone and if she was in school.

'She slept well,' I said. 'No wet bed. She's in school and loving her new school uniform.'

Meeting Susan

'So she was all right about going to school?' Jill asked. 'The referral said Aimee refused to go to school.'

'From what Aimee's told me I'm guessing she didn't go to school because she couldn't wake her mother in time to take her. Also Aimee had no friends at school because of her poor hygiene and her bad behaviour. But Jill, last night when I helped Aimee with her bath I saw she's covered in small bruises. She says she fell over, which is possible, but the designated teacher I was with this morning told me they'd seen bruises on her before. Apparently they have been raising concerns about Aimee with the social services since she was in nursery – over four years ago. They are upset that Aimee wasn't taken into care sooner.'

'Join the queue,' Jill said, meaning that everyone connected with Aimee's case was upset that Aimee hadn't been taken into care sooner. 'I'll speak to the social worker about the bruises. And Aimee's behaviour?' Jill asked. 'Is it manageable? She sounded like a real demon in the referral.'

'Aimee is used to having her own way and needs boundaries and routine,' I said. 'She's obviously got a lot of anger in her, which will have to come out. We'll see; it's early days yet.'

We discussed Aimee's first night for a while longer and then Jill made an appointment to visit Aimee and me the following Tuesday after school. 'And if you need any help or advice over the weekend you know to phone our out-of-hours number,' Jill finished.

'Yes, I will.'

I said goodbye to Jill and then half an hour later Kristen telephoned. Jill had spoken to her and I now told Kristen more or less what I'd told Jill.

'When I speak to Susan later today I'll ask her about the bruises,' Kristen said. 'I suppose it's possible Aimee got them from falling over. Let me give you the details of the arrangements for contact.'

I reached for a pen and paper. 'Go ahead,' I said.

'Contact is just with Mum at present,' Kristen began. 'She doesn't live with Aimee's father and they aren't speaking. He will need to apply for contact separately, which he hasn't done yet. We'll consider his application if and when it arises. As you know, contact with Aimee's mother is on Monday, Wednesday and Friday. It will start at three forty-five, which should give you enough time to collect Aimee from school and drive to the family centre.'

'Yes, it should,' I said. 'School finishes at three fifteen.'

'Good. Contact will end at five thirty. Telephone contact will take place on those nights Aimee doesn't see her mother: Tuesday, Thursday and the weekend. You will need to phone Susan's mobile number, as she doesn't have a landline, beginning tomorrow, Saturday. Susan's number should be in the essential information forms but I'll give it you again.' I wrote down the mobile number Kristen now gave me and read it back to her. 'That's correct. I suggest you make the call about six p.m. or soon after. I will be telling Susan your phone will be on speaker and you will be listening to and monitoring the call. Susan won't be happy but she'll have to accept it if she wants phone contact.'

'All right.' I knew it was a legal requirement to tell a parent if the phone call was being monitored.

'I think that's all for now,' Kristen said, winding up the conversation. 'I'll be on the case for another week and then I'll be passing it to the children in care team. Not sure which social worker will be taking over yet. Well, good luck when you meet Susan at contact tonight. A contact supervisor will be on hand if there's a problem. Have a good weekend.'

'And you.'

* * *

Meeting Susan

That Friday afternoon I collected Aimee from school and she came out in a positive frame of mind, saying she liked school, and then talked non-stop about school as I drove to the family centre. Eventually I had to ask her to save her news until we arrived at the centre, as it was difficult for me to concentrate on driving. But as we pulled up outside the family centre, before Aimee got the chance to tell me more of her news her attention was distracted.

'There's Mum!' Aimee yelled. 'Oh my god, she's angry!'

I cut the engine and looked over to the stick-thin woman with unkempt frizzy hair who'd come out of the main door and was now rushing down the path towards us. Her face was contorted with anger and her mouth open and closed with screamed obscenities. I pressed the interior locking system on the car.

'Someone's in for it,' Aimee yelled, and I had the feeling that someone might be me.

Susan arrived at my car, tried the door handle and, finding it locked, banged on the roof. At the same time her face appeared outside my window as she shouted: 'What the fuck do you think you're doing telling that bleeding social worker I've been beating my girl? You wait till I get hold of you. I'll show you what beating is! I'll teach you to make up lies about me.' So I guessed Kristen had told Susan about the bruises I'd seen on Aimee and possibly asked her how she got them, with the implied suggestion that Susan might be responsible.

I looked at the face distorted by rage just outside my window. Susan's skin was deathly white and there was no flesh on her face, which accentuated her nose, cheekbones and chin, making them jut out like those of a witch, not helped by a wart on the side of her nose. She appeared to have no back teeth and a few broken teeth at the front, which hollowed her cheeks even more and caused her to hiss and spit as she spoke.

'Mum!' Aimee shouted, now banging on her side window and compounding the noise. 'Shut up! Do you hear? Stop screaming. You're doing my bleeding head in!'

Susan took no notice of her daughter and continued to bang on the roof and shout obscenities at my window. I knew from the essential information forms that she was forty-four but she could have been four hundred, so ravaged and lined was her face. I thought if ever there was an image that portrayed the harm drug abuse can do it was her face.

I was about to start the car and drive away when a contact supervisor appeared from the centre.

'Susan!' she shouted at the top of her voice. 'Stop that now or there'll be no contact tonight!'

'Do you hear that, Mum!' Aimee yelled from the back seat. 'Shut the fuck up or you won't be seeing me!'

'Aimee, don't swear,' I instinctively cautioned.

'What the fuck are you going to do about it?' Aimee shouted at me. 'Let me out of this bleeding car now! I want to see me mum!'

'You've just lost ten minutes' television time for swearing,' I said, feeling I needed to keep some form of control. I sounded calm, although I felt far from it; I felt threatened and my heart was racing.

Aimee looked slightly surprised that she'd just lost television time, and didn't answer me back as I'd expected. A second female contact supervisor appeared from the centre and ran down the path to join the first. Together they approached Susan.

Susan's face disappeared from the window and the banging on the car roof stopped as she turned to shout at them: 'She' – meaning me – 'told the bleeding social worker I've been beating me kid,' Susan screamed. 'I ain't done nothing of the sort.'

Clearly that wasn't what I'd told Kristen. I'd reported the bruises I'd seen on Aimee as I was supposed to. I assumed that either Kristen had handled the situation very badly when she'd asked Susan about the bruises – implicitly accusing her – or Susan had gone on the defensive and had heard criticism where there was none.

'Calm down and come into the centre,' one of the contact supervisors said to Susan. 'Then you will be able to see Aimee. Otherwise we'll have to tell Cathy to take Aimee home and contact will be cancelled for tonight.'

'Ain't going home with you!' Aimee cried, kicking the back of the seat but now close to tears. 'I want me mum. Why did you tell the social worker my mum hit me? She didn't.'

I released my seatbelt and turned to look at Aimee. She was angry but also looked very sad and confused. I felt for her, I really did. I reached out to hold her hand and offer some reassurance but she snatched it away. 'Aimee, I didn't tell Kristen your mum hit you,' I said. 'I told her that when you were in the bath I noticed bruises on you which you said had been caused by falling over.'

Aimee shrugged but accepted what I'd said. 'Mum's always getting it wrong and then flying off on one,' she said. So I guessed Aimee was used to her mother's volatile temper – not that it made it any easier. Loss of control is always frightening to witness, especially for a young child.

The contact supervisor continued to talk to Susan, reassuring her that she would see Aimee in the centre as soon as she was calm. After about five minutes Susan stopped shouting, although I could see she remained very twitchy and agitated; how much of that was her normal disposition I didn't know. One of the contact supervisors then went with Susan into the centre while the other came round to my car door. I released the central locking system and opened the door.

'Give us a couple of minutes to get Susan a glass of water,' she said. 'And then bring Aimee in.'

'I want to see me mum now!' Aimee demanded from the back seat.

'We'll do what the supervisor says,' I said.

'I want to see me mum now,' Aimee said again. Then, without the central locking system on, Aimee flung open her car door, jumped out, and rushed up the path to the family centre, before I had a chance to stop her.

'Let her go,' the supervisor said. 'I'll see to her.'

'Are you sure?' I asked, feeling Aimee was my responsibility.

'Yes, you go home and then come back to collect Aimee at the arranged time. We've got your mobile number if we need you, but hopefully Susan will calm down now.'

'All right, if you're sure,' I said.

I watched as the supervisor walked up the path and joined Aimee at the main door of the centre. She said something to Aimee. Aimee nodded and then the supervisor buzzed and the door opened. They disappeared inside, and I returned to my car and then sat for a moment staring after them. Little wonder Aimee's behaviour was bad, I thought, with Susan as her role model. I'd never seen a parent so angry and out of control. I would meet Susan later when I collected Aimee at the end of contact, when I hoped to be able to introduce myself properly, and even talk to her. It's always better for a foster child if the child can see their parent(s) working together with the foster carer: they settle more easily and are less anxious. But my hope of talking to Susan was short-lived.

Chapter Nine
'He's Horrible'

When I returned, the receptionist at the family centre told me which room Aimee was in and that I should go straight through and collect her, which was normal practice at the end of contact. I went down the corridor and knocked on the door of the contact room before slowly opening it.

Each of the six contact rooms at the centre is furnished like a sitting room with a sofa, table and chairs, carpet and curtains, and shelves stacked with books, puzzles and games. Aimee was sitting on the sofa next to her mother, eating a bag of crisps, while the contact supervisor sat at the table making notes about the contact. I smiled as I entered the room and said a quiet hello. I then stood unobtrusively to one side, preparing to wait while Aimee finished her crisps and said goodbye to her mother. But as soon as Susan saw me she jumped up and, with her eyes blazing and her fist raised, rushed towards me.

'Get the fuck out of here!' she yelled in my face. 'This is my time with my daughter. Get out!'

I quickly backed out of the room as the supervisor looked over but made no attempt to intervene. The door slammed shut behind me and, shaken, I returned along the corridor and to reception. 'I'll wait here for Aimee,' I told the receptionist. 'Susan is very angry.'

'Does the contact supervisor know you're waiting here?' she asked, still inputting into her computer.

'I should think so,' I said. 'It was pretty obvious I couldn't collect Aimee from the room.'

She nodded. I sat in one of the chairs in reception and my pulse began to settle. I hate aggression; I believe situations should be discussed rationally, although I could appreciate how upset and angry Susan must be, with the last of her six children now having been taken into care. I hoped that if she didn't calm down sufficiently to talk to me rationally then the contact supervisor would tell her to wait in the contact room while she brought Aimee to me. I didn't want another scene in front of Aimee and also if I'm honest Susan's temper scared me.

Five minutes later Aimee appeared, holding her mother's hand, with the supervisor following a couple of steps behind. Susan's face was set and pinched, and before she opened her mouth I knew she was looking for trouble. The supervisor was young and I guessed inexperienced. Contact supervisors vary enormously in the competency with which they do their job.

'I'll report you!' Susan shouted, advancing along the corridor towards me. I stood. 'If my daughter wants biscuits you give them to her. Do you hear? Do as Aimee tells you or you'll have me and her father to answer to.'

I looked at the supervisor to see if she was going to intervene but she didn't. She just stood to one side, watching, which gave Susan permission to continue. Aimee was smirking, clearly revelling in her mother's anger towards me.

'What do you think you're doing forcing her to have a bath and hair wash?' Susan continued angrily. 'No one washes my girl except me. Keep your bleeding hands off her! I say when she needs washing, not you!' It crossed my mind that clearly Susan hadn't regularly washed Aimee; otherwise she wouldn't have arrived in the state she had.

'And where are her clothes, the ones I sent her in?' Susan now demanded. 'Have you stolen them? I'll report you to the police. They're her clothes and she wants them. You give them back.'

'They're at home,' I said. I didn't have a chance to say anything further, for Susan had moved on to her next complaint. As she spoke her chin jutted out, just as Aimee's did when she was angry.

'Don't you dare force my girl to sit at a table and use a knife and fork,' she yelled. 'She don't sit at the table and she can't use a fork.' As with Susan's other complaints she had clearly been told this by Aimee, and I was saddened that Aimee appeared to have spent most of contact complaining to her mother about me and was now basking in the result. 'And what did you put on her toast?' Susan now demanded. 'She said it was disgusting.'

I was about to say butter when the centre's manger, roused from her office by the noise of Susan shouting, appeared.

'Susan,' she said, 'calm down and we'll go somewhere quiet to talk in private.' Then to me: 'Have you got a minute to discuss Susan's grievances?'

My first reaction was to say that Susan's grievances were so ludicrous that they didn't merit discussion but I knew that wasn't the right answer. 'Yes,' I said. 'If it will help.'

'If you think I'm going to sit in a room with her,' Susan sneered, jabbing a finger in my direction, 'forget it.'

Fine, I thought, but didn't say.

The centre manager, used to dealing with upset and angry parents, took this in her stride and produced plan B. 'All right, Susan,' she said calmly. 'Say goodbye to Aimee and then we' – by which she meant Susan, the manager and contact supervisor – 'can go into my office and discuss what's wrong.'

This seemed to pacify Susan a little and with a brief goodbye to Aimee she turned to the manager.

'Come on, let's go home and get some dinner,' I said gently to Aimee.

'No!' Aimee said in a good imitation of her mother. 'I ain't going with you. I'm staying with me mum.'

'See!' Susan said, her temper flaring again. 'My girl don't want to go with that woman. Who can blame her, forcing her to wash her hair and sit at the table.' It was almost laughable, except it wasn't.

'Why don't you want to go with Cathy?' the supervisor now asked, bending down towards Aimee and inviting further complaints about me.

'She's horrible,' Aimee said, eyeing her mother. 'I'm not allowed to do what I want at her house.'

'There!' Susan said. 'Told you!'

'What do you mean, you're not allowed to do what you want?' the supervisor persisted.

'I'm not allowed to eat biscuits,' Aimee said. 'And she makes me eat horrible food and forces me head under the tap.'

'There!' Susan said again triumphantly.

The manager and the contact supervisor looked at me for an explanation and I hid my upset and anger. I was doing my best for Aimee, as I did for all the children I looked after, yet I was being blamed and ridiculed. Like the victim of a kangaroo court, I felt I'd been put on trial and I knew the only person who was going to defend me was me.

'Aimee ate a good meal last night,' I said positively, addressing Susan, the manager and supervisor. 'As usual we ate at the table and I helped her use a knife and fork. Then I helped her with her bath, and this morning I washed her hair under the shower. Now, if there's anything else you wish to discuss I'd prefer it if it was done in private with the social worker and my support worker present, and away from Aimee.' For I could see that Aimee, far from being uncomfortable, was glorying in the disagreement.

'He's Horrible'

The manager looked slightly taken aback by my closing statement, but as an experienced foster carer I knew that what I'd suggested was correct procedure. I felt sorry for any new carer put in the same position.

'That seems reasonable,' the manager said. 'Susan, say goodbye to Aimee, and then we'll go into my office and I'll write down what you want to say. I'll send a copy to your social worker and he can arrange a meeting.'

Lured by the prospect of having her grievances committed to paper Susan called goodbye to Aimee and trotted off with the manager and contact supervisor. Aimee, with her audience now gone, looked deflated. She also looked at me, clearly wondering what I was going to say and if I would tell her off.

'Come on,' I said gently, offering her my hand. 'Let's go home and get some dinner.' Aimee looked slightly relieved, ignored my hand but followed me out of reception and into the car park, where I opened the car door and she climbed in.

'What's for dinner?' she asked as I got in and started the engine.

'Spaghetti bolognaise,' I said. 'Most children like that.'

'I like it,' she said quietly.

I glanced at Aimee in the rear-view mirror. She looked sad and lost now her bravado had gone, and my heart went out to her. How strange and vulnerable she must feel, I thought: she had been loyal to her mother's ways for eight years and now she was suddenly expected to conform to a whole new way of life with very different standards and expectations. It wasn't her fault she'd complained to her mother about me; she'd only told her mother what she thought she wanted to hear. I knew that with Susan's history of battling with the social services over her older children for twenty-five years she was going to be difficult to work with, especially if Aimee continued to work against me.

'Aimee,' I said gently, as I drove, 'I know it's difficult for you coming into care and having to leave your mother and live with me. But making up stories about me won't help. It will just upset your mother and make her angry.'

'It will help,' Aimee said quietly. 'Mum's older kids got moved from their foster carers when Mum complained, and that will happen to me.'

'I doubt it,' I said. 'I've never had a child move from me before as a result of complaints, and I've looked after lots of children.'

'How many?' Aimee asked.

'Over a hundred.'

Aimee went quiet for a moment and then asked reasonably, 'Where are all those kids now?'

'Some children returned to live with their parents. Some went to live with relatives, and some were found new mummies and daddies and were adopted.'

'I'm going to live with my mum as soon as she's bought me a bed,' Aimee stated categorically. 'That's what she has to do.'

'Who told you that if your mother bought a bed you could go home?' I asked.

'Mum,' Aimee said.

It's always difficult if a child comes into care with preconceived notions of when and what criteria need to be met to allow them to return home. The day comes and goes, or the goal is obtained, and their frustration mounts as they stay in care and nothing appears to be happening. This is especially true for a child like Aimee, who on the balance of probability wouldn't be returned home by the judge.

I glanced at Aimee in the rear-view mirror. 'Aimee,' I said carefully, 'we don't yet know what the judge will decide. But it's not just about the bed. Did your social worker explain to you about the judge?'

'Yes.' Aimee nodded. 'She said he was like a wise owl. He reads all the reports from all the professionals and then decides what is best for me.' Well done, Kristen, I thought.

'That's right, but it will take a long time for the judge to read all those reports and decide what is best for you. Maybe even a year. The judge will have to be certain the right decision is made because you are very important. During the time he is deciding I will look after you. But we'll have a fun time. It's November now, so Christmas isn't far away. I love Christmas. Do you?'

Aimee folded her arms over her chest and scowled. 'I don't like Christmas. Last Christmas was horrible. I had to stay at Craig's house.'

'Oh yes? Who's Craig?' I asked, again glancing in the mirror. There'd been no mention of Craig in the referral.

'He's one of Mum's friends,' Aimee said. 'Mum has a lot of men friends. Some are nice but Craig's not.'

When a child tells me she doesn't like a person I try to find out more. It may be nothing, but sadly fostering has taught me that a story of abuse often lies behind a chance remark or throw-away comment like the one Aimee had just made.

'Why don't you like Craig?' I now asked.

'Me and Mum stayed with him at Christmas and he gave us corned beef for dinner. I didn't like it. He shouted at me really loud. He said I was a rude little bitch. Then he grabbed me by the throat and belted me all over with his fist. It hurt and I had lots of bruises for ages. It wasn't a good Christmas.'

How quickly one's world can change! A moment before I'd been thinking of the spaghetti bolognaise we were going to have for dinner, and Christmas; now I was hearing Aimee disclose abuse. I'd just pulled into the top of my road and I didn't say anything further until I'd parked outside the house, for I needed to give Aimee my full attention. I released my seatbelt and turned in my seat to face her.

'It was very wrong of Craig to hit you. Have you told anyone – your social worker or teacher?'

'No. Mum said I mustn't. She said if I told anyone I'd be taken into care. I didn't tell, so how did the judge know?'

'Aimee, you were right to tell me,' I said. 'You were brought into foster care for many reasons, not only that Craig hit you.' In fact, as far as I was aware Craig's assault hadn't been part of the case for bringing Aimee into care, I assumed because no one knew about it. While the social services hadn't ruled out the possibility that Aimee had been abused, she'd been brought into care for severe neglect; there'd been no firm evidence of abuse, until now. I needed to find out as much as I could, so that I could inform the social worker the following day.

We were still in the car and I could see Aimee's face by the light of the street lamp. 'Aimee,' I said. 'Last Christmas was a long time ago – eleven months. Have you seen Craig since?'

Aimee nodded. 'We see him all the time. Mum and me stay at his place and he stays at our place. He's horrible. His cat had kittens and he strangled them all.'

'What? He did that?' I asked, confused and disturbed. The referral had stated that Aimee had committed that shocking act of cruelty.

'Yes. There were six kittens,' Aimee said. 'They were only a few days old and their eyes were closed. They were in the shed at the bottom of his garden. He said he wanted to show me something nice and he took me into the shed. I stroked the kittens and then he picked them up and pulled back their necks. I heard a click and they went all floppy. He said they were dead and he threw them in the dustbin. I cried. It was horrible.'

'That's dreadful,' I said. 'Absolutely horrible. Where was your mother while Craig was doing this?'

'In the house, in bed asleep. She never wakes up until the afternoon.' Which I knew from the social services to be true.

'This was at Craig's house?' I clarified.

'Yes.'

From Aimee's description it sounded as though Craig had broken the kittens' necks, not strangled them, but that wasn't the point. Susan had told the social services that it had been Aimee who'd killed the kittens; there'd been no mention of Craig. Was Aimee blaming Craig to hide her own evil act, perhaps even making up the very existence of Craig in a bid to pass on responsibility? I didn't know, but her next comment convinced me she was telling the truth.

'You know all those bruises you saw on me in the bath?' Aimee said.

'Yes.'

'Craig did them.'

Chapter Ten
Poor Role Models

We stayed in the car. I didn't want to go inside and risk breaking the rapport that had formed in the close and intimate atmosphere of the car. Aimee was disclosing abuse and it was important I learnt all I could.

'When did Craig make those bruises?' I asked, still turned in my seat and watching her carefully.

'Last weekend. We always go to his house at the weekend. He stays with us during the week and we go there at weekends.' So why weren't the social services aware of Craig's existence, I wondered? There'd been no mention of him in the referral and there should have been, as clearly he'd played a part in Aimee's life.

'How long have you and your mother known Craig?' I asked. 'Do you know?'

'A long time. Two Christmases,' she said. It was November now, so that would make nearly two years at least, maybe longer.

'Aimee, can you tell me how you got those bruises?'

She nodded. 'He' – by which she meant Craig – 'said I was a rude bitch and I shouldn't answer him back. He said I needed to be taught a lesson and apologize. So he grabbed a lump of my flesh, like this.' Aimee demonstrated by grabbing her underarm and pinching it. 'Then he squeezes really hard until I scream and say I'm sorry. Then he lets go.'

I looked at Aimee and my eyes welled. Although as a foster carer I'd heard many accounts of cruelty to children it never became any easier to hear. The bastard, I thought, but didn't say. Aimee was calm and I needed to stay calm and objective too.

'And this happened last weekend?' I clarified.

'Yes, but he does it all the time. Mum says I'm always covered in his fingerprints. That's one of the reasons I don't go to school.'

It was then I realized, with a shudder, what had struck me as odd about the bruises: they were all the same size and shape – round and the size of a small coin. I now realized they were finger- and thumbprints. They were all over her body, including her bottom, the tops of her thighs and across her lower stomach, close to her private parts. I knew Aimee's abuse was now a matter for the police and that once I'd told the social worker she'd call child protection; I therefore had to be careful that I didn't ask her 'leading questions', which could contaminate her evidence. But I also knew from experience that children often disclose when they feel safe and comfortable with a foster carer.

'Aimee, love,' I said, 'you've done very well telling me this, but why didn't you tell me last night when I asked you about the bruises? You said you'd fallen in the playground.' I knew this would be one of the first questions the social worker would ask: why had Aimee changed her mind? Was she making up the story about Craig?

Aimee's reply was simple and plausible: 'I feel safe with you,' she said. 'Last night I thought Craig might come to your house and hurt me. But at contact Mum said she didn't know where you live, and the social worker won't be telling her. So I thought if she doesn't know then she can't tell Craig.'

'I understand, love.' I smiled. 'And yes, you are safe with me. On Monday morning I'll phone your social worker and tell her what you have told me, and she will decide what to do for the best. It's possible you will have to speak to a police lady, but don't worry: I'll explain all about it nearer the time.' I knew there was no point in phoning the out-of-hours duty social worker now (Friday evening) or over the weekend, because Aimee was in care and therefore removed from her abuser she wasn't at risk from further harm, so it wouldn't be classified as an emergency. I would be told to wait until Monday and speak to her social worker. That was normal practice. However, Aimee's bruises could have faded by Monday, so my evidence would be crucial. As soon as I got the chance during the evening, I'd write up my log notes detailing what Aimee had told me.

'Will Craig be punished?' Aimee asked, standing in the well of the seat and peering at me. 'Will he have to say sorry like he made me say sorry to him?'

'I hope so, love. He certainly should do.'

'Will my mum have to say sorry too?' Aimee asked.

'For what?'

'For letting Craig hurt me. I think she should have stopped him, don't you?'

I swallowed hard. 'Yes, love. I do. Hopefully she'll say sorry too.'

That evening as I was seeing Aimee into bed she asked if she could watch some television. Although it was her bedtime we didn't have to get up for school in the morning, so I said she could as she'd been good.

Aimee looked at me sheepishly. 'Are you sure?'

'Yes, of course. Why do you ask?'

'You said I'd lost ten minutes' television time for swearing in the car at contact.'

With all that had happened in the interim I'd forgotten, but Aimee had remembered and reminded me, which was a good example of how much children appreciate boundaries – they're safe and reassuring. I didn't feel like punishing Aimee, given all that she'd told me about Craig, yet I knew I couldn't simply let her off either – it would have undermined my authority.

Quick thinking from years of fostering saved me: 'You've earned back your lost television time,' I said, 'because you sat at the table and ate your dinner nicely.'

Aimee grinned. 'That's good.' And just for a moment I thought she was going to reach out and hug me, but the moment passed.

Saturday morning saw no sign of the vulnerable and engaging child I'd established a rapport with the evening before. From the moment Aimee got out of bed she was rude, confrontational and verbally aggressive.

It began with the clothes I'd taken from my emergency supply and laid on her bed. She didn't want to wear them; she wanted to wear her school uniform – indeed she demanded it. I explained that she'd only wear these clothes until we'd been shopping and bought her new clothes, which we would do that morning, and that her school uniform had to be kept for school. But Aimee persisted in her demands, folding her arms across her chest defiantly and refusing to dress. As a compromise I suggested she might like to choose her own clothes from the ottoman in my bedroom and eventually she agreed to do so, stomping off round the landing with giant steps that made the floor shudder, so that I reminded her to tread more quietly.

'Won't!' Aimee shouted.

The skirt and top she chose from my emergency supply were too small but rather than risk further confrontation over something relatively minor, I decided they'd do for now. Then Aimee didn't want to brush her hair and she refused to allow me to brush it either.

'We'll do it after breakfast, then,' I said, hoping she'd be in a better humour after she'd eaten.

Downstairs she demanded biscuits for breakfast, adding: 'If you don't give me biscuits I'll tell me mum!'

'You can have a biscuit later with a drink of milk,' I said, ignoring the threat. 'For breakfast you have a choice of cereal, toast or egg.'

'Nothing!' she growled, arms folded and glaring at me, which I ignored. Then a few minutes later: 'Cereal.'

'Good. Would you like cornflakes, wheat flakes, Rice Krispies or porridge?' I asked politely.

'Give me porridge,' Aimee demanded rudely.

'Could I have porridge, please,' I corrected, while taking the packet from the cupboard.

'Porridge!' she said gruffly, and plonked herself at the table, where she began kicking one of the chairs.

'Don't kick the chair, please,' I said. 'You'll damage it.'

'Can if I want to,' Aimee said, her eyes blazing defiantly.

'If you continue to kick the chair you'll lose your television time,' I said evenly.

'Hate you,' Aimee said, but the kicking stopped.

Aimee had every right to be angry, having been badly neglected and abused, and an abused child's anger isn't selective – indeed they are often most angry with those they feel safe with and who they know won't retaliate and hit them.

Ignoring Aimee's ill humour as best I could, I finished making her porridge and placed the bowl with a spoon in front of her.

'Yuck,' she said, screwing up her face. 'I ain't eating that muck.'

'Don't be rude,' I said. 'It's the porridge you asked for. Now eat up and then we can go shopping to buy your new clothes.'

Aimee sat at the table scowling for a while longer while I concentrated on eating my own cereal; then she finally picked up her spoon and began eating. A few minutes later her bowl was clear. 'That was nice,' she said quite pleasantly, smacking her lips. 'I'll have porridge again tomorrow.'

'Good. It's nice to try new things,' I said. 'Now let's go upstairs and clean your teeth and brush your hair.'

'Later,' Aimee said.

'We need to do it now, so we can go shopping,' I said.

'I'll do it after shopping,' Aimee said, used to having her own way.

I didn't say anything but busied myself in the kitchen. Aimee watched me for a while and then asked, 'I thought you said we were going shopping?'

I looked at her surprised. 'I did, love. I said we'd go shopping just as soon as you'd cleaned your teeth and brushed your hair.' I continued with what I was doing as though Aimee's refusal was of no consequence and it didn't matter if we went shopping or not. Having met Susan, I guessed Aimee and her mother had thrived on the drama of confrontation and I wasn't going to be drawn down that path. Aimee needed to learn to do as the adult looking after her asked, as it was for her own good.

Aimee watched me for a while longer and then muttered, just loud enough for me to hear, 'Come on, then, I'll do it. You always get your own way.'

'That's because as an adult I usually know what's best for you,' I said with a cheerful smile.

'My mum don't,' Aimee said, following me out of the kitchen. Which was doubtless the truth.

Upstairs Aimee brushed her teeth nicely and then let me help her brush her hair. Once we were ready we left Paula and Lucy in bed for a Saturday morning lie-in, and I drove into town.

Buying clothes was a whole new experience for Aimee, and one that she had to learn. I'd parked the car in the multi-storey and we went down the stairs and into the high street.

'I want to go in that shop,' Aimee said, drawing me to a halt outside a charity shop.

'Why? It sells second-hand clothes,' I said. 'I'm going to buy you new clothes.'

'Oh,' Aimee said, dumbfounded. 'Mum and me always go in the charity shops. They don't put security tags on their stuff so the alarm won't go off.'

'You mean you stole things from the charity shops?' I said. I'd fostered children before who'd stolen but not from charity shops.

'It's not stealing,' Aimee said. 'The stuff was for me.'

'It's stealing,' I said. 'It doesn't matter who it's for. If you take something from a shop without paying for it, it's stealing, and it's wrong.'

Aimee gave a dismissive shrug. 'Say what you want but I believe my mum and dad and they say it's OK to take stuff for me. How else am I supposed to get me things?'

'We pay for them,' I said, drawing Aimee along the pavement and away from the charity shop. 'People work hard and get paid money which they use to buy the things they need.'

'My dad don't,' Aimee said. 'He can do as he likes.'

'No one can do exactly as they like,' I said, and continued into the clothes shop.

It wasn't Aimee's fault she'd had such bad role models as parents; she was only repeating what she'd been brought up to believe, and it would take a long time for her to change. In most big towns and cities, there exists a parallel society; drug-fuelled and feral in its existence, such societies defy the normal rules of a civilized society. Many of the children who come into care come from these backgrounds. It's a different world but the only one Aimee had known.

Once inside the shop, Aimee entered into the spirit of choosing and trying on new clothes, although she told me more than once that she didn't see the point in buying the clothes when they could easily be taken. She was an expert on security tags, pointing out how, and the ease with which, a security tag could be removed. In fact her expertise dominated her choice of clothes. 'We don't want that one,' she would say, returning an item to the rail. 'The tag's in the arm and the hole will show when you pull it off. This skirt's OK – the tag's on the label. Have you got scissors in your bag so we can cut it off in the changing rooms?' I dreaded to think what other shoppers were making of Aimee's comments, and the sales assistants who were dotted around the store.

Eventually, nearly three hours later, we had all the items Aimee needed, including a new winter coat, casual clothes for weekends, trainers, school shoes, pyjamas, vests, pants, socks, dressing gown and slippers. We were laden down with bags but on the way back to the car Aimee asked, disappointed: 'Is that it? Aren't you getting stuff for you? Mum always did.'

'That's sweet of you, dear,' I said, touched. 'But I don't need anything at present, and I've spent enough for this week.'

'If you've run out of money we could go to the charity shop and take it,' Aimee suggested.

'No,' I said firmly. 'I will save up for what I need.'

'OK,' Aimee said. 'I thought you might say that so I got you this.' Thrusting her hand into her jacket pocket she took out a necklace, still on its card, and pushed it at me.

I looked at it, horrified, and stopped dead in the middle of the pavement. There was no need to ask where the necklace had come from: it still had the shop's price tag affixed. 'After everything I've said about stealing, Aimee!' I exclaimed. 'And you've taken this!' I'd no idea how or when she'd slipped it into her pocket. She was clearly an expert on thieving.

'Stay cool. It's not for me, it's a present for you,' Aimee said, as though this justified it. 'Mum and me always got each other a present when we went shopping.'

'By stealing it! Aimee, you didn't pay for this,' I began. 'Therefore you stole it. It doesn't matter who it is for. We don't steal, as I've told you over and over again this morning. Now, we're going to take the necklace back to the shop, and you're not to do it again. Understand?'

Aimee shrugged. Touching her arm to indicate follow me, I turned and led the way back to the shop. Inside my first inclination was to return the necklace to one of the cashiers at the checkout, but the shop was very busy and there was a long queue at the tills. I didn't want to wait in the queue; I wanted to get this over and done with as quickly as possible. Also I didn't want to shame Aimee in front of other shoppers – she was, after all, an eight-year-old girl who didn't know any better and I didn't want to humiliate her; but neither could we keep the necklace. I spotted a young sales assistant wandering aimlessly between the lines of garments without a lot to do and I went up to her. Aimee followed, not meekly or repentant, but interested in what I was going to say.

'Excuse me,' I said to the assistant. 'I'm afraid my daughter has accidentally taken this without paying for it.' I showed her the necklace. 'Can you return it to the display, please? She's very sorry and promises it won't happen again.' I quickly dropped the necklace into the assistant's hand, turned and left the store, thinking it would be a long while before I returned.

'What a waste!' Aimee said outside. 'I could have given it to me mum.'

I sighed. 'Aimee, while you are with me you won't be taking anything without paying for it. I shall give you pocket money, if you're good, so you can save up and buy things, not steal them.'

'Cool,' Aimee said. 'Pocket money.' Then she looked at me thoughtfully. 'In that shop you said I was your daughter. Why?'

'It was easier than giving an explanation as to who you were.'

'OK,' she said, shrugging. 'Just as long as you know you ain't me mum. Although I guess it would have been better for me if you had been.'

Chapter Eleven
The Phone Call

Once home we had lunch and then Aimee helped me hang and fold her new clothes into the drawers and wardrobe in her bedroom. I could see from the expression on her face that she was pleased with all her new things, but she didn't tell me and she wasn't grateful. I didn't expect her to be. I thought she probably resented the fact that I had provided for her when her parents had not; in her eyes this would have underlined their failure to look after her, and her loyalty to her parents would have dominated.

Saturday afternoon passed reasonably amicably with only a few minor scenes, as a result of my refusal to allow Aimee to watch television all afternoon and not give in to her constant demand for biscuits. She had two chocolate biscuits after her lunch but she was used to eating the whole packet in one go (for lunch), so two were not enough to satisfy her craving for sugar. I explained again to Aimee why too many sweet things were bad for us but her response was: 'Don't care!' or 'I'll tell me mum.' She appeared to be addicted to sugar and this was something else I would be mentioning to the paediatrician when Aimee had a medical.

Instead of letting her watch television for hours I provided Aimee with a steady selection of games and puzzles. I played some board games with her but I encouraged her to do the very simple puzzles for herself. She wasn't familiar with any of the games or puzzles that one would expect a child of her age to be, so I showed her what to do, and I was pleased when she understood relatively quickly.

'Did you have any games or toys at home?' I eventually asked her as she stared blankly at the boxed game of Snakes and Ladders I was just opening.

'Dolls,' Aimee said. 'But I broke them when I got angry, and Mum said she wouldn't get me any more.'

'So what did you do all day?' I asked. 'You didn't go to school much.'

'I watched television,' Aimee said, confirming what her social worker had previously told me. 'I like ...' and she reeled off a list of adult television programmes, some of which she'd mentioned before, and all of which were unsuitable for children. 'I've told me mum you won't let me watch them here,' Aimee threatened, as though this would force me to change my mind and allow her to watch inappropriate programmes. I ignored the threat and concentrated on the game, praising Aimee as we played.

After a while of playing simple board games and helping Aimee with the puzzles I suggested she might like to do some colouring and she agreed she would. I fetched the crayons and crayoning books and spread them on the table in the kitchen. Aimee grabbed a crayon enthusiastically and held it in her fist as a toddler would, and then made a very uncoordinated attempt to colour in a large picture of a dog. The coloured lines she made strayed all over the page instead of staying inside the outline of the dog. It was incredible (but not unheard of) that a child could reach her age and not have learned how to colour in. Most children of this age are holding a pencil and writing sentences, but Aimee, as a result of a lack of school and no encouragement at home, couldn't even hold a crayon properly.

'Try holding the crayon like this,' I said, picking up another crayon and showing her how to hold it like a pencil.

'No,' Aimee said adamantly. 'I do it my way.' She turned the page and began scribbling over the next picture.

'You'll find it is easier to draw if you hold the crayon like this,' I said, and began colouring in the picture on the adjacent page. 'It gives you better control.'

'I'll do it how I want!' Aimee said. But a minute later I saw her change the position of her crayon and hold it as I'd suggested, which as I'd thought proved easier for her and therefore she produced a neater picture. I wanted to help Aimee, but at present she wore a protective cloak designed to keep me out, which meant that her immediate reaction to anything I suggested was to reject it and me.

Paula and Lucy had been out for most of the afternoon and returned for dinner, which we ate at six o'clock. Aimee pulled a face when I set the plate of fish, chips and peas in front of her and predictably demanded biscuits. Then she said she'd just eat the chips as long as she could have tomato ketchup.

'You can have some tomato ketchup,' I said, and passed her the squeezy bottle.

We all began eating, Aimee's chips swimming in tomato sauce. But throughout the meal I was acutely aware that once dinner was over I'd have to phone Susan for Aimee's supervised telephone contact. I wasn't looking forward to it. Although Susan would be safely at the end of a phone and not in person, I was pretty certain she wouldn't let the phone call pass without having a go at me, as she'd been so angry the previous evening at contact, especially in respect of my reporting Aimee's bruises to the social worker. Susan wouldn't know that Aimee had since told me it was Craig who'd assaulted her and that she (Susan) hadn't protected her. It wasn't for me to tell Susan, but I wondered if Aimee would, and what Susan's reaction would be.

The Phone Call

Aimee hadn't mentioned Craig again during the day and it was probably better she didn't say anything to her mother, but if she did I couldn't stop her: my role was to monitor the telephone contact, not direct the content.

Aimee ate all her chips, laden with tomato ketchup, very quickly and then put down her knife and fork.

'Eat your fish and peas,' I encouraged. 'They're good for you and will help your body grow and stay healthy.'

'Don't want my body to grow and stay healthy,' Aimee grumbled. 'Can I have biscuits now?'

'Not until you've eaten your dinner.'

'Hate you,' she said.

'Mum only wants what's best for you,' Paula said.

I smiled at Paula, grateful for her support, while Aimee folded her arms across her chest and sat back in her chair, scowling.

'Come on, finish your dinner,' I encouraged. 'Then we can phone your mother.'

With a huff and sigh Aimee leant forward and, picking up her knife and fork, began eating the fish. 'Won't have to eat this stuff when I go home,' she said.

I knew from Kristen that the chances of Amy being returned home were slim to non-existent, but it wasn't the right time to start explaining this to Aimee. When Aimee had been with me for longer and was used to being in care and away from her mother I would, as I had with other children I'd fostered, gently introduce the possibility that the judge might decide she would be better off being looked after in care rather than living with her mother. It's always a difficult conversation to have with a child, and strictly speaking the child's social worker is supposed to discuss this with the child, but more often it is left to the foster carer, who often has a better relationship with the child than the social worker does. Children in foster care have so much to cope with and their lives aren't made any easier by the care system, which often seems to follow the 'letter of the law' while disregarding the realistic and compassionate.

Aimee squirted another liberal helping of tomato ketchup on to her plate, which allowed her to eat the rest of her fish and peas. Once we'd finished eating, I left Paula and Lucy to clear the table while I took Aimee into the sitting room to phone her mother.

'Have you ever used a telephone before?' I asked, reaching for the phone and setting it between us on the sofa.

Aimee nodded. 'Me mum's mobile,' she said.

'This phone is a little different and it has a loudspeaker. You won't have to put it to your ear when you talk to your mother. I press this button and we will both be able to hear what your mother is saying, and she'll be able to hear us.' I gave a demonstration of the phone on speaker by pressing the 'hands-free' button. We could hear the dialling tone. 'I'll key in the numbers and tell your mother who it is, and then you'll speak to her,' I said. Aimee nodded.

Opening my fostering folder, I found the form with Susan's mobile number and keyed in the digits. We heard her phone ringing and then after about six rings Susan's voice answered.

'Hello,' she said, sounding very tired. I wondered if she'd been asleep.

'Hello, Susan,' I said. 'It's Cathy, Aimee's carer. I have Aimee beside me, ready to speak to you.'

Susan didn't say anything and Aimee didn't either.

'Say hello to your mum,' I encouraged Aimee.

'Hi, Mum,' Aimee said in a similar small voice to her mother's.

'Hi, love. How are you?' Susan asked.

Aimee didn't reply.

'Tell your mother you're OK and what you've been doing today,' I suggested.

The Phone Call

'Nothing,' Aimee said. 'I ain't been doing nothing.'

'Haven't you?' Susan exclaimed, her voice rising as she latched on to her daughter's complaint.

'Tell your mum we went shopping,' I said quietly to Aimee. 'Then we played games all afternoon.'

'I haven't been doing anything all day,' Aimee said again. 'I'm so bored.'

I didn't want Susan thinking her daughter had been left all day doing nothing. Apart from it not being true it could have been upsetting for Susan to hear.

'We went shopping this morning,' I said. 'And then Aimee has been doing puzzles and playing games all afternoon.'

'No I haven't,' Aimee said defiantly.

'Who asked you?' Susan demanded of me. 'This is my phone contact, with my daughter, so keep your bleeding nose out.'

Aimee grinned. 'That's right, Mum. You tell her!'

I could have quite happily cut the phone call there and then but as a foster carer I knew I couldn't do that. The judge had ruled that Aimee should speak to her mother on the phone and I should facilitate this. Aimee telling her mother lies about me or her mother swearing at me didn't justify ending the phone contact.

'Talk to your mother, then,' I said evenly to Aimee as she fell silent and Susan was silent too. 'Tell her what you've been doing.'

'I want to come home,' Aimee said. 'I'm unhappy.'

'I knew you were unhappy,' Susan said, seizing on another possible complaint. 'What's that woman been doing to you?'

'I can't watch television all day,' Aimee lamented.

'That ain't fair,' Susan sympathized.

'She won't let me watch the programmes I want,' Aimee continued. 'You know, the ones I used to watch with you.'

'I'll report her,' Susan said, ignoring the fact that I could hear her. 'She's not stopping you watching television, it's inhuman.'

'And I have to eat yucky food,' Aimee persisted, winding up her mother even more. 'And she won't give me biscuits until I've eaten it.'

'That's cruel,' Susan responded. 'She ain't feeding you proper.'

'No, she ain't,' Aimee agreed. 'You report her, then I can come home.' Despite my already explaining to Aimee that complaining about me wouldn't return her home she persisted in this belief.

Aimee's complaints were so ridiculous that they could have been laughable, expect of course it wasn't funny. I was quietly seething and upset.

'Of course I'm feeding Aimee,' I said to Susan, unable to sit there any longer and just accept it. 'She's had three good meals today, and pudding and some biscuits. She's also had some fruit.'

'Who asked you?' Susan snapped down the phone at me.

Aimee smirked.

And so the conversation continued, with Aimee making untrue allegations about my care of her and Susan fuelling the situation by reacting to them. I didn't interrupt to protest my innocence again or correct all the lies Aimee was telling her mother; there was no point. Susan wanted to believe what her daughter was saying and my interrupting would just make her angrier. I was therefore forced to sit by for another twenty minutes and listen to Aimee and her mother criticizing me, my home, my care of Aimee, my daughters, the food I cooked, and the routine and boundaries I'd put in place for Aimee's good. Aimee avoided saying anything positive, including the fact that I'd bought her a wardrobeful of new clothes that morning and I'd spent all afternoon playing with her. I knew why she was saying these things – the psychology that lay behind it; I'd seen it before in other children I'd fostered. In Aimee's eyes as well as possibly getting her moved (although not home) if she criticized me it lessened the significance of the inadequate care her mother had given her. No child wants to believe that their parents have failed and that a stranger is now looking after them better than their parents did. Criticizing me, in Aimee's eyes, raised her mother's status. But while I understood the psychology behind Aimee's denigration of me, it didn't make hearing it any better. Foster carers invest a lot in the children they look after and take criticism of the care they give the child personally.

Eventually Aimee ran out of derogatory comments and complaints, which gave Susan a chance to tell her that their dog, Hatchet, which I knew to be a Rottweiler, had bitten another dog in the park that morning and the owner had called the police. Mother and daughter seemed to find this very amusing.

'I won't be going to that park for a while,' Susan said, laughing.

'No,' Aimee chuckled. 'You might get caught.'

Finally Susan said she had to go and I breathed a sigh of relief. The length of phone contact is sometimes stipulated in the care plan but it hadn't been in Aimee's case, so that I had to let their conversation run its course. They'd been on the phone for about thirty minutes.

'You have to phone tomorrow,' Susan told Aimee before they said goodbye. 'It's Sunday and you have to phone me.'

'Do you hear that?' Aimee demanded rudely of me.

'She'll phone at about the same time,' I confirmed to Susan.

'Right. And make sure you give her the biscuits she wants and stop starving her. I don't want her losing weight.' Aimee needed to lose some weight but I wasn't going to say that to Susan. Mother and daughter said goodbye and I was finally able to press 'hands-free' to end the call.

I stayed where I was on the sofa, with Aimee beside me. She'd fallen silent now and was looking at me a little sheepishly. I guessed she was wondering what my reaction would be now her mother had gone.

'You can't hit me,' she said. 'You're not allowed to.'

'Of course I'm not going to hit you,' I said. 'I never hit anyone, let alone a child. But why did you tell your mother all those things that weren't true?'

Aimee shrugged. 'I don't know.'

'I do and it won't help. I know you love your mum and want to be with her but the judge has decided you should be looked after by me for the time being. We don't know how long that will be but making up lies won't help.'

'Yes it will,' Aimee said defiantly. 'I'm not listening to you any more.' She pressed her hands over her ears and screwed up her eyes so that she couldn't hear or see me.

I returned the phone to the corner table and, standing, left the room. I went into the kitchen, where Lucy and Paula were leaning against the worktops talking quietly. As I entered they both looked at me, concerned, so I guessed they'd overheard some of what Aimee had said to her mother.

'Are you all right, Mum?' Paula asked.

I sighed. 'I guess so.'

'Shall I talk to Aimee?' Lucy offered. 'Point out the error of her ways.' She smiled.

'No, don't worry yourself. It's early days yet. She's got a lot to cope with. She's angry. Things will improve, I'm sure.'

Both girls came over and gave me a big hug – we call it a group hug, where we hug in a small circle. Adrian used to join in when he was younger and lived at home, and most foster children join in eventually. I felt the warmth of their embrace and it was just what I needed to get me back on track and ready to face Aimee again. Tomorrow was another day.

Chapter Twelve

Craig

Sunday evening's phone contact was no better than Saturday's. Despite the fact that Aimee had had a good day, which had included a visit to our local park, where she'd fed the ducks (a new experience for her), followed by a hot chocolate in the park's café, which she liked even more than feeding the ducks, Aimee couldn't find a single positive thing to tell her mother and made up more complaints. Susan reacted as she had done the previous evening by over-reacting, and reassuring Aimee she would be reporting me to the social services, her solicitor, Aimee's father and I suspected anyone else who would listen. The only positive element in the phone call was that, having spoken to her mother on the phone the previous evening for over thirty minutes, once Aimee had reassured her mother that she'd been bored all day, had been forced to have a wash and had been force-fed 'muck', while being denied biscuits and television, she ran out of things to say. Susan told Aimee that Hatchet had bitten her that afternoon but that he hadn't meant to as he'd only been playing. Aimee agreed Hatchet wasn't to blame and remembered all the times he'd bitten her and how they'd made sure the social worker didn't know. Susan seemed to finish the conversation quickly then; I guessed she was concerned at what else Aimee might remember and I would hear and pass on to the social worker. Susan told Aimee she'd see her the following evening at contact and they said goodbye.

As soon as I'd pressed 'hands-free' to sever the call Aimee clapped her hands over her ears so that she couldn't hear the lecture about lying she thought I would give her. She needn't have bothered, for I didn't intend repeating myself by saying what I'd already said the previous evening, although I was sad Aimee had told her mother more untruths. I consoled myself that fortunately Aimee's complaints were so ludicrous that if Susan did report me as she'd threatened, no one would take her seriously – or so I thought.

The following day after I'd taken Aimee to school I went straight home, with the intention of phoning Jill and advising her of the disclosures Aimee had made on Friday about Craig abusing her and being responsible for the bruises. Jill would then phone Kristen, who would contact the police.

It was 9.30 when I arrived home and, grabbing a coffee, I went through to the sitting room. I took my fostering folder from the shelf and, opening it, sat on the sofa with my coffee within reach, ready to make the call. But before I had a chance to key in the numbers the phone rang. It was Jill.

'I was just about to phone you,' I said.

'I'm not surprised, after what Aimee has told her mother,' Jill said, her voice serious. 'It's just as well you're an experienced carer and we know you well or we would have been forced to remove the child.'

'You're not serious?' I gasped, my mouth going dry and my heart starting to pound. 'You're never taking Susan's complaints seriously?'

'The complaints are coming from Aimee, through her mother, so we need to investigate. I know how that makes you feel, Cathy, but Susan has had kids in care for twenty-five years and she knows how the system works. She knows her rights and she knows which buttons to press to cause maximum trouble. She was on the phone to Kristen first thing this morning and Kristen's manager has asked for some explanations.'

I was shocked and hurt. I'd assumed that Aimee's/Susan's complaints would be dismissed for what they were: an angry and upset mother and child making a desperate bid to be reunited. Now I was having to defend myself.

'Let's deal with the television first,' Jill continued evenly. 'Aimee has told her mother that you do not allow her to watch any of her favourite television programmes. Why?'

'Jill!' I said, my voice rising. 'Her favourite programmes aren't children's programmes. They're adult programmes which are shown late at night and not at all suitable for a child of eight.' I then reeled off a list of programmes that Aimee had told me she'd regularly watched with her mother and were her favourites, all of which were unsuitable.

'OK, slow down. I'm writing this,' Jill said.

'And Susan allowed Aimee to watch adult DVDs,' I added, without pausing. 'Bloody horror movies and ones portraying sado-masochistic sex!'

'Susan didn't mention DVDs.'

'No, but I am.'

'All right, calm down. I'll make a note.' Jill wrote while I took a deep breath and tried to control my anger. Not only were my honesty and integrity being called into account but so were my parenting and fostering skills. Of course Aimee could watch television, but only what was age appropriate. Young minds can so easily be damaged by watching cruel and violent images.

'Now the food?' Jill continued. 'What's causing Aimee so many problems?'

I took another deep breath. 'Jill, as you know when Aimee was at home with her mother her diet consisted of dry toast and biscuits. She appears to be addicted to sweet things, especially biscuits, and demands them continuously. She's used to eating a packet of biscuits at one sitting instead of a meal. I'm rationing her intake of sweet things and she has one or two biscuits after her meal.' I stopped while Jill wrote.

'And the meals you're providing?' Jill queried. 'Aimee told her mother she doesn't like the food and you're forcing her to eat it.'

'Jill! For goodness sake!' I exclaimed. 'You surely know me better than that. I'm giving Aimee the same meals I cook for the rest of us. I encourage her to eat them but I don't force her!' But to Aimee, who'd done exactly as she'd wanted to before coming into care and had never been asked to sit at a table and eat a meal, it could have seemed as though I was 'forcing' her.

'Cathy, I'm sorry,' Jill said, 'but Aimee has made the complaint, so I have to ask the questions. Tell me exactly what you've given her to eat and then I can tell Kristen, who can reassure Susan.'

Silently fuming, I thought back and recalled what I'd given Aimee to eat since she'd arrived, and I told Jill. I also said that I'd told Aimee she could have a biscuit once she'd eaten her meal, and that although Aimee had moaned about the food on her plate, once she'd tried it she'd found she liked it and she hardly left anything.

'Thanks,' Jill said. She then went on to the next complaint, which was about washing – that I was forcing Aimee to get into the bath against her will.

'I help her in,' I said, 'because she's not used to a bath, having never had one at home.' I then explained in detail how I ran the bath to the right temperature and helped Aimee climb in while Jill, on the other end of the phone, made notes. After that Jill moved on to the next complaint, which was that I was putting

Craig

Aimee to bed very early, in the afternoon, and so the list continued. As patiently as I could I answered each allegation, explaining and justifying what I was doing to help Aimee. In all the years I'd worked with Jill it was the only time I'd been annoyed with her, and it crossed my mind that Susan had already succeeded in setting the professionals involved in her case against each other.

Some twenty minutes later Jill finally came to the end of her list. 'Thank you, Cathy. I think that's it,' she said.

'Fantastic,' I said, not bothering to hide my sarcasm. 'Can I now tell you why I was going to phone you?'

'Sure, go ahead,' Jill said lightly.

'Aimee has been abused by her mother's boyfriend, Craig. The bruises she has all over her body were caused by him.'

'What!' Jill exclaimed. 'You should have said sooner.'

'You didn't give me a chance. You were too busy with Susan's complaints.'

'Point taken,' she said. 'So what exactly has Aimee told you?'

I looked down at the fostering folder in my lap and, opening it, was finally able to tell Jill of Aimee's disclosures. I began by setting the scene, saying that Aimee had told me in the car after contact on Friday. I explained we'd been talking about Christmas when Aimee had said last Christmas hadn't been nice for her. Using Aimee's words, which I'd written down, I said that Aimee had told me she and her mother had stayed at Craig's over Christmas and Craig had given her corned beef for dinner. When Aimee had said she didn't like the food Craig had shouted at her, called her a rude bitch, then grabbed her by the throat and 'belted me all over with his fist'. I continued with Aimee's account of how Craig had killed kittens in front of her by breaking their necks.

I heard Jill gasp. 'Susan said Aimee did that.'

'I know.'

107

I then brought Aimee's disclosures of abuse up to date by telling Jill that Aimee had said Craig had made all the bruises she now had by pinching her flesh between his thumb and forefinger.'

'Bastard,' Jill said. 'The poor kid.'

'When I first saw the bruises I thought there was something odd about them,' I said. 'Aimee said they were from falling over but they're all the same size and shape. Now I know they were his thumb- and fingerprints and couldn't possibly have been made by falling over. Aimee was scared of him, but now she knows she's safe she felt able to tell me.' My anger and upset about all the complaints Susan had made had gone now that I was focusing on Aimee and my concern for her.

'But who is this Craig?' Jill asked. 'There was no mention of him in the referral, and I'm sure Kristen didn't mention him, did she?'

'No, not to me. Yet according to Aimee he's been part of her and her mother's life for up to two years — she remembers two Christmases with him.'

'So why weren't the social workers aware of him?' Jill asked, thinking aloud. 'They certainly should have been. Aimee was on the child protection register. She and her mother would have been monitored and regularly visited by social workers.'

'I know,' I said.

'And Susan was aware he was abusing Aimee?'

'Yes. She was present, for some of it at least.'

Jill fell silent before she said, 'I'll phone Kristen now. She'll want to talk to you later. It will be a police matter. Can you email me a copy of your log notes and I'll forward them to Kristen. I think all Susan's complaining could be a "smokescreen" to cover up what's really been going on.'

'Pity Kristen's manager didn't think that,' I said cynically.

'Sorry, but we do have to investigate all complaints.'

Craig

'I know.'

Jill and I said goodbye and I drank my now cold coffee, and then took my fostering folder through to the front room, where I switched on the computer. I was still annoyed and upset that Susan had been allowed to cause so much trouble, but I concentrated on typing up my log notes as Jill had asked. I was halfway through when the phone rang and, answering it, I recognized the female voice as Kristen's.

'I'm just typing up the log notes now,' I said. 'I should be finished in about ten minutes.'

'Thank you. Jill's just phoned and told me what Aimee said. But I'm sure Aimee is wrong. We've never heard of a Craig. I think Aimee is confusing Craig with her father, Shane. She's made allegations about Shane in the past, although they were never substantiated.'

Now I was confused. 'But the name Craig sounds nothing like Shane,' I said. 'And Aimee always refers to her father as Dad.'

'I didn't mean that Aimee is confusing the names,' Kristen said, a little tersely. 'I meant that she's getting the incidents mixed up. She thinks it was Craig, who we've never heard of, who assaulted her, while it was really her father.'

'Oh,' I said, no less confused. 'But Aimee was quite adamant that it was Craig. Why would she make him up?'

'To protect her father? Or maybe her mother has put her up to it?'

It was possible, although I wasn't convinced. Aimee had been very clear who her abuser had been. But I knew Kristen would want more than my belief in Aimee: she would want evidence. 'Shall I talk to Aimee tonight after school and find out some more details?' I asked.

'Yes please. See if you can get a description of Craig, and ask her if she knows his surname and address. She says she stayed with him, so she might know his address or at least the area in which he lives. I'm not going to alert CP' – the police child protection unit – 'until I hear back from you.'

'All right. I'll speak to Aimee tonight, but I'd be very surprised if she is confusing Craig's actions with her father's,' I persisted.

'Cathy, she's an eight-year-old girl who's just come into care; it's understandable if she is confused.' I thought that Kristen was rather hoping this would be the case, for it would look very bad on the social services if Aimee had been abused by a man the social services weren't aware of, while she'd been on the child protection register and being monitored by social workers who were supposed to keep her safe.

Kristen and I said goodbye and I returned to typing up my log notes, although my concentration kept wavering to the possibility that Aimee had made up Craig, in which case it would be difficult to know what to believe in future. Once I'd finished typing I emailed the document to Jill, who would keep a copy for her agency's records and forward a copy to Kristen. With a bit of time to spare I stayed at the computer and put the finishing touches to a presentation I was giving the following week for prospective carers at an introduction to fostering evening. Since my own children had grown up and were largely self-sufficient I'd broadened my role in fostering. I sat on various committees connected with fostering and adoption; gave presentations to prospective carers; ran training courses for carers; and participated in a mentoring scheme that gave support and advice to other foster carers. I enjoyed all aspects of my role, although I was always a little nervous before going into a room and having to address a new group.

Once I'd finished the presentation I had some lunch and then spent some of the afternoon practising it, out loud and in front of the mirror in the front room. Anyone chancing to peep in would have wondered what on earth I was doing, but after half an hour I was nearly word perfect and felt more confident. Then it was soon time to drive to school to collect Aimee.

I parked in a side road, glanced around for any sign of Susan before getting out, and then waited in the playground for the bell to ring. Aimee came out with her class and was accompanied by Heather, her teaching assistant.

The first thing Heather said to me was: 'Doesn't Aimee look smart in her new coat and school uniform?' I smiled and Aimee looked pleased. 'Aimee's had a good day,' Heather continued. 'She completed some nice work, and enjoyed playing in the playground after lunch. She's got some reading and writing homework in her bag.'

'Thank you,' I said.

'I can't do me homework tonight,' Aimee put in. 'I'm seeing me mum, so there won't be time.'

'My mum,' Heather and I both corrected, trying to improve Aimee's poor diction.

'There'll be plenty of time to do the homework after contact,' I said to Heather and Aimee, although it was true her time would be limited. I knew from my experience of previous children that when children have been at school all day and then have contact, they arrive home tired and emotionally exhausted, and find concentrating on homework very difficult. But Aimee, having missed so much school, had a lot of catching up to do. 'We'll do what we can,' I said to Heather.

'Enjoy your evening,' she said.

'And you.'

Aimee and I crossed the playground and left the school.

I wasn't sure if I should raise the matter of Craig with Aimee, as Kristen had asked me to, before or after contact, but given my questions were relatively simple and straightforward I decided to approach the subject now. Once we were in the car and before

I started the engine, I turned in my seat to look at Aimee. 'You remember what you told me on Friday about all those bruises you had?'

Aimee nodded. 'Yeah, I've still got some of them.'

'I know. How did you get them?'

'I told you,' she said, puzzled. 'Weren't you listening? Craig pinched me all over. He's always doing it. I hate him.'

'I remember what you said but Kristen, your social worker, has asked me to ask you again. It was definitely Craig? It couldn't have been your father?'

Aimee looked at me oddly and I thought she had every right to. 'I know the difference between me dad and Craig,' she said. 'I ain't stupid.'

'I know you're not, but I understand you told a social worker that your dad had hurt you too.'

'That was ages ago. Another time. I know who me dad is and it ain't Craig.'

'I believe you. Can you describe Craig? Can you tell me what he looks like?'

'He's big and fat with tattoos on his arms. My dad is short and thin with tattoos on his legs. My dad ain't got teeth. Craig has big teeth and he picks food out of them and sometimes bites people.'

'Did he bite you?' I asked, aware this could be a new disclosure.

'Sometimes. Can we go to contact now?'

'In a minute.' I made a mental note to add Craig biting Aimee to my log when I got home. 'Aimee, you told me about some kittens that were hurt? Who hurt them?'

'Craig! I told you,' Aimee said, becoming annoyed with me.

'It was definitely Craig and not you?'

'What?' Aimee exclaimed. 'No! I wouldn't do that. It's cruel. I cried when Craig killed them.'

Craig

'I believe you.' As indeed I'd believed her when she'd first told me. I felt awful appearing to doubt her now, but Kristen had asked me to find out as much as I could and to try to verify what Aimee had said before she phoned the police child protection unit.

'Good girl,' I said. 'Do you know Craig's surname? It would help the police to find him.'

'What's a surname?' Aimee frowned, puzzled.

'It's your last name. Like yours is Mason and mine is Glass. Do you know Craig's last name?'

'No. Mum never said. I just call him Craig. Or pig, or shit head when he hits me.'

I had to smile. Despite all that had happened to Aimee she had spirit and a sense of humour.

'OK, but don't swear. One last thing before we go to contact: do you know where Craig lives?'

'I don't know the name of the road because I can't read. But it begins with the letter C. We went on the 121 bus. It's one of those roads behind the old gas tower.'

I knew exactly where Aimee meant. Over on the far side of town was a disused gas tower, redundant for over thirty-five years since the introduction of North Sea gas. The tower dominated the surrounding streets of terraced Victorian houses and I thought there couldn't be that many roads there beginning with C.

'He lives in part of a house,' Aimee added. 'He has the top floor and another man lives downstairs.' So I thought it was a house converted into two flats, as some were in that area.

'Well done,' I said, turning to the front and starting the car's engine, ready to drive to contact. 'You have got a good memory.'

'Yeah, better than yours,' Aimee said. 'I told you a lot of that already. Are you getting old?'

113

Chapter Thirteen

More Trouble

I didn't see Susan at the start of contact that night; she was already in the contact room. Following the centre's normal practice I said goodbye to Aimee in reception and the contact supervisor took Aimee through to her mother. I returned to my car, but before I started the engine I took my mobile phone from my coat pocket and phoned Kristen. She was at her desk and I told her what Aimee had just said, including the description of Craig and where he lived. Kristen went very quiet.

'So Craig definitely exists,' I said, making sure Kristen appreciated there could be no doubt. 'Aimee's father is a completely different person.'

'We'll have to investigate,' Kristen finally said, sounding subdued and clearly aware of the implications. 'I don't understand why this wasn't picked up sooner. As you know, I only took over this case a couple of months ago.' I didn't point out that Craig's most recent assault on Aimee had happened just before she'd come into care and on Kristen's watch. Social workers carry huge workloads, and unfortunately errors and oversights do occur. The problem is that in child protection oversights and errors can't be allowed to happen because a child's life could be in danger or at the very least their welfare damaged.

'I'll type up what Aimee has just said as soon as I can,' I added.

'Thanks, Cathy. I'll be in touch.'

I had enough time to go home for half an hour and prepare dinner, before I had to return to collect Aimee from contact. Following normal practice I waited in reception for Aimee to be brought out by the contact supervisor. Parents are encouraged to say goodbye to their child(ren) in the contact room, as current thinking suggests it usually makes for a less stressful separation. But if parents insist on coming into reception with their child to say goodbye, the supervisor usually allows this rather than risk causing a scene.

Presently Aimee and the contact supervisor appeared through the door leading into reception, with Susan following close behind. As soon as Susan saw me she began complaining; possibly that was the reason she'd come into reception – to complain. 'That coat you bought Aimee is the wrong colour!' she said in a loud voice and coming right up to me. 'She doesn't like it. Change it. And that school skirt you got her is too long. And she's got food down her shirt. It's filthy. You should be ashamed of yourself, sending her to school like that. And she needs socks, not tights. She can't put tights on!'

Susan paused for breath and the contact supervisor looked to me for an explanation of what appeared to be sub-standard fostering.

Calmly, and choosing my words carefully, I dealt with the last complaint first. 'Aimee has learnt how to put on her tights,' I said in an even tone. 'She learnt very quickly and I thought tights would be warmer than socks for winter. Her coat is the right colour for school and I've brought her a jacket for weekend and casual wear. Her shirt was clean on this morning. I expect she dropped some food down it when she had her dinner.' I didn't get a chance to explain further, for Susan was now shouting.

'Are you saying my girl doesn't know how to eat proper?' she demanded right in my face.

I took a step back. 'No, many children have accidents with their meals, especially when they're learning to use a knife and fork.' I realized it was the wrong thing to say as soon as I'd said it.

Susan's eyes blazed. 'I've already told you to stop forcing my girl to use a knife and fork! She can use her fingers like she always does. It ain't for you to change her. You do as you're bleeding well told!'

Susan's voice had risen to such a pitch that the centre's manager now appeared and, as she had done previously, placated Susan with the suggestion of going into her office and the promise of writing down all her grievances. Susan was so keen to do this that she forgot to say goodbye to Aimee. The two of them disappeared into the office and the door closed, while the contact supervisor went down the corridor, which left Aimee and me alone in reception.

'Come on, let's go home,' I said, offering Aimee my hand, which she refused.

'What's for dinner?' she asked, falling into step beside me. She appeared to be used to her mother's rages and didn't seem too badly affected by them, while my heart was pounding heavily and I felt quite shaken. Contact had been set at three times a week, so I would be seeing a lot of Susan. I hoped she calmed before too long. I also hoped that the centre's manager, when she'd finished recording Susan's complaints, took the opportunity to talk to Susan about her attitude towards me. For seeing her mother so negative and angry wasn't going to help Aimee settle into foster care, but then of course that was what Susan intended, I thought unkindly. Kristen had warned me right at the start that Susan had made so many allegations about the foster carers of her older children that eventually they'd all had to be moved to new foster homes, repeatedly, which was very disruptive for the children, and of course the allegations hadn't had the desired effect of returning the children to Susan.

Aimee was very talkative in the car on the way home and told me all about the many sweet things her mother had given her at contact. 'I was allowed to eat all the biscuits and sweets I wanted!' Aimee repeated, in case I hadn't grasped it the first time. 'Mum said I could.' There was a challenging defiance in Aimee's words: she was making the point that she'd been allowed to eat unlimited sweet foods at contact with her mother while I rationed them at home. I was used to foster children trying to play off their parents against me (the foster carer) and I'd found it was best ignored. Another good reason for the child's parents and carer working together is that it limits the times the child can manipulate the situation.

However, when Aimee repeated for a fifth time that her mother had given her lots of sweets, I simply said, 'I'm glad you had a nice time with your mother.' Which wasn't what Aimee wanted to hear at all.

'You're not listening!' she accused. 'I said my mum let me eat lots and lots of sweets and biscuits – all of them!'

'I heard you,' I said, 'but when you are at contact your mother sets the rules and when you are at home with me I set them. If your mother is happy for you to eat lots of sweet things so that your teeth go rotten that's up to her. I'm trying to keep you healthy by limiting your sweet foods and giving you a good diet.' I didn't want Aimee thinking I was rationing her sweets out of spite – it was for her own good.

She didn't answer and I hoped she appreciated what I'd said.

* * *

We arrived home and had dinner – roast chicken, potatoes and carrots – which Aimee ate after the usual protestations of saying she didn't like it and wanted biscuits instead. After dinner I told Aimee it was time to do some homework and I would help her. She didn't want to do her homework but wanted to watch television instead. I explained how important it was to do well at school and that she had some catching up to do.

'Not catching up!' Aimee scowled, folding her arms defiantly across her chest. 'And you can't make me!'

I was getting used to Aimee rejecting all my requests: it was spontaneous, and a prerequisite before doing as I'd asked. But Lucy and Paula sighed with exasperation.

'Here we go again,' Paula said quietly under her breath.

'I know you've had a busy day,' I said to Aimee. 'So we'll just spend a quarter of an hour reading, and then you can watch some television before bed.'

'I want television now,' Aimee demanded. 'Or I'll tell me mum.'

Lucy and Paula left for their bedrooms while I continued to explain to Aimee the advantages of learning to read and write. But Aimee didn't want to know. I suspected she was unsettled from seeing her mother and being reminded of life before she came into care, where the focus was on immediate gratification rather than long-term goals: Aimee wanted to enjoy watching television now rather than doing some homework which would help her in the future.

'Aimee,' I said finally, 'in my house we always do our homework first before we watch television. It's one of our rules. Where do you think Paula is now?' I added for good measure.

'How should I know?' Aimee shrugged.

'She's in her bedroom doing her homework. Then when she's finished she'll watch her television.' I omitted to mention that Paula often did her homework with her television on and with her iPod in her ears. She was seventeen and that was the way she studied, and it worked for her.

Aimee thought about this for a moment and then asked, 'What about Lucy and your boy who ain't here? Are they doing their homework?'

'Adrian is doing homework at university,' I said. 'And Lucy did homework until she was eighteen. She got the qualifications she needed, so she doesn't have to do homework now, but she still likes to read.' Nothing like labouring the point, I thought! But it was so important that Aimee got into the right mindset for making the most of her schooling and learning.

The message began to sink in. Aimee sulked for a while longer, glared at me (just as her mother did), and then, having thought about it a bit longer, and probably swayed by the examples of my grown-up children, she plonked herself on the sofa next to me. 'You always get your own way!' she huffed. 'You said quarter of an hour, that's all. Then I'm having me television on.'

'Excellent. Deal done,' I said with a cheery smile.

But Aimee couldn't read the time so I managed to stretch the fifteen minutes' homework to thirty minutes before, tired after a day at school and contact, she began to yawn and lose concentration.

'Well done,' I said. 'That wasn't so painful, was it?'

She almost agreed but not quite.

Aimee watched some children's television and then with the usual protest that she wanted to stay up later and watch more (adult programmes) I saw her up to bed. I tucked her in and asked her if she wanted a goodnight kiss or a hug but she didn't.

Having said goodnight I came out, closed the door and went downstairs, where I wrote up my log notes. I then spent some time chatting to Lucy and Paula before I went to bed soon after ten o'clock, exhausted. My weekday routine had begun. The following day we had school and phone contact; then on

Wednesday we had school and face-to-face contact. Thursday was school and phone contact again, and then Friday school and face-to-face contact. My routine with Aimee would continue largely unaltered until the final court hearing, possibly a year away, when the judge would decide who should look after Aimee. During that year the legal cogs would turn slowly in the background, with reports being written, assessments and observations being completed, and Aimee's progress monitored. As with all the children I'd fostered Aimee would be part of my family for the time she was with me and I would care for her as I did my own children. Aimee certainly wasn't the easiest child I'd fostered, but her behaviour was manageable, if not a little wearying. I was more concerned about the physical and emotional distance she kept between us. It was as though she thought that to allow me close was a sign of weakness. I hoped that in time she would put her trust in me, as long as there was time and Susan's complaints didn't lead to Aimee being moved.

I took Aimee to school the following morning and after school Jill visited as arranged, but it was only a brief visit – to meet Aimee – as Jill was on her way to another carer, whose teenager kept running away. After dinner I took Aimee to the sitting room for telephone contact but when I phoned Susan's mobile it wouldn't connect, and an automated message said that her phone was off and to try again later. My phone was on speaker and Aimee, who was sitting beside me ready to talk to her mother, could hear the recorded message and was angry.

'Silly cow! Why isn't she answering?' Aimee stormed.

I reassured her that sometimes mobile phones didn't connect and we would try again later. I tried twice more over the next half an hour but received the same automated message. Now Aimee was very angry – with me, believing it was my fault her mother's phone was switched off. I explained that I had no control over the number we dialled, but Aimee was not convinced and thought I was stopping her from speaking to her mother. In Aimee's view this would be preferable than having to accept that her mother's phone was off and she wasn't waiting for her daughter to call. It was only when Lucy came downstairs and confirmed what I'd said about mobile phones that Aimee finally accepted there was nothing I could do to connect the call. Our whole evening had been disrupted by not getting through to Susan on the phone and as a result Aimee wasn't in the right frame of mind to learn, so I read her some stories.

The following morning I took Aimee to school and as I left the playground my mobile began to ring. It was Kristen. 'Susan's just called me. She's very upset. Why didn't Aimee phone her last night?'

I sighed wearily and explained what had happened: that we'd tried to phone three times but Susan's mobile had been switched off.

'Are you sure her phone was off?' Kristen asked. 'Susan says her phone was on all evening and she was waiting for your call. Perhaps you dialled the wrong number?'

'What? Three times. No. It was the right number. I explained to Aimee these things happen sometimes with mobile phones and it wasn't her mother's fault.'

It was Kristen's turn to sigh. 'All right, I'll try and explain this to Susan. But she's very angry and pointed out that phone calls are part of the court order. She threatened to take us' – the social services – 'back to court for breaking the order.' It sounded as though Kristen was holding me responsible.

I stopped where I was on the pavement and moved to one side. 'Kristen, there's nothing I can do if Susan's phone is switched off.'

'No, but she says it wasn't. Look, if it happens again keep trying.'

'What? All evening?'

'Well, more than three times.'

'All right, if you insist, but it's very disruptive to Aimee.'

'I appreciate that but Susan's out to make trouble.' At the expense of her daughter, I thought. But I knew why Kristen was so eager to placate Susan, for at this stage in the legal proceedings the parents had the 'upper hand'. In court the judge had granted the social services the care order with certain stipulations, one of them being that telephone contact should take place four times a week. This had to be upheld, and if it wasn't Susan could go back to court and possibly make a case for having Aimee returned to her. Kristen had previously said that the social services had been forced to agree to a high level of contact, as otherwise they wouldn't have been granted the care order. In my view one of the elements of the child protection service I would remove is the adversarial nature of the proceedings where the social services and the parents are battling on opposite sides of a courtroom instead of around a table, working for the good of the child.

'I've spoken to child protection about Aimee's allegations against Craig,' Kristen said, moving on. 'Detective Constable Nicki Davies will interview Aimee at school on Thursday.'

'Do you want me to be present?' I asked. 'I'm happy to be if it will help.'

'No, I'll be there,' Kristen said, 'and Aimee knows Nicki. She's been interviewed by her before.'

'Has she?' I asked, surprised. This was news to me. Children are only interviewed by a child protection police officer when there is a specific incident of abuse; the police don't provide a monitoring service as the social services do. 'Can I ask in what connection?' I said.

'Certain things Aimee said before coming into care – about her father, and others,' Kristen said vaguely, not knowing or not wanting to tell me.

'Do you want me to talk to Aimee about Thursday so she's prepared?' I asked.

'No, don't say anything. We don't want her changing her mind.'

'I'm sure she won't do that,' I said. 'You'll let me know the outcome so I can deal with any questions Aimee might ask?'

'I won't personally, but I'll put a note on the file for someone to phone you. As you know, Aimee's case will be going to the children in care team after Thursday. So if I don't speak to you again, goodbye.'

'Goodbye,' I said, and returned my phone to my pocket.

I took one step along the pavement and was about to continue round the corner to the street where I'd parked my car when I felt a heavy tap on my shoulder. I turned, to see Susan standing directly behind me. Stick thin, pale and drawn, with blood-shot eyes and dilated pupils, she looked dreadful. Her hair was dishevelled, as though she'd just got out of bed, and she looked very angry. She had a large dog on the end of a short thick chain lead, which I took to be Hatchet.

I didn't have a chance to say hello and try to defuse her. The dog barked as she jabbed a finger at me and said: 'If you go making trouble for me and my girl, you'll be sorry.'

The dog barked again and she yanked its lead; then, turning, she headed back along the pavement, the dog at her heels, while I continued quickly around the corner and to my car. I got in, pressed the internal locking system, and then sat for a moment while my heart settled. It was only the week before that Susan had been escorted off the school premises when Lynn had called the police, and now here she was again, this time outside the school and threatening me. She knew I'd be here at the start and end of school each day and I had no doubt that unless I put a stop to it Susan would approach and threaten me again. There are many good elements in fostering but angry and irrational parents aren't one of them.

Retrieving my phone from my pocket I pressed Kristen's number. She answered straightaway. 'It's Cathy. Susan has just come to school and threatened me.' I told her what Susan had said.

'I guess she's angry about the allegations Aimee has made against Craig,' Kristen said. 'I didn't tell her, but apparently the police asked Susan for Craig's address.'

'So can you warn her off approaching me again, please?' I said. 'Susan's very threatening, especially with that dog.' The last time I'd been threatened by a parent the social worker had taken my concerns seriously and had told the woman that if it happened again the social services would take out an injunction. But social workers vary in the level of support they give their foster carers and Kristen was about to leave the case.

'I don't like that dog either,' she said. Then: 'I won't have time to raise this with Susan today, so I'll put a note on the file for whoever takes over.' There were going to be a lot of notes on the file, I thought. 'Must rush, I'm in a meeting soon.' And she was gone.

Not satisfied with a note being left on the file, and concerned for my safety, even if Kristen wasn't, I now pressed Jill's number. It might seem that I was making a fuss over what was in effect one incident but given Susan's generally aggressive attitude towards me I thought that if I left it unchecked she'd escalate her threats. Often foster carers have to speak up and make a fuss to safeguard themselves, as no one else does.

Jill answered and I told her what Susan had said and Kristen's response.

More Trouble

'Not good enough,' Jill said. 'I'll email Kristen now. Best to have it in writing.'

True to her word, Jill did as she promised and an hour later she phoned and said Kristen had spoken to Susan and had told her not to approach me again in the street. But of course telling Susan not to do something was like 'a red rag to a bull'. That evening at contact Susan was furious with me, and so too was Aimee.

Chapter Fourteen

Keep Asking

I hadn't seen Susan when I'd taken Aimee to contact, as she was already in the contact room, but when I collected Aimee at the end of contact Susan came out with Aimee and the supervisor.

It was Aimee who spoke first. 'You've upset my mummy! She likes to go to my school, and I like to see her.' I hadn't said anything to Aimee, so I assumed Susan must have told Aimee that I'd complained about her being outside the school that morning, while omitting to mention why I'd complained.

'There! Told you so,' Susan said to the contact supervisor. 'My girl likes to see me at school, and that woman is trying to come between us.'

'Yeah, I like seeing me mum through the railings at play-time,' Aimee agreed. So it appeared that Susan going to the school had become a regular occurrence since Aimee had come into care. A public footpath ran down one side of the school with only a railing fence separating it from the playground. I'd seen children in the morning call goodbye to their parents through the railings, so I guessed that was where Aimee had been meeting her mother at playtime.

Aimee and Susan glared at me while the contact super-visor looked at me coolly and said nothing. I didn't know the supervisor and she hadn't introduced herself. It was a different supervisor to the one of the week before and while she should really have intervened and stopped Susan from lambasting me I knew that wasn't going to happen. Susan was a formidable woman when angry and this contact supervisor, like the last one, wasn't going to cross her unless it was absolutely essential. Susan was therefore allowed to continue unchecked.

'She's got new bruises on her legs,' Susan said to me, accusingly. 'Craig couldn't have done those, could he? Aimee hasn't seen him for two weeks.'

'No, Craig didn't make the bruises,' Aimee agreed.

'So who made them?' Susan asked me. The contact supervisor opened her notepad and began writing.

'I wasn't aware Aimee had any fresh bruises,' I said to Susan. 'Perhaps she fell over at school. Have you asked Aimee how she got the bruises?'

'No, I'm asking you!' Susan said, stabbing her finger at me.

'I've no idea,' I said. 'Did you fall over at school?' I asked Aimee.

'I don't know,' Aimee said with a shrug. 'But Craig didn't do them.' I wondered what conversation had taken place in contact about Craig bruising Aimee and what effect it would have on Aimee's testimony the following day when she was interviewed by the child protection police officer. I'd been told not to discuss the matter with Aimee, and Susan shouldn't have discussed it either, but clearly something had been said.

As the supervisor wasn't going to intervene and stop Susan's diatribe against me, it was left to me, so I said what the contact supervisor should have said. 'Susan, if you have any concerns you need to raise them with your social worker, not here.'

'Don't you worry, I will!' she snapped at me.

'Are we ready to go, then?' I said to Aimee.

'No!' Aimee said.

'Say goodbye to your mum,' I encouraged Aimee.

The contact supervisor stopped writing and I hoped she might help and encourage Aimee to say goodbye to her mother, which was part of the contact supervisor's role, but she didn't.

'Not going with her,' Aimee said, folding her arms across her chest and scowling at me.

'Dinner is ready and waiting,' I tried. 'I bet you're hungry.'

'Don't want dinner,' Aimee scowled. 'I'm full of sweets.'

There was a few moments' silence when I wondered how long we were going to stand here in this impasse before the contact supervisor decided to intervene and help. Then Susan spoke, and what she said left me speechless. The supervisor looked shocked too.

'Aimee, go with Cathy and have your dinner,' Susan said quietly, all signs of anger gone.

I wondered if I'd heard right, and so too did the supervisor, who was staring at Susan, as well as looking somewhat relieved. 'Come on, say goodbye, love,' Susan said, taking a step towards her daughter to hug her.

I continued to look at Susan, amazed at the sudden change. There was no sign of her previous anger; as she concentrated on Aimee she just looked very tired and old. Then I noticed she was sweating; beads of perspiration stood out on her forehead and the skin on her cheeks and chin glistened, despite it being a cold winter's day. The heating in the centre was on but it wasn't especially hot – not enough to make you sweat. I also noticed that Susan was shaking, her hands trembled as she reached out to hug Aimee, and she kept licking her bottom lip and swallowing. Either Susan was ill or badly in need of her next fix. For it now occurred to me that Susan was showing classic signs of drug withdrawal.

'Give me a kiss,' Susan said to Aimee, agitated and clearly in a hurry. Her hand trembled on Aimee's shoulder as she bent forward to hug her daughter. And just at that moment, as they hugged and kissed goodbye, I felt sorry for Susan. How and when had her life gone so badly wrong? She hadn't started life intending to lose all her children into care, and I feared if she didn't get off drugs soon she'd lose her life too.

'Bye, speak on the phone tomorrow, and see you on Friday,' Susan said, easing her daughter away from her and towards me. I saw the desperation in Susan's eyes and I think she knew I'd seen it.

'Bye, Susan,' I said. 'Take care, and we'll phone tomorrow.'

'Thank you,' she said quietly, as though she was ashamed.

Aimee came compliantly to my side and we left the building. She had gone quiet and didn't say anything until we were in the car. Before I started the engine I turned in my seat to look at her. All anger towards me had gone and she just looked sad and also worried.

'Are you OK?' I asked gently.

She shrugged. 'I wish Mum wouldn't go to Craig's. I don't like him.'

I didn't understand the connection but assumed Aimee just needed some more reassurance. 'You're safe with me now,' I said. 'Craig can't hurt you.'

'No. You don't understand,' Aimee said, peering out of her side window for any sign of her mother. 'Mum *has to* see Craig or she gets ill.'

I turned in my seat to look at her, aware she hadn't finished what she wanted to say. 'Mum was starting to get ill in contact,' Aimee continued. 'She'll be very sick soon if she doesn't see Craig.' It was then I realized that Aimee was probably referring to the effects of drug withdrawal and that she too had seen the signs in her mother, just as I had. Living with her mother Aimee would be more familiar with them than I was.

'Why does she go to Craig?' I asked, half guessing her reply.

'He gives her Big H,' Aimee said, using the street name for heroin. 'Well, he doesn't give it to her – she has to pay him. A lot. He takes all our money and he's horrible to me and my mum.'

From which I deduced Craig was Susan's main supplier. That Aimee knew all this was shocking. She was still staring out of her side window, watching for her mother to come out of the family centre. 'I wish my life could have been different,' she said wistfully. 'I wish I was at home with my mum and dad, and my brothers and sisters. I wish my mum would stop doing drugs and being ill.'

'Aimee, love,' I said, watching her carefully, 'I know how difficult it is and I wish things could have been different for you too. I know you worry about your mum, and maybe having you taken into care will give your mother the shock she needs to get her off drugs.'

'Maybe,' Aimee said, looking at me. 'But I don't think the judge will send me back home even if she does. Mum's had all these years – since before I was born – to get clean, but she hasn't done it. Even if she says she's clean I don't think the judge will believe her, do you?'

My heart ached for Aimee. She was so young and yet showed the wisdom of an adult. The poor child couldn't read or write but intuitively knew the outcome of her court case. She was right: given her mother's long history of drug addiction and failure to look after and protect her older children, of course a judge wouldn't make an order to return her home. Susan had had twenty-seven years to turn her life around! In this respect it was too late and Aimee deserved an honest response.

'I think you're right, Aimee,' I said gently. 'I think the judge will want to make sure you're safe and well looked after while you are a child. You are too precious to risk being hurt again.'

Aimee gave a small nod and then said: 'It was bad at Mum's, and Dad's, and all the other houses we had to go to. It was dark, and strange and scary people came into the house at night. No one told me but I knew what they were doing.'

'What?'

'Buying and selling drugs, and not just Big H. There was other stuff.'

'Where were these other houses you had to visit? Do you know?'

Aimee shook her head. 'They were all over the place, some in our town and some in a different town. It was better when we stayed at Craig's. There was a blanket on the floor and I hid under it while Mum went with Craig. Sometimes my mum had to go with Craig when she didn't have the money for the drugs,' Aimee explained. 'And sometimes she had to go with other men. I didn't know them. Then she got the drugs and we left.'

I knew prostitution was rife among addicts and that sex was a common form of currency for paying for drugs when the money had run out. I looked at Aimee and hesitated before asking, 'Do you know what your mother was doing when she went with Craig or the other men?'

'Having sex,' Aimee said easily, pulling a face of disgust. 'Sometimes they went to a different room to do it, but sometimes they didn't. You let men do anything if you need drugs. You even let them hurt you.'

A cold chill ran down my spine. Whatever had this poor girl witnessed in these drug dens? 'Was your mother hurt?' I asked.

'Can't tell you,' Aimee said, and she grimaced. And I knew the memories of her mother very likely being sexually abused in return for drugs were far too painful for Aimee to share with me now.

'Did those men ever hurt you?' I asked. I should find out what I could for the social worker.

'They tried,' Aimee said, 'but Mum usually stopped them. She said I was too young.'

'Usually?' I asked.

Aimee didn't reply.

'All right. Tell me when you are ready,' I said. 'You're safe now.' If Aimee had witnessed sexual acts, as it now appeared, it could explain her sexual awareness, which was inappropriate for a child her age, but it was also possible she'd been sexually abused by the men who had abused her mother. I would pass this on to her social worker but for now Aimee just needed reassurance.

'Thankfully you are safe now and will continue to be safe, and happy.'

'But Mum still loves me,' Aimee said. 'I hope she always will, even if I don't go home.'

I felt my eyes fill. It was at moments like this that I dearly wished I could change history and make everything OK, so that Aimee could return home to two loving parents and live happily ever after, but I knew that wasn't going to happen. 'Your mum loves you,' I said, 'and I'm sure she always will.' And while I believed this to be true, part of me said that Susan should have shown her love by getting off the drugs so she could parent her children.

'And I will always love my mummy,' Aimee added.

'Good,' I said, smiling. 'But it's OK to like me a little as well, you know?'

'I wish my mum could be like you, and not do drugs,' Aimee said as I turned to the front, ready to start the car engine. 'You don't do drugs, and you're happy – well, most of the time, apart from when you tell me off.'

I smiled at her in the rear-view mirror. 'I don't tell you off that often,' I said. 'But I do care about you, and part of caring for a child is helping them do the right thing so that they grow into really nice people. Now let's go home and get some dinner. I'm starving.'

'Me too,' Aimee said.

I smiled at her again and started the car's engine, but before I pulled away the doors to the family centre flew open and Susan came out. Eyes down, she hurried along the path with little jerky steps, clearly agitated and, if Aimee and I were right, now desperate for her next fix.

'Look! There's Mum!' Aimee cried, tapping on her window to try to attract her mother's attention.

But Susan had only one thing on her mind: getting the drugs her body so badly craved. She continued past our car without even seeing Aimee, sweating and shaking, her need for drugs again overriding the needs of her daughter, just as it had always done.

'I'm never doing drugs,' Aimee said, as her mother turned the corner and was out of view. 'Never. Ever.'

'I know you won't. You've seen the damage they can do. You'll be happy without them.'

'Like you.'

That evening at home Aimee was quieter and less confrontational than usual. She ate her dinner without making a scene over not having biscuits and barely complained when I said we should do fifteen minutes' homework. At bedtime she didn't protest at having to wash, and then let me brush her hair. I guessed that seeing her mother in the state she'd been in had reminded Aimee of just how bad things were at home, and that perhaps life with me wasn't so bad after all. Lucy and Paula noticed the change in Aimee too.

'Aimee was quiet,' Paula said later, when I was in the sitting room writing up my log notes.

'Long may it continue,' Lucy added.

I explained to the girls how Susan had been at contact and that Aimee had talked about the drug dens and what had gone on there.

'Poor kid,' Lucy said. 'I'll forgive her for waking me up this morning.'

'I'm glad you stopped smoking, Mum,' Paula said. 'Smoking is a drug and I used to worry about you smoking.'

'I'm sorry, love,' I said, feeling about two inches tall. I'd stopped smoking many years before and this was a harsh reminder of what children remember and worry about. 'I won't start again,' I confirmed. 'It was silly to ever begin. And I know you two won't ever smoke,' I added for good measure.

The following morning Aimee was still a little subdued but I thought that might be no bad thing. She was being interviewed by DC Nicki Davies, the child protection police officer, that day at school, and if Aimee was still reflecting on her life before coming into care, then I hoped she would be in a good position to answer DC Nicki Davies's questions and detail the abuse she'd suffered, which should lead to prosecutions.

I didn't tell Aimee that she was gong to be interviewed, as Kristen had instructed me not to, so I took Aimee to school as usual, waited in the playground until the bell rang, and then said goodbye (Aimee still didn't want a hug or kiss goodbye) and I went home.

Half an hour later, with a mug of coffee within reach and my fostering folder containing my log notes open on my lap, I telephoned Jill. I related what Aimee had said after contact the evening before – about visiting the drug dens, Susan's anger towards me, and that both Aimee and I had thought we'd seen signs of drug withdrawal in her mother. Jill thanked me for being so vigilant, said she felt very sorry for Aimee – having been forced into that life, and confirmed she would pass the information to Kristen. I also told Jill that I was getting fed up with Susan's anger and complaints and perhaps Kristen could ask Susan to try to control herself.

'I'll certainly ask.' Jill said lightly. 'Although I doubt it will do any good.' Her dismissiveness niggled me slightly, as I didn't think Jill fully appreciated the effect Susan's anger and aggression was having on me.

'I don't expect Susan to be grateful,' I said. 'But if she could stop shouting complaints at me in front of Aimee, it would help.'

'All right, I'll see what I can do.'

I didn't hear anything further from Jill (or Kristen) that day and when I collected Aimee at the end of school she told me she'd had to leave one of her lessons to see Kristen and a strange lady, whom she remembered seeing once before. I guessed the 'strange lady' was DC Nicki Davies. Aimee said the lady had asked her questions but she didn't know many of the answers, which didn't sound very positive. Aimee was vague about the whole meeting and didn't want to talk about it, so I didn't press her. She was in a bad mood all evening, made worse by her mother not answering when we rang for phone contact. I tried four times, over an hour, and even let Aimee key in the numbers to make sure they were right, but each time we listened to the automated message – *It has not been possible to connect this call*. After the fourth attempt I gave up and didn't try again. Aimee stamped her feet, cursed her mother, cursed me and generally made herself very disagreeable, so that I was glad when it was time for her to go to bed. On the way to bed she objected to and complained about everything; she refused to wash, brush her teeth and hair, change into her pyjamas and go to her bedroom, until I said she'd lose television time the following evening if she didn't do as I'd asked. Aimee's confrontational attitude and anger was just like her mother's and this was another reason Susan needed to control her anger – Aimee copied her.

Finally Aimee was in bed and I breathed a sigh of relief. 'Goodnight,' I said, leaving the room and starting to close her bedroom door.

'Hey! Haven't you forgotten something?' she demanded rudely.

I eased open the door. 'What, Aimee?'

'You always ask me if I want a hug and kiss goodnight. But you didn't tonight.'

'No, because you never want to. Why? Do you want a hug and kiss tonight?' I asked, amazed. Aimee had been so angry with me all evening I'd have thought it was the last thing she would have wanted.

'No, I don't,' Aimee said bluntly. 'But I want you to keep asking me. It's a sign of caring to keep asking.'

Despite myself, I laughed. Aimee had such a streetwise charm, and stated things simply as she saw them. All my annoyance caused by the hard time she'd given me that evening vanished, and I would have loved to wrap her in my arms and hug her.

'Are you sure you wouldn't like a hug and kiss goodnight?' I asked, going back into the room.

'Quite sure,' she said. 'But keep asking and one day I will.' She smiled and her face lit up, just as an eight-year-old's should.

'Good. And when that day comes I'll give you the biggest hug and kiss ever, and I'll be so happy.'

'Me too,' Aimee said dreamily. ''Night, Cathy.'

'Goodnight, love.'

Chapter Fifteen
Quiet and Withdrawn

Jill phoned on Friday afternoon and asked if I'd heard yet from Aimee's new social worker. I said I hadn't heard anything, so Jill said she'd phone the social services on Monday, speak to someone in the children in care team and find out who was taking over. She then asked if Aimee had given me any feedback on the interview she'd had with DC Nicki Davies the day before. I said she hadn't, other than telling me she'd seen Kristen and a 'strange lady' who had asked her questions she didn't know the answers to. Jill laughed at the 'strange lady' but, like me, was concerned the interview might not have been very productive. She then said she'd spoken to Kristen before the interview and told her what Aimee had said about visiting drug dens with her mother, and that it was possible Susan could have been under the influence of drugs while at contact. Kristen had said she wouldn't have time to look into it now as she was leaving the case after the child protection interview, but she would leave a note on the file for the next social worker.

'And did you have a chance to ask Kristen to speak to Susan about trying to control her anger towards me?' I asked.

'I did,' Jill said. 'And Kristen said she'd try to raise it with Susan before she passed on the case.'

'Fantastic,' I said. 'Because I think another complaint from Susan will soon be on its way. We couldn't get through for phone contact last night, despite trying four times.'

Another Forgotten Child

'Oh dear,' Jill said, sighing. 'Fingers crossed Susan takes on board what Kristen tells her.' But I could hear the scepticism in Jill's voice.

As usual I didn't see Susan at the start of contact that Friday afternoon, as she was already in the contact room, but at the end of contact she came out with Aimee and the contact supervisor, and as usual she was furious. Not only because we hadn't phoned – 'She won't let my daughter speak to me!' – but also because I was 'forcing' Aimee to wash, brush her teeth and hair, being 'horrible to her' and making up lies about Susan to the police. I was slightly surprised by this last reference – to the police – but I suspected it was in some way connected to the interview Aimee had had with DC Nicki Davies, but I didn't know how or what I was supposed to have said. I hadn't been at the interview and hadn't spoken to Nicki Davies or any other police officer. Perhaps Susan was referring to the fact that I'd reported Aimee's disclosures about Craig abusing her in the first place. Susan didn't elaborate on this point and continued with her diatribe of largely illogical complaints, so that again I was forced to stand in reception at the family centre and listen to a torrent of abuse, while the contact supervisor stood by watching. Sometimes contact supervisors intervene if a foster carer is facing a difficult parent and try to calm the parent, thereby offering some support to the foster carer, but more often, wanting to stay on the good side of the parent, whom they have to see regularly at contact, they say nothing. There was no sign of the centre's manager who had intervened before and there was no sign of Susan relenting. I thought this could go on all night.

Eventually I'd had as much as I could take and said to the contact supervisor: 'We need to go,' Then to Aimee: 'Say good-bye to your mother, please. Good girl, then we can go home.'

'No! Shan't!' said Aimee rudely.

I looked at the contact supervisor. 'I think it's best if I wait outside in my car and you bring Aimee out to me,' I said.

'You can't do that,' the contact supervisor said. 'You're supposed to collect the child from inside the centre.'

'So tell me how I can do that?' I asked, not bothering to hide my irritation.

The contact supervisor looked very uncomfortable and then looked at Susan. 'Do you think we might –' she began, but didn't get any further.

'Don't you start!' Susan said, rounding on her. 'What the fuck do you think you're doing writing down that I was on drugs at contact?' Which I thought was interesting. This wasn't the same supervisor who'd supervised the contact on Wednesday, when Susan appeared to be withdrawing from drugs, so it appeared there'd been another occasion when this supervisor had spotted signs of drugs in Susan.

The contact supervisor looked more uncomfortable, but said nothing.

'Aimee, say goodbye to your mother,' I tried one last time.

'No,' Aimee said defiantly.

'I'll be waiting in the car,' I said to the supervisor, and turning, I left the centre.

I went down the path and to my car, where I got in and closed the door. My heart was racing and my breath was coming fast and shallow; I was stressed and upset. I'd never given up on a child before but I couldn't put up with this three times a week, every week for a year. Susan had played a game of having her older children repeatedly moved from foster carer to foster carer and I could see how it had happened. I was someone who avoided confrontation and I prided myself on usually being able to establish a good working relationship with the parent(s) of the child I was fostering, but Susan was impossible to deal with. Unless I got some support from the contact supervisors I could see a point coming in the not too distant future where I would have had enough.

Thirty minutes later, after the family centre had officially closed for the day, the contact supervisor finally appeared with Aimee. Susan wasn't in sight. I got out of the car and opened the rear door so that Aimee could get in. She didn't look at me but I could see that her eyes were red from crying. I didn't know if there was a specific reason for her crying or if she was just upset, and the contact supervisor didn't tell me. Indeed the supervisor treated me very coolly. Having brought Aimee to the car she turned and went back into the centre without even saying good-bye. Perhaps she blamed me for leaving her to Susan's rage, but she had her manager and the other centre staff to look out for her while I just had me.

'Are you OK?' I now asked Aimee as I leant in and checked her seatbelt.

She nodded and sniffed. I put my hand lightly on her shoulder to comfort her but she pulled away. Closing her car door, I went round and climbed in the driver's seat, and began the drive home. Aimee didn't speak during the journey and every so often I glanced in the rear-view mirror and asked her if she was all right, to which she gave a small nod. But as I pulled up outside our house she broke her silence and said: 'I don't want dinner. I've got tummy ache.'

I guessed it was a result of the upset at contact. I knew how she felt; my stomach was still in a tight knot.

'I want to go to bed,' she added plaintively.

Cutting the engine, I turned in my seat to look at her. She looked very sad and withdrawn, almost depressed. 'Aimee,' I said with a reassuring smile. 'When children first come into care it's always very difficult for everyone, but it does get better, I promise you. Very soon you and your mum will be in the routine of seeing each other at contact and having a nice time and then saying goodbye. Your mum will be less angry and it will get easier for both of you, and me. I've looked after many children and know this always happens.' This was true, although I did wonder if this would happen with Susan.

'So please try not to worry,' I continued, trying to give Aimee the reassurance she so badly needed. 'Enjoy the time you spend with your mum at contact and then enjoy your time at home with me. It's Saturday tomorrow and I'm planning on taking you to the cinema. Have you ever been to the cinema before?'

Aimee shook her head. 'No.'

'You'll love it. A film called *Madagascar* is showing. It's a lovely cartoon film about animals who run away from a zoo and have lots of adventures. We'll have some sweets and popcorn too.'

Aimee's face finally lost its downcast expression and lit up, although I suspected it was more because of the promise of sweets and popcorn than anything else I'd said.

'Cor,' she exclaimed. 'I've heard the kids at school say they've been to the cinema and had sweets and popcorn. Now I'll be able to say I have too.'

I smiled. 'Yes, you will. You'll be able to join in.' Here was another sad indication of the life Aimee had lived: that she'd reached the age of eight without ever going to the cinema. True, it wasn't life-threatening neglect or abuse but in a developed society it's reasonable for a child to benefit from what society has to offer and share similar experiences to those of their peer group.

'We'll have a great time,' I said.

'Yes, we will,' Aimee agreed, brightening. 'I'm looking forward to it.'

* * *

That evening Aimee was exhausted; it was the end of the week and I also suspected she was emotionally exhausted from the ups and downs of seeing her mother. She did eat dinner, and with virtually no complaints, and was too tired to object to having a wash and brushing her teeth, which made the bedtime routine a lot easier. Once she was in her pyjamas I saw her into bed, and I said she could sleep in the following morning, as we didn't have to get up early for school.

'Good,' she sighed, snuggling beneath the duvet. 'I'll have a long, long sleep. I like my bed here. It's nice and warm and comfortable. Not like that smelly mattress at home.'

I smiled and tucked her in. 'I'm pleased you like your bed,' I said. 'Would you like a goodnight kiss and a hug?'

Her face wrinkled to a cheeky grin. 'No thank you, but keep asking.'

'I will.'

That evening, as usual, once I'd finished clearing up I wrote up my log notes, including the scene that had taken place at contact. As I wrote I felt the heaviness of what had happened descend on me again – Susan's anger and Aimee's upset. Goodness knew what thoughts went through Aimee's head when she was alone in bed at night and ran through the day's events. Because of the distance she was keeping between us she didn't share her fears and worries with me, as other children I'd fostered had, and as far as I knew she didn't share them with anyone else, so they were 'bottled up'. Aimee didn't have face-to-face contact over the weekend, but she did have phone contact, and I dearly hoped Susan wouldn't use it as a vehicle for making more trouble. I was looking forward to a pleasant and relaxing weekend.

The following morning we all had a lie-in and then once up I cooked a full English breakfast, which was a weekend tradition in our house: eggs, bacon, sausage, tomatoes and fried bread. Adrian, my son who was away at university, telephoned during the morning and said he was up in the Lake District with a couple of his friends for the weekend. Their return journey, the following day, would take them within a few miles of our house and he was thinking of stopping by to see us – was that OK?

'Of course,' I said. 'We'll look forward to it. Do you all want dinner?'

'Yes please. It'll give me a chance to meet Aimee too.'

'Yes,' I said, hesitantly. 'It will. But you'd better explain to your friends that Aimee hasn't been with us long and is still settling in.'

Adrian gave a small laugh. 'OK, Mum, but don't worry. I'm sure she'll be on her best behaviour.'

'Hopefully,' I said.

As soon as Adrian and I had finished talking on the phone and having said goodbye, I went through to the kitchen to make sure there was enough food in the fridge for the weekend. Three big lads would need feeding well and I took a large joint of meat out of the freezer to defrost. I then told Lucy and Paula that Adrian would be stopping by with a couple of friends for Sunday dinner and they were pleased. I also told them I was planning to take Aimee to the cinema that afternoon for the five o'clock performance of *Madagascar* and, never too old for animated cartoons, they both wanted to come too.

When I told Aimee that Adrian and two of his friends were coming on Sunday she said, 'Oh goody. Lots of men, just like at my mum's.'

'I don't think so,' I said. 'What do you mean?'

'Nothing.' She shook her head and refused to say any more.

I also told Aimee that Lucy and Paula were coming with us to the cinema. 'Are Adrian and his friends coming too?' Aimee asked with no conception of time.

'No, they are coming tomorrow – Sunday. Today is Saturday, and we are going to the cinema.' As I'd done previously with Aimee (and also other children I'd fostered who'd struggled to understand time and the days of the week) I pointed to the large colourful children's calendar pinned to the wall in the kitchen.

'Here is today,' I said, pointing to Saturday on the calendar. 'And here is tomorrow, Sunday. Sunday is after one sleep. We are going to the cinema today, and tomorrow, after one sleep, Adrian and his friends are coming.'

'And how many sleeps to school again?' Aimee sensibly asked.

'Two – tonight and tomorrow.'

She nodded and I think she understood.

Aimee was thrilled to have Lucy and Paula accompany us to the cinema and wanted to sit between them to watch the film, which was fine with them. I'd already explained to Aimee what would happen in the cinema – how we'd sit in a row of chairs with other people and the lights would go down and then the film would come on a very big screen, much bigger than the television. But when the lights dimmed and the cinema darkened Aimee squealed and grabbed the girls' arms, which sent popcorn everywhere. 'Don't worry,' I laughed. 'It's an occupational hazard at the cinema. You've got plenty more.'

The four of us had a nice afternoon and we all enjoyed the film (and the sweets and popcorn); the only downside for me was the thought of the phone call I had to make when we got home. We'd be phoning Susan a bit later than usual – I estimated we'd be home from the cinema at about seven o'clock, and we'd phone straightaway. We usually phoned between six and 6.30, so it wasn't much later than normal and I (naively) hoped Susan wouldn't object, as her daughter had benefited from going to the cinema.

Quiet and Withdrawn

As I had estimated, we arrived home at seven o'clock and with Aimee on the sofa beside me we phoned straightaway, but as soon as Susan answered and Aimee said 'Hello, Mum,' she began – at Aimee.

'You're late phoning,' she said. 'I've been waiting for ages for you. I'm not well, and this has made me feel worse. Where have you been?'

Aimee's previous enthusiasm for telling her mother all about her trip to the cinema vanished, and she looked at me to give her mother the explanation.

'Susan, Cathy here,' I said, moving closer to the mic in the phone. 'I'm sorry we're phoning a bit later than usual but I took Aimee to the cinema to see –'

'I'm not talking to you,' she snapped rudely. 'This phone call is between me and my daughter.' Then, addressing Aimee: 'Aimee, don't phone late again, do you hear? It makes me ill. I've been in bed all day.' And Susan continued telling Aimee about her stomach cramps, diarrhoea and sickness, which according to her had been made worse by our later-than-usual phone call.

Clearly I didn't know if Susan had been unwell that day or if us phoning slightly later than usual had compounded her illness, but the result was instant and effective. Aimee gave up all thoughts of telling her mother what a good time she'd had at the cinema and, feeling guilty for upsetting her, listened, sympathized and then apologized.

'I'm sorry, Mum,' she said. 'I should be at home to look after you. Tell the social worker you need me there.'

'I will.'

Most emotionally responsible parents wouldn't worry their children with their own ailments but make light of them or not mention them at all, but Susan was emotionally immature and very needy, probably as a result of her own upbringing. She treated Aimee as a confidante or surrogate mother figure and offloaded. So that after another ten minutes of listening to her mother's symptoms and suffering (which were really quite minor) Aimee was sad and anxious.

'Will you be all right alone tonight?' she asked fretfully.

'I'll manage. Craig's coming later. He'll look after me.'

I saw the colour drain from Aimee's face at the mention of her abuser and she also looked very confused. 'Why's he coming?' she asked in a small voice.

'To look after me, silly. You know how he looks after me.'

I didn't know what game Susan was playing but it was a cruel one, for here she was telling her daughter that her abuser was a good man who looked after her when she was ill, while her daughter wasn't there for her. I saw the confusion, upset and rejection on Aimee's face and decided it was time to step in. Lowering my voice away from the mic I said quietly to Aimee, 'Tell your mother you went to the cinema and then say goodnight.'

'Bye, Mum. I hope you're better soon,' Aimee said, omitting her news.

'Are you going already?' Susan asked, her voice rising.

'Yes. Cathy says I have to.'

'Why? What's it got to do with her?'

Aimee looked at me, very worried, and didn't know what to say.

'Susan,' I said, again moving closer to the mic, 'as you know I've been asked to monitor these calls and intervene if necessary. I don't think it's appropriate to be talking about Craig, given the allegations that have been made against him, and the police investigation. It's also upsetting for Aimee. So if you'd like to say goodbye we'll phone again tomorrow at the usual time. You can discuss my decision to shorten this call on Monday with your social worker.'

'You bet I will! When I find out who the new social worker is.'

'Say goodbye to your mum,' I now said to Aimee so that Susan could hear.

'Bye, Mum,' Aimee said. 'Please don't let Craig come round. I don't like him. He'll hurt you.'

'Don't be so silly – of course he won't hurt me,' Susan said. 'He's my friend. Make sure you phone on time tomorrow. Goodbye.' And she hung up.

Aimee sat beside me on the sofa, confused, sad and upset. I could see she didn't know what to think about Craig and her mother, and was riddled with guilt and self-doubt. Susan would make a complaint next week that I'd cut short the call but I knew my action had been justified – to protect Aimee. I reasoned that if I couldn't end a call when I saw fit there was no point in monitoring these phone calls, and I hoped the new social worker would agree and support my decision.

'It's my fault Mum has to see Craig,' Aimee said after a moment.

'Of course it's not,' I said firmly. 'Your mum is an adult. She makes her own decisions about who she sees. You're not responsible for her.'

'But if I'd looked after her better when I was at home I wouldn't be in care. If I'd cleaned the house and cooked and gone to school when I should, I would be at home with Mum and she wouldn't need Craig to look after her. I shouldn't have told you about Craig – it's made Mum upset.'

Susan had succeeded in punishing Aimee and making her feel guilty for disclosing Craig's abuse.

'Aimee, love,' I said, turning to her on the sofa, 'you are not responsible for your mother and you did right to tell me what Craig did to you. Parents should protect their children and look after them. It's not the child's job to cook and clean and get to school. It's the parents' job, and unfortunately your mother couldn't do it, which is why you're here with me. I'm sorry your mother feels she has to see Craig, and I can understand why you're worried, but it is your mother's decision. It's a pity she mentioned Craig on the phone and when I speak to the new social worker I will explain what has happened. All right?'

Aimee shrugged despondently, any residue of delight in our outing to the cinema completely gone.

'Come on, cheer up,' I said. 'Can I give you a hug?

Aimee shook her head.

'Can I hold your hand, then?' I asked, feeling the need to offer her some physical comfort.

She gave a small nod and I gently lifted one of her hands, which was resting on her lap, and took it between mine. It was the first physical contact I'd had with Aimee apart from washing her hair, and her hand felt stiff and resistant. Children who have been physically abused are very wary of physical contact, as experience has taught them it usually hurts. I continued to gently stroke Aimee's hand as she stared straight ahead; then she slid her hand from mine and asked if I'd read her a bedtime story.

'Of course,' I said. 'Choose some books from the shelf.'

She left the sofa and gathered a selection of young children's storybooks from the bookshelf, which I read with her sitting next to me on the sofa. After we'd finished I told her it was time for her bath and I began the bedtime routine. She was still subdued and for the second night in a row didn't object to washing or cleaning her teeth. And while this made life easier for me, I hated seeing her so quiet and withdrawn and would have preferred the feisty child who objected to everything. I asked her a few times what was wrong and she said, 'Nothing.'

I finally tucked her into bed and said goodnight. She was lying flat on her back and staring at the ceiling. And just for a moment as she stared, unseeing and distant, I caught another glimpse of Jodie who, as a result of horrendous abuse, withdrew so far into herself she became impossible to reach. It had been dreadful to witness and I knew it must never happen to Aimee.

Chapter Sixteen
Serious Allegation

I didn't sleep well that night. Thoughts of Jodie flashed through my mind and I checked on Aimee three times, but she was always fast asleep. It was a long night and I was very relieved when Aimee woke the following morning and sprang out of bed, her usual objectionable self. 'I ain't having me hair washed today!' were her first words – she was aware I always gave her hair a good wash and fine-tooth comb on a Sunday morning.

'Aimee, before we debate the merits of washing your hair, there's something I need to say to you.'

'Yeah?' she said quizzically, standing by her bed. 'You know you can talk to me.'

I smiled at the phrase I sometimes used, sounding quaint when spoken by a child. 'Aimee, I wanted to make sure you know that you can talk to me about anything that's worrying you. It often helps to talk about the things that worry us, to share a problem. And I won't be shocked or upset.'

'Like what?' she said, eyeing me cautiously.

'Well, I don't know exactly,' I said, perching on the bed. 'Only you know what could be worrying you. But I think things could have happened before you came into care, which you now realize were bad and could be worrying you. I want you to feel you can tell me. I don't want you to keep worries to yourself and "bottle them up" because that can make them worse. I also want you to remember that whatever happened before you came into care wasn't your fault. Do you understand?' Abused children often blame themselves, feeling they should have stopped the abuse, or that they deserved it because they were naughty, or even encouraged it by being 'a tease'.

'Can I have egg and bacon for breakfast?' Aimee said, changing the subject.

'Yes, but will you remember what I've told you? And try and share any worries you have with me or another adult you trust, like your teacher?'

'I'll try,' she said. 'Egg, bacon, beans and fried bread, please.'

'Fine. Would you like your hair washed before or after your breakfast?' I asked, relying on the closed choice.

'After,' she said, not realizing she'd agreed to a hair wash.

'Excellent.'

And that is what we did. I cooked Aimee the breakfast she wanted and once she'd finished eating she kept her part of the bargain and allowed me to wash her hair – with, of course, her usual protestations, which I didn't mind. The old Aimee was back and I was pleased.

However, when Adrian and his two friends arrived just after one o'clock it soon became obvious I was going to have to keep a watchful eye on Aimee to make sure they weren't embarrassed.

'Cor, they're nice,' Aimee said, sighing, as the lads stepped into the hall and we greeted each other. 'Much better-looking than me mum's men.'

Lucy and Paula had heard Aimee's remark and looked at me, worried, but I didn't think Adrian and his friends had heard. But once we were in the sitting room Aimee snuggled herself cosily in between the lads on the three-seater sofa and then gazed up at them adoringly.

'Aimee, come and sit with me or the girls,' I said, going over. I took her hand and led her off the sofa. 'There's not enough room for four on there.' Aimee was about to object but thought better of it, and joined Paula and Lucy on the two-seater sofa. The girls knew why I'd moved Aimee, and Adrian might have done too, while his friends simply thought I'd moved her to give them more room.

I made drinks and then we all sat in the sitting room while the dinner cooked and chatted – about the lads' trip to the Lake District, university, and what the girls and I had been doing. Aimee sat between Lucy and Paula and tried to join in the conversation. Most eight-year-olds would find adult conversation boring and prefer to be off playing, but Aimee, having never been allowed a carefree childhood, was used to living on the edge of her parents' adult word. I was slowly teaching her to play as a child should but there was still a long way to go.

When I had to leave the room to check on dinner I suggested to Aimee that she might like to come with me and help, but she wanted to stay in the sitting room. Lucy and Paula knew to watch her if I wasn't in the room, and when dinner was ready I set a place at the table for Aimee between Paula and me, and on the opposite side of the table to the lads. But she had clearly taken a fancy to Adrian and stared at him adoringly throughout the meal. I would like to say it was the adoration of a younger sibling towards an older brother but it was more than that. Aimee batted her eyelids and threw him flirtatious looks designed to catch his attention, which Adrian either ignored or didn't see. Every so often I said, 'Come on, Aimee, concentrate on your meal,' to redirect her attention, but whenever she regained concentration it was short-lived.

I knew that Aimee had watched a lot of adult films before coming into care and she'd said she'd seen her mother go with men in return for drugs, so it was possible she was imitating

what she'd seen, but it was also possible Aimee's sexual awareness was a result of sexual abuse. Clearly Aimee had secrets and
had been living in an environment where she could have been
sexually abused, but I wouldn't know for sure unless she told
me.

After we'd finished eating everyone helped clear the table,
and a short while later Adrian said he and his friends should be
going, as they had a lengthy drive to university and the temperature was set to drop to freezing that night. The girls and I went
to the front door to see them off and we kissed each other goodbye. Aimee, as part of our family, was included in this and the
lads bent down so that she could reach their cheeks to kiss them
goodbye, which she did appropriately. But once they'd gone she
then spent the next hour with a silly grin on her face talking
about the 'three big boys' she'd kissed. I knew that taken out
of context and repeated to a third person her comments could
sound highly inappropriate, so eventually I said, 'Aimee, in our
family we always kiss each other goodbye on the cheek. It's
nothing to be silly about, so just forget it.'

'I'm not silly,' Aimee said. 'I know about kissing. I kissed lots
of men at me mum's.'

'Did you?' I asked with assumed nonchalance, pausing from
what I was doing.

'Who were they?'

'My mum's friends. We did lots of kissing.'

'What, on the cheek?'

'Sometimes, and sometimes we kissed on the mouth like
this.'

I looked at Aimee and she parted her lips and demonstrated
a lingering open-mouthed kiss on the back of her hand. 'Who
did you kiss like that?' I asked.

'Can't remember,' she said, perhaps now realizing it wasn't
appropriate for men to kiss a young girl like that.

'Are you sure you can't remember?'

She nodded. 'My mind's a blank.'

'Well, if you do remember, please tell me,' I said. 'A grown man shouldn't kiss a young girl like that.'

I'd have to note this in my log, for clearly if what Aimee had said was true, adults kissing a young girl in this manner was another abuse. Adrian was due to return home from university for Christmas in three weeks' time and I hoped that by then Aimee would have learnt how to behave appropriately when around him so that I wouldn't have to watch her the whole time. It is always difficult fostering a child who is sexually aware beyond their years and has come from a background where sexual abuse was possible. You want to give the child love and affection and make sure they felt included in the family but at the same time you are aware you have to protect your own family. For this reason all foster carers have a document called 'A Safer Caring Policy', which includes how to kiss, touch and hug the foster child appropriately. It's sad that this is necessary, but children who are sexually aware or have been sexually abused view affection very differently from the average child, so that even the most innocent gesture can be misinterpreted.

That evening at 6.30 I called Aimee to the sitting room, ready for phone contact. As usual we had the phone between us on the sofa and I pushed the hands-free button to set it to speaker-phone. I dialled Susan's number, hoping she had recovered from her stomach upset of the day before and that there'd be no mention of Craig.

Susan answered almost immediately and sounded a bit brighter. 'Hi, how are you?' she asked Aimee pleasantly.

'I'm all right, Mum. I've had a nice day.'

'Have you?' Susan asked, sounding slightly surprised. 'What have you been doing?'

'Kissing boys,' Aimee said, and giggled.

'What do you mean?' Susan asked, her voice even.

'Cathy has a big boy and he and his friends came to the house and we all kissed goodbye.'

Although the emphasis was on kissing it was a reasonable explanation and I waited for Susan's reply. I didn't want to jump in with further explanation if it wasn't necessary. If I spoke to Susan on the phone it always made her angry.

A moment later Susan said, 'OK, so what else have you been doing?' So I assumed that no further explanation was required.

Aimee couldn't think what else she'd been doing and I quietly prompted her to say she'd been playing lots of games, had watched some television, and had spent a relaxing day at home, all of which she repeated. Then she added, 'And I had to have me hair washed. I don't like having me hair washed. I was forced to.'

Susan sympathized. 'I know you don't like having your hair washed. I never made you wash you hair at home, did I?'

'No,' agreed Aimee. 'You were nice. You didn't make me wash my hair and I could eat lots of cakes and sweets, and watch television with you all night.' And their conversation continued on the merits of Aimee's life at home with her mother, in which she could do whatever she wanted to and never had to go to school or wash or eat a healthy diet, compared with the life she led with me where I 'forced' her to do all sorts of things that were good for her. However, on a positive note, Susan didn't mention being ill, or Craig, so that by the end of the phone call I felt that compared to previous phone calls, it could have been a lot worse. I was getting used to Aimee and her mother criticizing me during the phone contact, and while I would note what had been said in my log I tried not to react or take it to heart. I knew that Aimee felt she had to show loyalty to her mother and this was exacerbated because of Susan's hostility towards me.

That evening when I tucked Aimee into bed I asked as I usually did: 'Would you like a hug and kiss goodnight?'

'No, but keep asking,' Aimee said with that cheeky little grin.

I smiled, said goodnight and came out. Paula, who was on the landing and had overheard what had become a nightly refrain, said, 'I don't know why you keep asking her, Mum. She never wants a hug, from any of us.'

'No, but she will one day,' I said. 'You wait and see.'

The following day was Monday, and the week was set to be a busy one. Apart from the (time-consuming) school run and contact, I'd booked a dental appointment for Aimee for after school on Tuesday, for her to have a check-up. I'd also received a letter saying that I should take Aimee for a medical on Wednesday at 9.30 a.m., and an email had arrived from the Guardian ad Litem to say she'd like to visit me at 11.30 a.m. on Friday. I was also hoping to do some Christmas shopping. It was the end of November and many of the shops had their Christmas gifts on display; some were playing Christmas music. Aimee was looking forward to Christmas. Last Christmas, when she and her mother had stayed at Craig's, had been dreadful, and from what she'd told me her previous Christmases hadn't been much better. She'd never hung up a pillowcase on Christmas Eve, never had a proper Christmas dinner, or played party games; in fact she'd never known the sheer joy of Christmas. As with many children from deprived homes, for her Christmas was something you saw on television or that happened in other people's homes. I intended to change all that and give Aimee a Christmas she would remember for a long time.

Jill phoned at Monday lunchtime and, having asked if we'd had a nice weekend, said that the duty social worker at the social services had just phoned, having received a call from Susan. 'More complaints, I'm afraid,' Jill said. 'The duty social worker is dealing with it until a new social worker has been assigned to Aimee's case, which should be by the end of the week.'

I sat on the sofa and reached for my fostering folder, which contained my log notes. 'I'm ready. Go ahead. What's the matter now?'

'Well, we've got the usual complaints – that you're forcing Aimee to wash, eat fruit and vegetables, go to school, brush her hair, eat at a table, and you don't let her watch any television,' Jill said. 'I've reassured the duty social worker on these points but there are two new complaints: you stopped phone contact on Saturday, and on Sunday you let Aimee kiss some teenage boys in your house.'

I sighed. Apart from Susan's complaints being a huge waste of time for all the professionals involved, I was getting fed up with having to justify my actions, and I think Jill was getting fed up with having to ask me to. Fine, if the parent of a child in care has genuine concerns, but this was just spiteful trouble-making.

'I suppose Susan didn't mention that Aimee had a nice weekend and went to the cinema on Saturday?' I asked Jill cynically.

'No. She didn't.'

'Have you got your pen ready?' I said. 'Here goes. I stopped the telephone contact on Saturday because Susan started talking about Craig. She said Craig was going to her house to look after her. As you know, Craig is the man Aimee has accused of abusing her and he is under police investigation. Aimee became very confused and upset at the thought of Craig going to her mother's. She was worried that he would hurt her mother as he'd hurt her. I therefore made the decision to stop the phone contact. I told Susan why. Aimee was quiet for the rest of the evening and blamed herself for being taken into care. She also said she shouldn't have told me about Craig hurting her.'

'I hope you reassured her she did right to tell you?'

'Yes.'

'And the incident on Sunday? What's all that about? I told the duty social worker it was sure to be a misunderstanding.'

'Thank you. Adrian and two friends stopped by for Sunday lunch on their way back to university. They'd been to the Lake District for the weekend. Aware that Aimee can be over-familiar with boys and men, I kept a watchful eye on her. They weren't here for very long and when Adrian and his friends left, Aimee came with us into the hall to say goodbye. We all kissed each other on the cheek, just as we always do when saying good-bye, and Aimee was included. She was a bit silly about it after-wards and told me she'd kissed men on the lips at her mother's. I've written it all down.'

'And that's it?'

'Yes. Except Aimee told her mother on the phone that she'd been kissing boys.'

'According to what Susan told the duty social worker, Aimee made it sound like a game of kiss chase.'

'Ridiculous. That's Susan causing trouble,' I said. 'It's true Aimee said she'd kissed some big boys, but then she clarified it by saying she kissed them goodbye. I'll read you exactly what was said.' I looked at my folder and read Aimee's words, which Jill made a note of.

'Thanks, Cathy. I'll get back to the duty social worker and if I need any more detail I'll give you a ring.'

'There aren't any more details,' I said a bit curtly. 'That's all that happened. Susan's just out to make trouble.'

'I know.'

We said goodbye and, still irritated by all the trouble Susan was causing, I left the house and did a quick round of the local supermarket. I returned home and had just finished unpacking the shopping when Jill phoned, quarter of an hour before I had to leave to collect Aimee from school.

'I've spoken to the duty social worker,' Jill said. 'He and I both support your decision to stop phone contact on Saturday. He's told Susan that Craig must never speak to Aimee on the phone while he's under investigation, and it's better if his name isn't mentioned. But about the other matter – on Sunday – can you confirm there were three lads? Susan says there was a gang involved.'

'You're joking! Of course there were three: Adrian and his two friends.'

'And what are their ages? I know Adrian is twenty-one.'

'The other lads are about the same age. They're all in the same year at university.'

'Thanks. And can you confirm it was only Aimee's cheek they kissed?'

'They didn't kiss Aimee at all!' I said, my voice rising angrily, aware of just how easy it was to make an innocent gesture sound sinister. 'Aimee wanted to kiss the boys goodbye as Lucy, Paula and I were doing. She couldn't reach, so they bent down, and she kissed them on the cheek quite appropriately.'

'You're sure about that, Cathy? It's not possible one of Adrian's friends could have kissed Aimee on the lips?'

'No! Absolutely not. What are you suggesting? I was there. I saw what happened.'

'Sorry, but you appreciate I have to ask. Susan is saying one of the boys kissed Aimee on the mouth, an open-mouthed kiss, and she's threatening to report your family to the police for child abuse.'

My mouth went dry and a cold shiver ran down my spine. Although I knew Susan's allegations were ludicrous, I also knew other foster carers who'd had their lives ruined by unfounded allegations from angry parents. The police (if it becomes a police matter) investigate allegations of child abuse against a foster carer just as they would if it is a parent who has been accused.

The foster child is removed from the foster home and the resulting investigation can take many months. During that time the carers are not allowed to foster and if they have children of their own they can be placed on the child protection register. All parties involved are interviewed and have statements taken; sometimes employers and relatives are also interviewed. Approximately 35 per cent of all foster carers will have an allegation made against them during their fostering career, and often when they are cleared they are too upset to continue fostering and resign – all because an angry parent sought revenge for having their child taken into care.

Not for the first time since I'd started fostering I was grateful I'd kept detailed log notes, and I read out to Jill the details of Adrian and his friends' visit on Sunday.

'Thanks, Cathy,' Jill said. 'I'll tell the duty social worker and hopefully that will be an end to it. I've explained that Susan has a history of unfounded allegations against foster carers. As the duty social worker he didn't know. Try not to worry. I'm sure her allegations will be seen for what they are – malicious.'

I thanked Jill and said goodbye and then, anxious and angry, I left to collect Aimee from school. My dear son, Adrian, a lovely, trustworthy, sensitive, caring lad who'd always welcomed foster children into our home, and his two nice friends, had been accused of inappropriate behaviour and could be the subject of a child protection investigation. I was fuming and hurt. And while I hoped that, given Susan's history of allegations against foster carers, common sense would prevail and the matter wouldn't be taken further, I couldn't be sure.

I arrived at school preoccupied and with a very heavy heart. I stood in the playground in my usual place so that Aimee would know where to find me among the other parents when she came out. Yet despite my worries and anxieties, my spirits lifted a little as Aimee came out and I caught a glimpse of her face. She was grinning from ear to ear and I knew she had some very good news to tell me.

'Guess what!' she cried, bounding to my side. 'I've made some friends! You said I would and you were right. Now I'm not smelly and I don't have nits the kids want to play with me! I told them I went to the cinema. I'm so happy!'

I smiled. Despite my anger at her mother's lies, I was happy for Aimee. This was what fostering was all about – seeing a child's delight at some achievement you have helped them with.

'Fantastic,' I said. 'That's wonderful. Well done. I want you to tell me all about your new friends in the car on the way to contact.'

'I will,' Aimee said. And as we crossed the playground she slipped her hand into mine. It was the first display of affection she'd ever shown towards me, and it couldn't have come at a better time.

Chapter Seventeen

Problem Family

I thought Susan would be pleased to hear Aimee's news — that she'd made friends at school. I thought it might put her in a good mood, so that at the end of contact she might be a bit more pleasant and, if she didn't want to talk to me civilly, she might at least ignore me. But no, when I collected Aimee at 5.30 p.m. and Susan came with Aimee into reception she was as angry and aggressive as she always was.

'Look at the state of her top,' she began as soon as she saw me, pointing to Aimee's school sweatshirt. I could see the sweatshirt had a generous smearing of what looked like chocolate all down the front, some of which was also on Aimee's face. 'If I'd sent her to school like that,' Susan continued, 'I'd have had the social services on to me. So don't think you're getting away with it. I'll report you first thing tomorrow!'

Aimee hadn't gone to school in a dirty sweatshirt and indeed she hadn't gone into contact with one either, so the mess must have resulted from the chocolate Susan had given Aimee at contact. But I knew there was nothing to be gained from pointing this out to Susan so, trying to pacify her, I said lightly, 'Don't worry. It will wash out.' While the contact supervisor as usual said nothing.

'And what about those bruises on her legs?' Susan now demanded. 'How did she get those?' Aimee was wearing school trousers and Susan rolled up the right leg to reveal a small bruise on Aimee's shin, just like the bruises many children have from playing.

'I expect she fell while she was in the playground,' I said. 'Did Aimee tell you she'd made some friends?'

'She always had friends,' Susan snapped, and I wondered if it was this that had riled her. Perhaps Susan was jealous that Aimee had achieved something with me that she hadn't achieved with her mother. But I thought it was best to let this comment go, as I did her other negative comments, and not react. Susan continued with her list of what was wrong with Aimee's appearance, diet, and how I looked after her, most of which I'd heard before, while I stood patiently by and told myself Susan probably couldn't help it, and I should feel sorry for her, until she got to her last comment, when I finally blew.

'And tell your son and his mates to keep their hands off Aimee,' she said.

My pulse soared as my anger rose. 'I beg your pardon?' I demanded. 'How dare you!'

'Letting your boys smooch my little girl,' Susan continued. 'I've told the social services and they'll have you.'

I was so furious I didn't know whether to cry or hit her. 'I really don't understand you!' I blazed. 'I've tried working with you but you're impossible. Little wonder you've lost all your kids into care! I'm not having anything more to do with you, or your malicious lies. I'll be waiting in the car,' I said to the contact supervisor.

Trembling and with my cheeks hot and red I turned and, yanking open the outer door, let myself out. I went quickly down the path and to my car, where I got in and slammed the door. I stared, unseeing, through the front windscreen, my heart racing and my hands clenched in my lap. I was fuming. How dare she! How dare she say that about Adrian and his friends! I could and would have said a lot more to her had Aimee not been present. I'd dealt with difficult parents before but Susan was the extreme. As I sat there, seething and upset, a decision formed itself in my thoughts and was made. My family and I were in danger from Susan's lies, I'd had enough, and I wouldn't take any more. I didn't want to repeat what the carers of Susan's older children had done and give notice and have the child moved, but I would if necessary. I decided I would tell the social services that they'd have to find another foster carer to look after Aimee unless two assurances were made: one, that Susan retracted all her comments about Adrian and his friends, and two, that I never had to meet Susan again.

Having reached that decision I started to calm down. I felt sorry for Aimee but I had to think of my own family. I continued to wait in the car, playing through the various scenarios that might result from my decision. About ten minutes passed before the contact supervisor appeared from the centre with Aimee. Susan must have stayed inside. I got out, opened the rear door so that Aimee could climb in and then closed it again after her.

'I'll have to make a note of your comments in my report,' the contact supervisor said, as though I was the guilty party.

'Fine,' I said curtly. 'I'll be including what happened in my report too.'

Irritated by the contact supervisor's lack of support and attitude, I said an equally curt goodbye and climbed into the car. The contact supervisor returned into the centre and presumably to Susan. It had almost become a 'them and us' situation, with Susan and the supervisor on one side and me on the other.

'Are you all right?' I asked, turning to look at Aimee. Having fastened her seatbelt she was sitting very quiet and still – unusually quiet for after contact.

She nodded. 'Are you all right?' she said. 'I've never seen you angry before.'

'No, well, it takes a lot, but I'm very protective of all my children, including you. I won't have malicious lies made up about any of them.'

'I didn't say anything to Mum about Adrian,' Aimee said defensively.

'Good.' And I left it at that. Whether or not Aimee had fuelled her mother's anger during contact I didn't know, but there was nothing to be gained by pursuing it. Aimee was a confused and vulnerable eight-year-old while her mother was an adult and should have known better.

I drove home deep in thought while Aimee quickly regained her usual composure and told me all about the friends she'd made at school and the games they'd played in the playground. I was pleased for her, although my pleasure was tempered by what I knew I had to say to Jill and the social services.

That evening, once I had read Aimee a bedtime story and she was in bed, I went downstairs and turned on the computer. Opening a fresh email, I began compiling what I needed to say to Jill. I'd been thinking about it all evening yet the words didn't come easily. It was nearly 9.30 before I was satisfied with what I'd written and pressed 'send'.

Dear Jill

As you know Susan has made serious allegations against Adrian and his two friends, which of course are lies. Susan repeated the allegations tonight at the end of contact in front of Aimee, which made me angry. I said things to Susan I shouldn't have done but I've tried to work with her and it's impossible. I now have to think of my family. While I do not want to give up on Aimee I can see no alternative but to terminate Aimee's placement unless Susan retracts her allegations immediately. If she does and Aimee stays with me I want an undertaking that I

will not have to come into contact with Susan again until she
can speak to me civilly. As you will appreciate, I've put a lot of
thought into this decision. I think this is reasonable. Thank you.
  Kind regards
  Cathy

I went to bed with thoughts of Susan and her evil manipulative ways going through my head. I knew Jill would phone me as soon as she read my email in the morning, and I hoped she knew me well enough to appreciate that I hadn't taken these steps lightly. I'd been pushed into this position by Susan, and I guessed this was how the foster carers of her older children must have felt when their children had to be moved. It was a pity that with Susan's history of disrupting placements, more hadn't been done to protect me from the start, especially at contact. But I had the feeling that the contact supervisors were afraid of Susan and went out of their way to keep on the right side of her, which was why her angry outbursts and insulting behaviour had been left unchecked.

The following morning Aimee was in a bad mood and took a long while to get out of bed and dress. Once downstairs she demanded biscuits for breakfast and when I told her she could have one biscuit after she'd eaten her proper breakfast she stamped her foot, folded her arms angrily across her chest and glared at me spitefully, saying, 'If you don't give me biscuits, I'll tell me mum!'

I paused from rinsing out a cup. 'And what good do you think that will do, Aimee?'

'I'll be moved from here.'

'And that's what you want, is it? You want to live with other carers – strangers – and have to get to know someone new? Because if so I'll see if it can be arranged.' I was calling Aimee's bluff. I guessed she was caught up in her mother's games and was repeating what she believed her mother wanted to hear, without considering the effects a move would have on her.

'My brothers and sisters were moved,' Aimee said with less certainty.

'Yes. And that made them happy, did it? To keep having to move to strangers?'

Aimee looked at me and gave a little shrug. 'I dunno.'

'Think about it, Aimee. Think about when you tell your mother things that you know will make her angry, and think about having to keep moving. If you really want to live somewhere else, I won't force you to stay. It would be a pity if you left us, because we like having you here, and I think underneath you are happy here with us. When I stop you from eating lots of biscuits or make you have a bath and wash you hair, or go to bed at a reasonable time, it's because I care about you. It would be a lot easier for me to give in to your demands, but I care and I want what's best for you.'

Aimee was silent and appeared to be thinking about what I'd said. After a moment she unfolded her arms and, with less anger in her movements, sat at the table and began eating her wheat flakes. I went to the cupboard, took one biscuit from the tin and, going over, set it on the table beside the grapes that I'd already put there on a plate. I didn't like giving a child a biscuit as part of breakfast but looking after Aimee was all about compromise.

'Thank you,' she said politely, without looking up. Then: 'I don't think I really want to leave you.'

Immediately I felt emotion rise and would have dearly liked to reach out and hug her, but I knew she wasn't ready for that yet. Instead I said, 'Good, because I don't want you to leave. Neither do Lucy or Paula.'

'What about Adrian?' Aimee asked.

I purposely hadn't included Adrian, as I thought the less he was mentioned at present the better.

'I'm sure he would want you to stay as well,' I said a little stiffly.

'And what about his friends? Do they still like me?'

From which I guessed Aimee knew that what she'd said to her mother had caused trouble. 'They have no reason to dislike you,' I said carefully.

'I'm glad we're all friends again. I'll tell me mum,' Aimee said, and finished the last of her cereal. But I thought that anything Aimee told her mother – regardless of how positive it was – was likely to be purposely misinterpreted by Susan and used against me.

Each time I took Aimee to school or collected her I was on the lookout for Susan and her threatening dog, Hatchet. Although I hadn't seen her since she'd been warned not to approach me in the street I wasn't convinced she wouldn't reappear, so this morning as on the previous ones I scanned the area as I parked the car and was then watchful as I took Aimee into school. As usual I waited with Aimee in the playground until the bell sounded and then I said goodbye, and was vigilant again as I returned to my car. It was nearly 9.00 as I climbed in and closed the car door, but before I'd had time to start the engine my mobile rang. Jill's number showed on the display.

'Morning, Cathy,' she said as soon as I answered. Then, coming straight to the point: 'I've read your email and I'm sorry you've had to deal with all this. I'm going to phone the social services now, but first I wanted to find out what exactly happened last night at contact and what you said to Susan that you shouldn't have done? Best I know beforehand.'

I told Jill what Susan had said about Adrian and his friends. 'Then I told Susan she was impossible to work with,' I admitted. 'And it was little wonder she'd lost all her kids into care. I said I wasn't having anything more to do with her or her malicious lies, and I left the centre and waited in the car until the supervisor brought Aimee out to me.'

'And that's everything?'

'Yes. Jill, I've had enough of her complaints, threats and anger. Accusing Adrian and his friends is the last straw.'

'I understand,' Jill said compassionately. 'I'll speak to the social services straightaway and get back to you. Hopefully, they'll have appointed a new social worker to take over Aimee's case. It will be easier than dealing with the duty social worker.'

'Jill, I don't want to give up on Aimee but I can't continue like this.'

'No, and neither should you,' Jill said supportively.

We said goodbye and I drove home feeling that at least Jill was on my side, but aware there shouldn't have been 'sides'. I knew I couldn't continue to look after Aimee unless the situation drastically changed.

When Jill phoned two hours later it was clear she'd been very busy.

'Do you want the good or the bad news first?' she said, trying to inject some humour into my gravity.

'Good, I guess,' I said, not sharing her enthusiasm.

'You won't be seeing Susan again before or after contact.'

'Well, that's something,' I said, and my spirits lifted slightly.

'There is an agency social worker, Beth, dealing with the case temporarily,' Jill continued. 'Until the authority appoints a permanent member of staff. I've spoken to her at some length. Although Beth doesn't know Aimee's case she agreed with me that you shouldn't be put in the position you have been, and we've agreed these new arrangements: Susan will be in the contact room at the start of contact when you take Aimee, as I believe she has been recently, and at the end of contact you will stay in your car and the supervisor will bring Aimee out to you, while Susan remains inside the building. Beth has phoned Susan and the family centre and has explained the new arrangements. Susan wasn't pleased but she's been told she needs to abide by the new arrangements or else contact will be reviewed.'

'Thank you, Jill,' I said. 'That should help. And the bad news?'

'It's not so bad really – no more than I expected. You will still have to make the telephone contact, but if Susan becomes angry and threatening on the phone, or tries to manipulate Aimee, you can end the phone call. Beth has explained to Susan what she can and cannot say to Aimee.'

'OK,' I said.

'And on the matter of the allegations against Adrian and his friends,' Jill continued, 'Susan is refusing to retract her comments but the social services won't be taking it any further. Beth agrees that with Susan's history of falsifying allegations against carers this is simply troublemaking and the allegation is unfounded.'

'And that will be enough to clear Adrian's name?' I asked. 'I don't want something on file that could have repercussions later.'

'When a permanent social worker is appointed I'll speak to them and make sure the information on file is correct.'

'Thank you, Jill,' I said again. 'I feel a lot happier now.'

'Good. But there is something else, which I don't think is going to please you.'

'Oh no. What?'

'While I was talking to Beth I asked if she could look on the file and see if there was any news about the interview Aimee gave to DC Nicki Davies and the investigation into Craig.'

'Yes? I hope he's going to be prosecuted for child abuse,' I said.

'Unfortunately not. It seems Aimee wasn't at all clear when she was interviewed. There wasn't enough evidence to make a case against Craig.'

'Oh no! What about my evidence?' I said. 'I saw the bruises and I wrote down exactly what Aimee told me. Surely that must count?'

'Has anyone from child protection phoned you?'

'No.'

Jill paused. 'And you're convinced Aimee was telling the truth? I mean, she's not adverse to making up things if it suits her, is she?'

'There is no doubt in my mind that Aimee was telling the truth about Craig.'

'And you'd be willing to give evidence if necessary?'

'Absolutely. I don't understand why I wasn't asked.'

'OK. Let me give the social services another ring and I'll get back to you.'

'Thanks, Jill. You know I'll do whatever it takes to bring Craig to justice. Aimee was brave enough to tell me what he'd done and she needs to see her abuser brought to justice. Otherwise it gives her the message that adults can treat children how they wish.'

'I know. I'll get back to you.'

As I put the phone down I wondered why no one had asked me for my evidence and also if Aimee would have given a better – clearer – interview if I'd been present. Although I appreciated DC Nicki Davies was trained in child interview techniques, perhaps having me in the room, or waiting outside the room, might have given Aimee that extra confidence to detail Craig's abuse coherently. Children often find situations intimidating that adults would have little problem with.

When the landline rang an hour later I was expecting Jill but was surprised to hear a female say: 'This is DC Nicki Davies. Is that Cathy Glass?'

'Yes. Hello.'

'I've just had a phone call from the social services about the allegations Aimee made against Craig. You're Aimee's foster carer?'

'Yes.'

'I was sent a copy of your notes in respect of what Aimee told you about Craig and I read them carefully. Our problem is that Aimee couldn't substantiate in the interview what she'd told you. We tried for over an hour, but she was very confused. We can't make a case strong enough to take to court if Aimee won't give evidence and repeat what she told you. Also Aimee's made similar allegations before about her father, so her evidence can't be considered reliable.'

'Perhaps her father abused her as well?' I suggested, not understanding the logic.

'It's possible, but again we don't have the evidence to take it to court. Although Aimee is eight, she's well behind in her language development, so it's very difficult to interview her. I'm sorry, but unless new evidence comes to light, in respect of Craig or her father, I'm afraid we can't proceed.'

'I understand,' I said, disappointed but having to accept the police's decision.

'Will Aimee be visiting her father in prison?' DC Vicki Davies now asked.

'I didn't even know he was in prison,' I said. 'How long has he been in there?'

'A couple of months, I think.'

'What's he been convicted for, or can't you tell me?'

'I can tell you. It's not a secret. He received a custodial sentence for possession of class A drugs with intent to supply, and resisting arrest. He got five years.'

'I see. Well, hopefully the social services won't decide Aimee needs to see him. I once had to take a child to visit a parent in prison and it was an awful experience for everyone.'

'I shouldn't think they will,' DC Nicki Davies said. 'Aimee doesn't have much of a relationship with him, and as I said, she's accused him of abuse before. I really don't understand why Aimee wasn't removed from home sooner. The older children were, years ago. I've been involved with that family since I first started working in child protection, over ten years ago, and it was obvious back then that it was never going to get any better in that home. Aimee should have been removed at birth.'

'That's what everyone says,' I agreed.

DC Nicki Davies thanked me for my time and promised to let me know if there were any new developments in the case against Craig; then she wound up the conversation and we said goodbye. While Nicki Davies was clearly a pleasant lady who I assumed was good at her job, the fact remained that Craig would not be prosecuted for assaulting Aimee, and neither would her father, if he too had abused her. I telephoned Jill and told her what I'd just learnt, and we agreed that unless Aimee specifically asked about Craig I wouldn't tell her he wasn't going to be prosecuted, and neither would I tell her that her father was in prison.

Chapter Eighteen

Flashback

Aimee had a dental appointment for a check-up that afternoon straight from school and I wasn't expecting good news. I'd seen inside Aimee's mouth when I helped her brush her teeth and it wasn't a pretty sight.

The check-up didn't get off to the best start as Aimee bit the dentist – hard.

'Ouch! That hurt!' Mike, the dentist, exclaimed, glaring at me as if I was to blame.

'Sorry,' I said, moving a little closer to the chair. 'Aimee, please try to keep your mouth open.' The dental nurse had asked me to stand at the foot of the examining chair and although I couldn't see what Mike the dentist could, his expression as he examined Aimee's mouth confirmed my worst fears.

'I'm sure she did it on purpose,' Mike said, still smarting over the bite, and now examining the tip of his index finger rather than Aimee's mouth.

'It was an accident,' I confirmed. 'Aimee's not used to visiting the dentist.'

'No. I can see that,' he said a little unkindly, and exchanged a meaningful glance with his nurse.

Satisfied that the tip of his finger wasn't severed, or even bleeding, Mike returned – with some trepidation – to the inner caverns of Aimee's mouth. This time he sensibly used the metal probe and kept his fingers well away from her teeth, while Aimee, bless her, now concentrated so hard on keeping her mouth wide open that her face contorted into a gargoyle-like grimace, which made her look rather odd and a little frightening.

'Try and relax,' the nurse suggested.

'Good girl,' I encouraged.

I already knew Aimee's mouth wasn't the best Mike had seen in his dental career and his findings, which he now read out to his nurse, confirmed this. Mike looked about seventeen but clearly had to be in his late twenties to be a qualified dentist. He was well tanned and had a strong Australian accent, and was a temporary replacement for our usual dentist, who was on maternity leave. The word 'cavity' featured often in Mike's dialogue with his nurse as he went round Aimee's mouth with his probe. And it didn't take great insight to know that meant a lot of decay and therefore fillings. 'Thirteen has a cavity, fourteen has cavity ...' he continued. 'And finally the last one, twenty, has a deep cavity too,' he said.

The examination complete, Mike sat back in his swivel dentist's chair, sighed and glared at me. 'The child's diet has been appalling. Does she eat a lot of sweets and biscuits?'

'She did but I'm changing that.'

'Does she ever brush her teeth?' he asked.

'She didn't, but she does now. I make sure of it.'

He sighed again. 'Her teeth are in a dreadful state for a child of her age – the worst I've ever seen. Every tooth needs filling but that would be far too traumatic, so unless they cause her pain I shall leave the primary teeth untreated – they'll come out soon. But I do need to fill the two second teeth, as otherwise she'll lose those. You really must make big changes to her diet and make sure she brushes her teeth properly. The nurse will give you a leaflet on dental hygiene before you leave.'

It was then I realized that Mike might be thinking Aimee was my child and I was responsible for the appalling state of her teeth. I'd written 'foster carer' on the form when I'd registered Aimee, and had filled in what I knew of her medical history, but it was quite possible he hadn't read the form and, not knowing me personally, didn't realize.

'Aimee is a looked-after child,' I said. 'I am her foster carer and she has only been with me a month.'

'Oh,' he said.

'She's on a good diet now, and I always make sure she brushes her teeth, but the damage has already been done.'

'Oh, I see,' he said again, now reassured that I knew how to look after a child's teeth. 'Well, that's nice of you – to foster. Come up here and I'll show you what I mean.'

I moved carefully around the instrument panel and up to the top end of the couch where Aimee's head rested. I stood next to where Mike sat, his previous hostile attitude now replaced by something approaching admiration. Using his probe he went round Aimee's teeth, pointing out the cavities. I knew from helping her brush her teeth they were in a bad way but now with her mouth wide open I could see the full extent of the damage. Some teeth were missing and nearly all of those that remained had some decay in them; the back teeth were brown and crumbling. How any mother could let her child's teeth get into that state I'd no idea. NHS dental treatment is free for children in the UK.

'It's a form of child abuse,' Mike said, voicing my thoughts. 'Just as well she came to you when she did or she'd have lost her second teeth as well.'

'Like me mum and dad,' Aimee put in, her mouth closing awkwardly around the probe.

'Exactly,' I said. 'And you don't want false teeth, do you? So we need to make sure you brush your teeth well.'

Aimee nodded.

Mike finished by pointing out Aimee's two second teeth, both of which already had small cavities in them and which he would fill. He then reinforced to Aimee that she must look after her second teeth, as they had to last a lifetime. He raised the dentist's chair and praised Aimee for being a good girl and the nurse gave Aimee a sticker in the shape of a large gleaming white molar with a smiling face.

'I'll give her teeth a polish when she comes for her fillings,' Mike said to me as Aimee climbed out of the chair.

'I'll need to have the consent form signed by her social worker,' I said. 'As her foster carer I can't give permission for the treatment. I'll make the appointment as soon as I have the form signed.'

'As soon as possible, please,' Mike said. 'And Aimee, you make sure you don't eat too many sweet things, and brush those teeth well. All right?'

'I will,' Aimee said. 'Cathy makes me.'

'Well done, Cathy,' Mike said, and I wished Susan had been present to hear this.

We said goodbye and on the way out I collected the consent form I needed for her treatment from the reception desk. Once outside I took the opportunity to reinforce again to Aimee just how important it was to brush her teeth and not to eat too many sugary foods.

'I hope you now understand why I don't let you eat lots of biscuits and sweets,' I said. 'And why I make you brush your teeth.'

Aimee, subdued by the prospect of having fillings, gave a small nod, and then said, 'I think my mum should have done the same.'

'Yes,' I agreed quietly. I hoped Aimee was starting to appreciate that the guidance I gave her was for her benefit. 'And

Aimee,' I said lightly, with a small smile, 'the next time we see the dentist, please try not to bite him. He's only doing his job and you hurt him.'

'But I don't like having things shoved in me mouth,' she said. 'That's why I bit him.'

'I know it's not very pleasant but it doesn't last for long.'

'I didn't like it at me mum's either,' she added, frowning.

'But you didn't go to the dentist while you were living with your mother, did you? That was some of the problem.'

'No. I mean I didn't like having things shoved in me mouth at me mum's.'

'What sort of things?' I asked naively.

'You know,' Aimee said, elbowing me conspiratorially in the side. 'Man's things.'

I looked at her carefully and hoped I'd misheard. 'No, I don't know,' I said. 'Can you explain?'

'Man's thingies!' she said louder, frustrated by my ignorance. 'You know, dinglies.' And she pointed to her crotch.

I hadn't misheard. There was no doubt. It was a cold winter's day but that wasn't the reason I shivered. I slowed my pace. Aimee, walking in step beside me, slowed too. 'Aimee, love, I need you to explain exactly what you mean so I can tell your social worker.'

Aimee gave a little sigh at my apparent lack of understanding but didn't appear outwardly distressed by what she'd just divulged. 'When the dentist put his fingers in my mouth,' she began, 'it made me think of when I was at me mum's. It felt like when the man put his thingy in my mouth. That's why I bit him.'

Reeling from the new disclosures, I was silent for a moment. I wasn't sure if I should question Aimee and try to find out more about the abuse or leave it to the child protection police officer, for it would certainly be a police matter. But what I was sure of was that before I reported what appeared to be gross sexual abuse, I needed to clarify what I was reporting. 'Aimee,' I said carefully. 'Are you telling me that while you were at your mother's a man put his penis – his willy – in your mouth?'

'Yes. His thingy,' she said. 'Like they do in the films.'

'What films?' I asked, wondering if this was something Aimee had seen in an adult DVD.

'The film I watched with the man,' Aimee said. 'He showed me a video of a man putting his thingy in a girl's mouth. He said it was a game kids played with him and I had to do it. He said other kids liked his game but I didn't, so I bit him like I did the dentist.' Which sounded like the classic paedophile using pornographic material to groom the child he was about to sexually abuse.

'What happened after you bit him?' I asked, looking at Aimee, as we continued walking along the pavement in the direction of the car.

'He shouted I was a fucking bitch, and then slapped my face. I screamed and Mum woke up. He took his video and left.'

'Did you tell your mum what had happened?'

'Yeah, but she didn't believe me.'

'Do you know the man's name?' I asked.

'No, he was just one of mum's friends,' Aimee said matter-of-factly. 'I think he gave her Big H sometimes.'

'I understand,' I said, apparently more shaken by what Aimee had described than she was. 'Well done for telling me. You did right. Aimee, it was very wrong of that man to try and make you do that. It wasn't a game, it was abuse. I'm going to contact Nicki Davies. You remember her?' Aimee gave a small nod. 'I shall tell her what you've told me and she'll probably want to speak to you again. All right, love?'

'I guess so, but I ain't telling her what I told you.'

'You must,' I said. 'It's important. I can tell her but she will want to hear it from you too.'

'No,' Aimee said adamantly. 'I'll get into trouble.'

'With who?'

'That man I told you about.'

'No you won't. You're safe with me. You won't ever have to see him again.'

'Already have,' Aimee said smartly.

'When?'

'When we were shopping last week, we passed him in the street. He was with a woman and he winked at me. He's still around and I ain't telling, so you best forget what I told you.'

I stopped and drew Aimee to one side. 'Aimee,' I said, bending a little towards her to make eye contact. 'I can't just forget what you've told me – not as a mother or a foster carer. What the man did was very wrong and the police have to know so they can stop him doing it again.'

'No,' Aimee stated categorically, and I knew she wasn't about to change her mind.

We continued on our way home, with Aimee talking about school and her friends and me fretting over the new disclosures. Was there nothing this poor child hadn't been subjected to?

Once home I began dinner while Aimee watched some television. When Paula and Lucy arrived home Aimee told them she'd been to the dentist. Then, non-stop, she said that she'd got to have two fillings in her secondary teeth, but Mike wasn't filling her first teeth, although they had cavities, because it would be too traumatic, and she had to look after her second teeth, as they had to last a lifetime. Clearly while Aimee had been lying in the dentist's chair she'd been taking in everything that had been said and had remembered it, which was good. I'd noticed before that Aimee could pick up and retain information she'd heard very accurately, and I was using this to help her learn – repeating spellings and times table etc. out loud, rather than relying on the printed sheet. The downside of Aimee's good auditory perception was that she could repeat back to me, word perfect, conversations I'd had, including girly telephone conversations with my friends. So that if I had to discuss Aimee's case with one of the professionals involved I always made sure I was well out of earshot.

I knew there was no point in phoning Jill that evening about the sexual abuse Aimee had disclosed, for although there would be a member of staff in the Homefinders office in the evening, the social services offices would be closed. I also knew that Jill, the social services and child protection would ask me to put what Aimee had said in writing. So once Aimee was in bed watching a Walt Disney DVD, I typed up my log notes, using Aimee's own words as much as possible. I detailed the abuse, that Aimee didn't want to speak to Nicki Davies, and that she had seen her abuser while out shopping with me. I also included the outcome of Aimee's dental check. Jill would read the email in the morning and then forward it to the social services. Foster carers who work for independent fostering agencies as I do usually funnel information through their support social worker at the agency, who passes it on to the child's social worker.

That night when I went up to say goodnight to Aimee and switch off her television I asked her, as I always did, if she would like a kiss and hug goodnight.

'Not yet,' she replied with a cheeky grin. 'But I'm getting close. So keep asking!'

I smiled, blew her a kiss and came out. But I was troubled. Only a few hours previously Aimee had remembered a dreadful incident of sexual abuse, yet she'd been able to continue as normal, apparently unperturbed, while the image of what she'd told me had tormented me all evening. Children who have been badly abused often compartmentalize their memories, hiving off the bad thoughts and 'forgetting' them until something happens – like the dentist putting his finger into Aimee's mouth – when they get a flashback. The fact that she was doing this made me wonder about the true extent of her abuse while she'd been living at home. Her dreadful neglect had been well documented but what else was there? What other memories lay hidden in Aimee's subconscious, waiting to resurface? Which brought me back to the question on everyone's lips: why had she been left at home for so long? The Guardian ad Litem was visiting on Friday and I hoped she would have the answer. The Guardian is appointed by the court to represent the child and give an overview of what is in the child's best interest. He or she has access to all the files.

It was only when I was climbing into bed that night that I realized we hadn't phoned Aimee's mother as we were supposed to. I'd been so preoccupied with Aimee's disclosures about sexual abuse, the state of her teeth and getting dinner on the table that I'd completely forgotten. Aimee hadn't remembered either. It was nearly eleven o'clock, so far too late to do anything about it now. All I could do was admit my oversight and apologize the following day, but I knew this would spark another complaint from Susan and this one would be justified. I could have kicked myself and I made a mental note that tomorrow I would write 'phone Susan' in my diary on every Tuesday, Thursday, Saturday and Sunday until the end of the year so I didn't forget again.

The following morning Aimee had a medical scheduled for 9.30, and I'd told the school I'd take her in afterwards. All children coming into care in England have a medical, in addition to any emergency treatment they might need. I'd already explained to Aimee why she was having a medical – to make sure she was fit and healthy – and what to expect.

'Don't really need a medical,' Aimee now said, finishing her breakfast. 'I'm fit 'n' healthy, living here with you. Wasn't fit 'n' healthy at me mum's, though.'

I smiled. 'That's because I give you fresh fruit and vegetables,' I said, seizing the opportunity to reinforce the importance of a good diet. 'Fresh fruit and vegetables contain vitamins, which help keep you fit and healthy.'

'Yeah, I know,' Aimee said, sighing. 'You told me already. Pity they don't taste like sweets.'

We left the house at nine o'clock for Aimee's medical and while I was driving to the clinic my mobile rang. I left it to go through to voicemail as I drove and then, once parked at the clinic, I listened to the message. It was from Jill, confirming she'd received the email I'd sent the night before, and that she'd forwarded it to Beth, Aimee's temporary social worker. Jill asked if I thought Aimee would change her mind about being interviewed by DC Nicki Davies, as clearly her evidence would be crucial to any prosecution. She finished by saying she'd phone me later. I doubted Aimee would change her mind but now wasn't the time to ask her. Since I'd parked the car at the front of the clinic Aimee had become very agitated.

'Are you all right, love?' I asked, turning in my seat before getting out of the car.

'No I ain't,' Aimee said. 'I've been to this clinic before, with me mum.'

'It's quite possible. Children come to this clinic for all sorts of reasons: to have their eyesight tested, their hearing tested, for vaccinations and medicals.'

'I don't want to go in,' she said. 'They called the police last time.'

'Why?' I asked, now fully turned in my seat to look at Aimee.

'The doctor wanted me to take my clothes off and Mum said no. When the doctor said she couldn't examine me unless I did, Mum got angry and pushed her.'

'I'm not surprised the police were called,' I said. 'It was wrong of your mother to push the doctor. Of course the doctor had to examine you. Just as he or she will today. Why didn't your mother want the doctor to examine you?' I asked.

'Because I had lots of bruises and Mum said they would think she did it.'

'And did she?'

'No!' Aimee said, annoyed. 'My mum doesn't hit me. It was that other geezer.'

'Who? Do you know his name?'

'No,' Aimee said too quickly, breaking eye contact. So I guessed she did know but wasn't going to tell me.

'Well, if you remember let me know his name,' I said.

'Maybe,' she said with a shrug. And I had a nasty feeling that this abuser, just like Craig and the unnamed paedophile, would continue to walk free to abuse again for a long time.

Chapter Nineteen

Hatchet

'Sit down, Mrs Glass,' Dr Patel said as we entered her surgery. 'Aimee, there's a toy box for you to play with over there.' Welcoming but forthright in her manner, Dr Patel was, I guessed, in her late thirties. Fortunately she wasn't the same paediatrician Susan had pushed.

'I don't have any of Aimee's medical records,' Dr Patel declared as I sat down and she opened the file on her desk. 'The social services have sent me the form I have to complete for the medical, together with a stamped addressed envelope, which was generous, but that's all. Do you know where her medical records are?'

'I assume they must be with her last GP,' I said (referring to her general practitioner or doctor), silently annoyed but not surprised by this oversight. More often than not when I took a foster child for a medical, the paediatrician, who didn't know the child, had not been sent the child's medical records and therefore had no idea of the child's medical history. It was a negligent and unnecessary oversight on the part of the social services, which I knew from experience would result in a half-complete medical assessment.

Dr Patel read out Aimee's full name and date of birth and then asked for my address, which hadn't been included on the form. I gave her this, together with my telephone number.

'So Aimee is eight,' Dr Patel confirmed.

'Yes.'

'Does she have any siblings?'

'Five older half-siblings,' I said.

'Do you know their ages?'

'Not exactly. They are all in their late teens and twenties.'

'Do they live at home with the parents?'

'They were all taken into care, although the older ones will probably be living independently by now.' Aimee glanced up from the toy box. I hated talking about a child in front of them, as it's disrespectful, but as Dr Patel didn't have any of Aimee's history and the form she was filling in requested this information there was no alternative.

'Does Aimee see any of her half-siblings?' Dr Patel now asked as she wrote.

'No.'

'Do you know why?'

'No.'

'And her father? Where is he?'

'In prison,' I mouthed quietly under my breath so Aimee couldn't hear.

Dr Patel nodded. 'I'll write "absent",' she said, filling in the information that should have already been made available to her. 'Are the siblings healthy?' she asked.

'As far as I know, but I don't know really.'

'Was Aimee's birth normal?' she said, reading the next question on the form.

'As far as I know, but I don't know really.'

'Are there any congenital abnormalities in the family that you know of?'

'Not that I'm aware of.'

'Are Aimee's grandparents still alive?'

'I don't know. They haven't been mentioned, so maybe they're not.'

Dr Patel gave a small sigh and continued, 'Do you know if Aimee's vaccinations are up to date?'

'I don't know. That will be on her medical record, won't it?'

'It should be.' Dr Patel made a note and then asked: 'What's the social services' care plan for Aimee? Do you know?'

I saw Aimee look over. 'Yes, I know but I can't really discuss it now,' I said pointedly. 'The social services will be able to advise you.'

'I understand. But Aimee is happy with you?'

'I think so. She has had to make a lot of adjustments since coming into care. But yes, I think she's happy. Isn't that right, Aimee?' I added, including her in the conversation.

Aimee nodded. 'But I'm not happy when I have to go to bed at night instead of watching television,' she grumbled good-humouredly.

Dr Patel smiled. 'Does Aimee sleep well?' she asked.

'Yes.'

'I like my bed,' Aimee put in.

'Is she dry at night?' Dr Patel continued.

'Yes, although before coming into care she wasn't.'

'She was probably very anxious about what was going on at home. Why was she brought into care?'

'Severe neglect.'

'And abuse? Sexual abuse?' Dr Patel asked quietly.

I nodded.

'Poor child,' she said quietly, and made a note. Then: 'Does Aimee eat well?'

'Yes, but before coming into care she was on a very poor diet with far too many sweet things. She seems almost to be addicted to sugar and I'm limiting the amount of sugary food she eats. I'm also concerned that she might be vitamin or mineral deficient. She never ate any fruit or veg.'

'I do now!' Aimee called from across the room where she was playing.

'Good girl,' Dr Patel said. Then to me: 'I'll check for any sign of vitamin deficiency when I examine her. But as long as she's eating a good diet now, her body should recover quickly.'

'I like sweets!' Aimee added.

'They're bad for you!' Dr Patel exclaimed, more forcefully than was necessary. I saw Aimee scowl at her and without Dr Patel seeing she stuck out her tongue. I frowned a warning at her.

'Has Aimee ever been tested for HIV?' Dr Patel suddenly asked, looking up from the form and directly at me. 'Both parents are intravenous drug users, so it would be sensible to know.'

I was taken aback. 'I don't know,' I said. 'It's never been mentioned by the social services. Would Aimee have been tested for HIV at birth? She was on the child protection register.'

'The mother would have been offered the HIV test. In this country all pregnant women are, but tests on babies are inconclusive because of the mother's antibodies. A child has to be tested at about eighteen months before the results are conclusive.'

'I've no idea if the test was done or not,' I said.

'Ask the social worker. Although the HIV virus is only transmitted in bodily fluids and is therefore relatively difficult to catch, you should know for your own safety and that of your family.'

'We practise safer caring,' I said, and thought back over the weeks Aimee had been with us. Had I always been careful, for example wearing disposable gloves when I'd treated her cut knee when she'd fallen over? I thought I had but I couldn't be completely sure.

'Her parents are high risk,' Dr Patel said. 'So if a test has been done you should be told the result, not only for your own safety but for the good of the child. If she is HIV positive then her health can be monitored and with modern medication the outcome is usually very good.'

'I'll pass on what you've said to the social worker,' I said. 'Foster carers are only told information about the children they foster on a "need to know" basis. Often the social services take the view that the foster carer doesn't need to know the result of an HIV test because if the carer is practising safer caring – as they should be – then they are not at risk.'

Dr Patel raised her eyebrows. 'If I was in your position, I'd want to know,' she said bluntly, before moving on to the next question on the form. 'Do you have any concerns about Aimee's eyesight or hearing?'

'No,' I said. Dr Patel made a note.

Once she'd worked through the remaining questions on the form Dr Patel stood and said to Aimee: 'Now it's your turn, Aimee, while Cathy has a rest. Come over here, good girl.'

Aimee responded to Dr Patel's forthright but friendly manner by immediately standing, leaving the toy box, and coming to her side. The doctor took an otoscope from her pocket and first looked in Aimee's ears. Then she shone a penlight in her eyes, and looked in her mouth. 'Good girl,' she said to Aimee. Then to me, 'She's seeing a dentist?'

'Yes.'

'Good. Let's check your vision now, Aimee.'

The doctor positioned Aimee to stand some distance away from the Snellen eye chart that was fixed to the wall. She then asked Aimee to read the letters, which decreased in size, starting with the top line.

'Aimee doesn't know all her letters yet,' I said, realizing that not recognizing the letter shapes could be mistaken for Aimee not being able to see them.

'Don't worry,' Dr Patel said to Aimee. 'Start at the top line and read as many as you can.'

Aimee read what she could from each row and recognized a sufficient number of letters for the doctor to be able to confirm her eyesight was good.

'Excellent,' Dr Patel said, making a note on the forms. 'Now I want you to pop up on to the couch so I can examine you.'

Aimee did as she was asked and clambered on to the couch as the doctor took a stethoscope from her desk drawer. She then crossed to the couch, where Aimee lay flat on her back, and began by checking Aimee's reflexes on her legs. Then she looked at the skin on her legs and her arms and finally lifted Aimee's jumper and listened to her chest. 'Good girl,' she said. 'Now let's sit you up so I can listen to your back.'

Aimee sat forward and the doctor put the stethoscope on various places on Aimee's back. 'All fine,' she said. 'Lie flat again, please, and I'll have a feel of your tummy.'

Aimee obligingly lay down and, using the palm of her hands, Dr Patel felt all over her abdomen. Aimee was very good throughout the process and lay still and watched the doctor.

'Good girl, you can get down now,' Dr Patel said, helping Aimee to sit up and then climb off the couch.

Aimee grinned. 'Was I good?'

'You were,' the doctor and I said.

Aimee returned to the toy box as the doctor once again sat at her desk. 'Everything is fine,' she said to me, filling in the medical form. 'There aren't any obvious signs of vitamin deficiency, although Aimee is overweight for a child of her age and height. Keep doing what you have been doing and I am sure that will sort itself out.'

'Thank you,' I said, reassured. Then to Aimee, who I knew had been listening: 'That's good news, isn't it?'

'Does that mean I can have more sweets?' Aimee asked, seizing the opportunity.

'No,' Dr Patel said firmly. 'You've had too many sweets in the past. Do as Cathy says and you'll stay healthy.'

It was 11.20 when Aimee and I left the clinic; we'd been inside for nearly two hours. 'You'll arrive at school just in time for your lunch,' I said to Aimee as we got into the car.

'Good. I'm hungry,' Aimee said.

As I drove to school my thoughts returned to Dr Patel's comments about the possibility of Susan and therefore Aimee carrying the HIV virus. Susan was dreadfully thin and I'd often thought she looked ill; in fact if I was honest she looked as though she could actually have AIDS. I would ask the social services if Aimee or her mother had been tested for HIV as Dr Patel had advised, but whatever the outcome I would still look after Aimee. What Dr Patel perhaps didn't realize was that over half the children coming into care came from backgrounds where one or both parents had been drug users, so most children could be considered 'high risk'. The social services often didn't know if the parents or the child had had an HIV test, and if they did know they rarely told the foster carer. Informing foster carers of these test results remains a contentious issue and is usually avoided by the social services, so the foster carer just gets on with looking after the child and tries to remember to practise safer caring.

I took Aimee into school and returned to my car with the intention of stopping off at the social services' offices on the way home to deliver in person the consent form I needed signing for Aimee's dental treatment. The social services' offices were only five minutes out of my way and if I hand-delivered the form it would be signed sooner than if I sent it through the post. Aimee needed to have the fillings as soon as possible. I'd put the form in an envelope before I'd left home and it was in my handbag.

I pulled into the council office car park and parked in one of the visitor bays at the front of the building. I cut the engine and was about to open my car door and get out when I heard a loud bark which sent a shiver down my spine. Was I being paranoid or had I heard something familiar in the bark? I looked through the windscreen, over to where the bark had come from, and saw Susan coming out of the main entrance of the building and go to the cycle rack, where Hatchet was tethered. The dog barked loudly, pleased to see her, but not half as pleased as I was that I was still in the car and hadn't met her or the dog on the way in. I stayed in my car until she and Hatchet had left the area and were out of sight before I went inside. I assumed Susan had had some business with one of the departments in the council building – the social services or housing, for example.

At the reception desk I showed the receptionist my foster carer ID badge and explained that I wanted to leave a letter for the social worker of the child I was fostering. 'Her name is Beth,' I said, showing her the envelope on which I'd written 'Beth'. 'But I don't know her surname,' I said. 'She's an agency social worker.'

The receptionist checked on a printed list beside her keyboard. 'Beth Ridgeway,' she said.

'Thank you.' Using the pen on the desk, I wrote 'Ridgeway' on the envelope after 'Beth', and passed the envelope to the receptionist.

'I'll make sure she gets it,' the receptionist said.

'Thank you.'

I came out and returned to my car.

The reason Susan had been in the council officers was about to become clear, for as I climbed into my car my mobile rang and it was Beth phoning from inside the building. 'Susan has just been in to see me,' Beth said, sounding stressed, and not aware I was outside. 'She's very upset that you didn't let Aimee phone her last night. She's told her solicitor and she's threatening court action.'

Ridiculous! I thought but didn't say. 'I didn't stop Aimee from phoning,' I said. 'I forgot. We'd been to the dentist and then Aimee disclosed sexual abuse. There was such a lot going on I forgot.'

'Oh, I see,' Beth said as though she had believed I'd intentionally not let Aimee phone her mother. 'I'll tell Susan it was an oversight on your part, but can you try not to forget to phone her in future?' Which was clearly a daft request, for I hadn't intentionally forgotten.

'I won't forget again,' I said, giving Beth the reassurance she needed to hear. 'I've just come out of your building. I'm in the car park. I've left the consent form for Aimee's dental treatment at reception. Could you sign it now and I'll come back in and collect it?'

There was a pause. 'I think I need to ask Susan first if she would like to sign it.' Which I knew was considered good social work practice but would cause delay.

'The sooner Aimee has the treatment the better,' I said. 'The fillings she needs are in her second teeth, so they don't want to decay any longer.'

'I understand,' Beth said. 'I received your email in respect of what Aimee said about the man who supposedly sexually abused her. I told Susan when she came in and she denies it ever happened. She says Aimee is lying.'

'Well, she would, wouldn't she? I mean, it's not going to help her case if Aimee was abused while she was asleep on the sofa.' I thought that perhaps Beth was new to social work and therefore inexperienced, and perhaps a little naive.

'I'll have to talk to my manager,' Beth said. 'It can be very traumatic for a child to be interviewed by the police.'

'I could help prepare Aimee,' I said. 'And she knows Nicki Davies from when she was interviewed before.'

'Who?' Beth asked. 'What interview?' So I guessed that, like most temporary agency social workers, Beth hadn't familiarized herself with her cases.

'DC Nicki Davies is the child protection police officer who has interviewed Aimee before – twice to my knowledge.'

'I'll speak to my manager,' Beth said again. And was about to wind up the conversation.

'Before you go,' I said, 'there is one more thing.'

'Yes?'

'Aimee had her medical this morning and the paediatrician asked me if Aimee or her parents had ever had a test for HIV. I said I didn't know. Do you know?'

'No.'

'Would you look on the file and tell me if a test has been done and the result?'

'It's usually considered confidential information, but I'll ask my manager.'

'Thank you.'

At least I'd raised the matter.

That evening Aimee had contact after school and as usual I took her into the centre at the start of contact; then the new arrangements were to apply at the end of contact, when I was to wait in the car for the supervisor to bring Aimee out. But when I returned to the centre to collect Aimee, to my surprise a dog that looked remarkably like Hatchet was tethered to the railings outside. If it was Hatchet I thought that two sightings in one day was too much of a coincidence and I wondered how he had got there. Hatchet hadn't been there at the start of contact, and that he was tethered suggested someone had put him there, after contact had begun, for I doubted he could have tied himself to the railings.

The dog's identity was confirmed when Aimee appeared from the centre with the contact supervisor and without Susan. Recognizing Aimee, Hatchet barked and jumped up. Aimee went over and stroked him before the supervisor brought her to my car.

'How did Hatchet get here?' I asked Aimee once she was in the car.

'Craig brought him,' Aimee said, pulling a face at the mention of Craig's name. 'So Mum didn't have to walk home alone in the dark.' Which seemed a thoughtful gesture but one that didn't quite fit the picture I had of Craig.

'Did you see Craig?' I asked as I drove.

'Ugh, no! I don't want to see him. He's horrible. A lady at the centre came into the room and told Mum Craig had left Hatchet outside.'

'I see,' I said.

Then a few minutes later Aimee said: 'I don't like Craig using my dog to scare people.'

'Who does he scare?' I asked.

'People who haven't paid him for drugs. Mum always lets him use Hatchet but I've told her not to.'

'Hatchet bites, then?'

'Only when Craig winds him up. Craig trained Hatchet to bite when he tells him to. But he doesn't bite me.'

'Good. But why was Hatchet at the family centre tonight?' I asked, puzzled.

'To scare you, I guess,' Aimee said easily.

'Why does Craig want to scare me?' I asked, glancing at Aimee in the rear-view mirror.

'When I was at home, Craig told Mum if I was taken into care he'd set the dog on the social worker and the foster carer.'

I returned my attention to the front and tried to concentrate on driving home.

The following day Beth phoned to say she'd signed the medical consent form for Aimee's dental treatment, so I could go ahead and book the appointment. 'Shall I put the form in the post or do you want to collect it?' she asked.

I was impressed by her efficiency. 'I'll collect it,' I said. 'Thank you for dealing with it so quickly.'

'You're welcome,' Beth said. 'Susan refused to sign the form, so I asked my manager what I should do and he told me to sign it.'

'Why did Susan refuse to sign it?' I asked. 'The treatment is for Aimee's good.'

'She said fillings would hurt Aimee and Aimee would blame her. I tried to explain that as parents we sometimes have to make difficult decisions for the benefit of our children, but she just didn't get it. I guess she never did, which is why Aimee is in care.'

'Yes,' I agreed reflectively. 'It's not always easy being a parent.'

On Friday morning the Guardian ad Litem, or Guardian, as such people are referred to, was due to visit at 11.30. The Guardian is a qualified social worker who is appointed by the court in childcare proceedings for the duration of the case. He or she is independent of the social services and, with access to all the files, would be able to answer my questions, the first being why hadn't Aimee been brought into care sooner?

The Guardian's name was Eva and she arrived exactly on time and accepted my offer of coffee. Middle-aged, she had a warm but efficient manner, as most Guardians have. Eva thanked me for seeing her, admired my house, and then chatted lightly about the weather while I made the coffee. Once we were settled in the sitting room with coffee and biscuits, I asked the question: 'Why was Aimee left at home for so long?'

'I don't know,' Eva said. 'I was going to ask you the same question. I was shocked when I read the referral. It seems Aimee was forgotten.'

Chapter Twenty

'Father Christmas Didn't Come to My House'

'I haven't seen all the social services files yet,' Eva explained. 'I've requested them but they are with a manager. I hope to have them soon. When I've read the files I'll let you know the reason why Aimee wasn't brought into care sooner, if there is one.'

'Thank you,' I said. 'It's a question everyone is asking. Even Kristen, the social worker who was responsible for bringing Aimee into care, couldn't understand why Aimee had been left at home for so long. Especially when she was on the child protection register at birth. Why didn't someone notice what was going on?'

'I agree, it's shocking – more so when you consider the older children were all taken into care years ago. Obviously no one wants to see a family split up but there comes a point when the parents have been given sufficient chances to put their lives right and you have to say enough is enough and put the children first. Early intervention can and does save lives. It can give children a fresh start, but from what I've read so far Susan had a very bad start in life too. Did you know that?'

'No, I didn't,' I said.

Eva nodded. 'She was badly abused, sexually abused, from the age of five, through to her teenage years. She finally ran away from home at the age of fourteen and ended up living on the streets, where she was picked up by a pimp. He introduced her to drugs, as they do, got her hooked, and set her to work as a prostitute in exchange for the drugs she quickly got addicted to. I dread to think what life she led with him, which of course scarred her for life.'

I was silent for a moment before I said, 'How dreadfully, dreadfully sad. Susan didn't stand a chance.' And despite all the trouble Susan had been causing me, my heart went out to her, and my attitude towards her softened a little, for she, like many other parents of children in care, had been a victim just as Aimee had.

'Susan's had a lot of help and support from the social services over the years,' Eva said. 'And therapy. From what I know it seems the social services have tried to keep her children with her but it hasn't worked, so I now have to concentrate on what is best for Aimee. She can't possibly be returned home. I'm trying to work with Susan but she's very angry. She pushed me at our first meeting and I've told her if she does it again I will take out a summons. I understand she's causing you problems too?' I was impressed, for despite not having had access to all the files Eva had a good grasp of Aimee's case.

'Yes. Susan has been very aggressive towards me,' I confirmed. 'So much so that I no longer see her at contact.'

'And she's made an allegation against your son, I believe.'

I nodded. 'That's the most worrying aspect.'

'Don't worry,' Eva said. 'Susan's made so many allegations in the past – against the carers of her older children – no one will take this one seriously. She usually seizes on something her child says and then twists it.'

'That's exactly what happened with us,' I said. 'Adrian would be devastated if he knew what had happened.'

'You haven't told him?'

'No. He's away at university but I'll have to say something when he comes home for Christmas.'

'Which university does he go to?' Eva asked, making conversation. I told her, and we then spent a few minutes talking about universities, as her two children were also away studying at university. 'So how is Aimee settling in?' Eva then asked, bringing back the conversation to Aimee.

'Very well, considering her past,' I said. 'When I first saw the referral she looked like the child from hell, but she is responding well. I have to be firm, as she often challenges the boundaries. But Aimee is gradually understanding that when I ask her to do something, or stop her from doing something, it is for her own good.' I then gave Eva a resumé of Aimee's routine and the progress she'd made: the variety of foods she now ate, that she slept well, and that she was starting to learn at school and had made friends.

'Great,' Eva said, making a few notes. 'Now, in respect of the disclosures she's made – the sexual abuse she's saying happened at home. I've spoken to Nicki Davies and it's highly unlikely she will be interviewing Aimee again until she is confident Aimee is ready to talk about what happened.'

'I see.'

'It's possible that once Aimee is no longer seeing her mother and is settled with a permanent family she will feel able to name her abusers. When that happens the case will be reopened.'

'And with regard to who will look after Aimee long term, what will you be recommending?' I now asked, aware the Guardian's report was crucial to the judge's decision and where Aimee would go.

'The social services' care plan is for adoption,' Eva said. 'But I'm not so sure. At Aimee's age and with her experiences of severe neglect and abuse she comes with a lot of baggage. I wonder if a long-term foster placement with a very experienced carer wouldn't be more appropriate. It's something I shall be exploring. What do you think?'

'Father Christmas Didn't Come to My House'

'I'm not sure. It's difficult,' I said. 'It would be nice if Aimee could have a new family and a fresh start, but it would take a very special adoptive parent to put in the work Aimee needs. And what about her relationship with her mother? There is a bond there. If Aimee was adopted she wouldn't see her mother again.'

'No, although some adoptions allow for a child to see their birth parents once or twice a year. But whether that would be in Aimee's best interest, I don't know. Sometimes a clean break is best for all, if there is no chance of the child being returned home, as in Aimee's case. If Aimee does go to a long-term foster home rather than adoption she will see her mother regularly and it will be impossible for either of them to move on.' Eva sighed and rubbed her forehead. 'It's very difficult. I'm due to meet Susan again next week, and then I shall visit Aimee's father in prison the week after. If I can persuade them that adoption is in Aimee's best interest my decision will be a lot easier.'

I smiled weakly. 'Is that likely?'

'No. I doubt either of them will be able to put Aimee's best interest first.'

'Eva,' I said, 'given that there is no chance of Aimee going home, it seems cruel to continue with such a high level of contact. Aimee sees her mother three times a week and speaks to her on the phone the other nights.'

'I agree. I can probably have the phone contact reduced. Phone contact for children Aimee's age is often very difficult. But there's nothing I can do about the face-to-face contact. I know it seems cruel, but as the law stands that contact will have to continue at its present level until the judge makes his or her decision on where Aimee will live permanently, at the final court hearing, which could be a year away.' I knew this to be so but like a lot of social care law I felt it was something else that needed reviewing. 'And in the meantime, until the final court hearing,' Eva asked, looking directly at me, 'Aimee can stay with you?'

'Yes, I hope so. As long as the matter with Adrian is resolved. Although Aimee isn't the easiest child I've fostered, she is doing well. We all like Aimee and I hope that underneath she likes us too.'

Eva smiled. 'I *know* Aimee likes you and your family,' she said positively. 'Yesterday, when I was talking to the head of her school she said Aimee had told her teacher that she loved living with you, even though you make her wash, eat proper food and go to bed on time. Her words, not mine.'

'That's lovely,' I said, touched. 'And it's reassuring. Aimee keeps me at a distance.'

'It might be unfair to tell you this,' Eva now said, 'but Aimee has also told her teacher that if the judge decides she can't go home to live with her mother then she wants to stay with you forever.'

I felt my eyes mist. 'Really? Oh, bless her. How sweet of her! Yet she won't even let me give her a hug.'

'She will in time,' Eva said. 'Deep down she thinks a lot of you. I need to ask you: would you consider looking after Aimee permanently? Would that be an option?'

I looked at Eva carefully. 'I'd have to ask Adrian, Lucy and Paula for their views,' I said. 'It's a very big commitment and Aimee would have to change her ways around Adrian, but yes, I would.'

'Thank you.'

There was no need to thank me. I knew I was growing close to Aimee, and thought that Lucy and Paula were too. Aimee had 'attitude' and a lot of bravado, and regularly challenged the boundaries, but beneath that hard protective shell there was a little girl in desperate need of love and protection. My eyes welled every time I thought of the shocking life she'd led before coming into care; little wonder she was angry and defiant sometimes. I knew it would take time, patience and understanding to help Aimee put the past behind her and move on, so she could make the best of her life. I recognized that and I was willing to put in the work. I liked Aimee and I knew I could easily grow to love her. The biggest problem was her behaviour towards Adrian, and indeed men and older boys in general, because quite simply she flirted with them. We'd seen it with Adrian and his friends when they'd visited, and also with the older boys at school, and with my friends' husbands and their sons. Aimee hadn't met my father, brother and his son yet but when she did I knew I was going to have to watch her carefully until she learnt how to behave appropriately.

As it was Friday and we didn't have to be up early for school the following morning, Aimee stayed up past her usual bedtime and watched two Walt Disney DVDs back to back. Having lived on the edge of an adult world before coming into care she hadn't seen much children's television or films, and indeed had been scornful of them, demanding to see the adult soaps and late-night films she'd watched with her mother. I'd stopped her watching adult programmes immediately and had introduced her to children's films – classics like *Mary Poppins* and *The Lion King* and more recent titles like *Finding Nemo*. Tonight she had watched *A Bug's Life*, and with Christmas approaching I'd shown an old favourite of ours, *Santa Claus: The Movie*. It was nearly nine o'clock when the Christmas film ended and Aimee, who'd sat silently throughout, now looked at me, amazed and overawed.

'Wow!' she said. 'I wish I was that little girl with all those presents. Father Christmas didn't come to my house.'

Lucy, who'd been watching the film with us, said: 'He'll definitely come here, Aimee. Don't you worry.'

'That's right,' I said. 'We'll have a lovely Christmas. We always do.'

'He won't give me any presents,' Aimee said a little sulkily.

'Of course he will!' Lucy exclaimed with a small laugh. 'Father Christmas brings us all presents. We hang our pillowcases on the front door on Christmas Eve, before we go to bed, then in the night he comes and fills them. In the morning when we wake they are beside our beds.'

'Yes,' I said, mindful that it was Mummy Christmas who had to get up at 4.00 a.m. to fulfil this.

'He won't give me presents,' Aimee said again, her face now setting.

'He will,' I said. 'And don't scowl. Christmas is a happy time.'

'No he won't,' Aimee persisted. 'I won't get any presents because I haven't been good.'

'Yes you have,' Lucy and I said together.

'You're doing very well,' I added, wishing as I often did that I could give her a hug.

'No,' Aimee said. 'I meant before I came here I wasn't good. Craig said I was very naughty and I would never get any presents ever.'

'Forget what he told you,' I said. 'That was rubbish. Everyone has presents here.'

'Didn't you have any presents last year?' Lucy now asked Aimee.

'No. But I got a good spanking instead.' I had to stifle a smile, for although what Aimee had said was clearly sad, the way she'd said it was so quaint.

'You surely didn't get smacked at Christmas?' Lucy asked, shocked.

Aimee nodded. 'I did. Craig brought lots of beer and he and Mum drank it all day until they were drunk and all over each other, kissing. I kicked up because our Christmas wasn't like the ones I'd seen on television. Craig sent me to the bedroom with a packet of biscuits and told me to be quiet or else. I wasn't quiet, I kept kicking the door, which made Craig angry. He came storming into the bedroom and grabbed me by my hair. He put me over his lap, pulled down my pants and smacked my bottom hard. Whack whack whack. I could feel it stinging, so I bit his leg and he thumped me. I had so many bruises I couldn't leave the house for a week.'

Lucy stared at Aimee, horrified. Any humour was now gone. We'd fostered children before who'd been badly neglected and harmed on Christmas Day – as on most other days; indeed Lucy's own Christmases before coming into care hadn't been good, but what she had experienced was nothing compared to this. And the fact that Christmas should be a time of peace and happiness seemed to make Aimee's suffering all the worse. I was grateful Paula was in her bedroom listening to music and hadn't heard what Aimee had just said.

It was a moment before Lucy and I spoke. I could see Lucy's eyes glistening as she stared at Aimee. Then she reached out and, gently touching Aimee's shoulder, said quietly: 'That won't ever happen again. Shall I tell you about all the nice things we do here at Christmas?'

'Yes please,' Aimee said, recovering. She moved slightly closer to Lucy on the sofa without actually touching her and Lucy began.

'Well, about two weeks before Christmas,' Lucy said, as if telling a child a story, 'we all help to get the Christmas decorations down from the loft, where they're stored in boxes. Two big boxes full of Christmas decorations. There are lots of brightly coloured garlands and big glittery stars and snowflakes, which we hang from the ceiling. Then there's a golden angel that goes on the wall in the hall and a model of the Nativity, and a Father Christmas that goes "Ho ho ho" whenever anyone walks past.' Aimee smiled. 'We all go shopping and buy presents for each other, and because they are surprises we wrap them without anyone seeing. Then a week before Christmas we buy a Christmas tree and we all help to decorate it – with tinsel and baubles and chocolate novelties, which mustn't be eaten until Christmas, Aimee.'

Aimee grinned. 'Hmm, yummy, I like chocolate.'

I smiled. Aimee was enthralled, as a young child should be. As Lucy continued telling Aimee all about the build-up to Christmas, I slipped from the sitting room and went into the front room where I kept my fostering folder. I wanted to write up my log notes while Aimee's new disclosures about Craig were still fresh in my mind. These, together with what Aimee had previously told me, would help build up a picture which would, I hoped, eventually lead to a prosecution. So, as Lucy's voice drifted in from the sitting room and she told Aimee all about the promised joy of this Christmas, I wrote about the misery of Aimee's last one, and Lucy's words could not have been more of a contrast: as Lucy said, '... then on Christmas morning we all sit round the Christmas tree and give each other presents,' I wrote '... she had so many bruises she couldn't go out for a week.'

Perhaps it was because Aimee had been remembering her last Christmas before she went to bed that she had a nightmare that night. Just after midnight I was woken by the most horrific blood-curdling scream. With my heart racing, I shot out of bed and went round the landing to Aimee's room as Lucy and Paula came out of their rooms. Going in, I turned on the light. Aimee was sitting upright in bed, her eyes screwed tightly shut and her hands pressed over her ears, as though trying to shut out the horror of what she'd seen and heard. She stopped screaming as I entered but now sat rigidly upright, like a statue. I sat on the bed and placing my hands over hers I tried to ease them away from her ears.

'It's all right, Aimee,' I said gently. 'You're safe. Open your eyes. You've had a bad dream, that's all.'

Aimee stayed as she was, hands pressed against her ears and eyes shut tight, frozen in her nightmare.

I kept my hands on hers and felt her skin, soft and clammy. 'Open your eyes, Aimee,' I said again. 'You're safe. There's nothing to worry about now. Lucy and Paula are here too.'

Gradually Aimee opened her eyes and let me ease her hands away from her ears. She looked vague and disorientated, still partly in the nightmare world she'd inhabited. Then slowly reality returned and her gaze went to Lucy and Paula, who were standing by the door looking very worried, and then back to me. Aimee looked at me, scared.

'Please don't hit me,' she said quietly. 'I've wet the bed.'

'Of course I won't hit you. I've never hit anyone,' I said, as I'd said before. 'A wet bed doesn't matter.'

Aimee looked at me thoughtfully and then said, 'I was so scared at home sometimes, I used to wet myself.'

'Scared about what, love?' I asked gently, my hand now resting lightly on her arm. 'What scared you so badly?'

Aimee shook her head, signalling either that she couldn't remember or that she couldn't tell me the horror that had made her wet herself at home.

'You two go back to bed,' I suggested to Lucy and Paula. 'I'll soon have Aimee tucked up in bed again.'

Satisfied Aimee was going to be all right, the girls went back to their own rooms while I went to the airing cupboard along the landing and took out clean bedding and pyjamas. Returning to Aimee's room, I helped her out of bed and gave her a packet of wet wipes. 'You can have a bath in the morning,' I said to her. 'Just wipe yourself clean with these for now.'

While Aimee took off her wet pyjamas and used the wet wipes to clean herself, I changed the bedding. I always keep a waterproof mattress protector on the bed, so no damage had been done. I wondered what Aimee had been so scared of at her mother's that she'd wet herself, but now wasn't the time to press her. I hoped that eventually she'd be able to tell me this and all the other half-remembered incidents of abuse she'd begun to tell me about and then stopped. Still quiet, but in clean pyjamas, Aimee climbed back into bed, while I dumped the wet bedding in the bath to take down to the washing machine later.

I returned to sit on the edge of her bed and tucked the duvet under her chin. 'All right now, love?' I asked.

'Yes,' Aimee said quietly, her rounded eyes watching me.

'I want you to think of nice things now and try to go back to sleep. I'm going to my bed but if you need me call out.'

Aimee gave a small nod and then reaching out her arms, to my surprise said: 'Hug.'

I smiled and slipped my arms around her and felt her little body warm against mine. It was only a small hug before she pulled away, as though she didn't want to be too close for too long. But it was a start: we had crossed a bridge and I knew there would be more hugs to follow as Aimee slowly put her trust in me and allowed me closer.

Chapter Twenty-One
Going for Gold

I decided it was time Aimee met my parents who, although in their eighties, were healthy and active and looked much younger. They'd always been supportive of my fostering and went out of their way to make the child or children I was looking after feel included in the wider family. It never took long before the child was calling them Nana and Grandpa and enjoying their kind and patient attention. They always bought birthday and Christmas presents for the child and obviously missed them, as we did, once they'd gone. I'd put off introducing Aimee to my parents for longer than normal, as I wanted to feel confident Aimee's behaviour would be acceptable. I find it very stressful to have guests (even if they are my parents) if I have to spend all day correcting the child, issuing warnings and sanctions, and eventually tell them off and give them time out. I now believed Aimee was ready to meet my parents, so I telephoned them and asked them over for Sunday lunch.

'You come to us,' Mum immediately said. 'I'll cook you dinner for a change.'

'Only if you will let us all help,' I said, mindful of the work involved.

'All right. We'll all help. Look forward to seeing you on Sunday.'

* * *

So on Sunday morning I explained to Aimee where we were going and who we were going to see, and she seemed appropriately excited. Paula came with us, but Lucy had already arranged to go out with a friend for the day, and as she saw Nana and Grandpa regularly it didn't matter if she missed this time. 'Give them my love,' she called as we left.

'I will.'

We arrived as arranged at twelve noon and Mum and Dad greeted us at the door with hugs and kisses. I introduced Aimee, who'd held back from hugging, and we went in. Almost immediately – as soon as we were inside – Aimee began playing up.

'Where am I supposed to play?' she demanded rudely.

I shot her a warning glance. 'Through here, in the sitting room. I'll show you,' I said. I'd brought activities with us – colouring books and puzzles – and Mum always kept a well-stocked toy box in the sitting room.

I settled Aimee at the coffee table with various activities but a minute later she was saying she was bored and demanding: 'What else is there to do?'

I spread out more activities and re-settled her. Then a couple of minutes later she was away from the table and trying to jump on and off the sofa. I steered her back to the activities, but then a minute later she was off again, running upstairs and into my parents' bedroom.

I went after her. 'You don't go in other people's bedrooms,' I said, taking her by the hand and leading her out. 'They are private. Like our bedrooms at home.'

I took her downstairs and re-settled her with another puzzle, but no activity lasted longer than a few minutes before she was up running around, up and downstairs, in and out of the kitchen and then opening various cupboards or drawers. Even when she was occupied with an activity it was impossible to hold a conversation, as the moment attention switched from her and what she was doing, she interrupted us, loudly butting in. Using my 3Rs technique (detailed in *Happy Kids*) I told Aimee how she should behave and warned her of the sanction if she didn't behave, then began stopping television time. Half an hour later Aimee had lost all her television for that night and I was starting on the following day.

'Don't care,' Aimee said. 'I'll do as I please.' And she did.

'You've got your hands full,' Dad said quietly to me, clearly concerned at the strain Aimee's behaviour was putting on my family and me.

'I thought she'd got over this,' I said apologetically. 'She's been doing well at home until now.'

Eventually, after another rude interruption from Aimee, I gave her time out and sat with her in the utility room while Paula helped Mum serve dinner. When dinner was ready we sat at the dining table but Aimee continued with her rude, confrontational and defiant manner. She demanded a spoon, claiming she couldn't use a knife and fork. Mum fetched her a spoon and also cut up her dinner for her, but Aimee refused to eat any of it, saying it was yucky and she wanted biscuits instead. I told her off, told her she wasn't having biscuits, stopped more television, and then gave her more time out so we could finish our meal in peace. But I was silently fuming and at a loss to know why she was letting herself and me down so badly. Mum and Dad looked forward to our visits and Mum had put a lot of effort into Sunday dinner and I felt awful, although Mum told me not to worry. The day was a disaster and we left earlier than planned. I was exhausted and stressed, and Paula had run out of patience. I could see she was angry at the way Aimee had treated her dear Nana and Grandpa and we both apologized to my parents as we left and got in the car.

Unbelievably, as I started the engine Aimee said: 'That was nice.'

'Nice!' I exclaimed. 'I spent the whole day telling you off! You've lost all your television for the next two days. I'm shocked at your behaviour, Aimee, shocked and saddened.' I reversed off the drive and set my face to a smile as we waved goodbye to my parents.

'Aimee, whatever was the matter?' I asked once we were on the road. 'When we go to someone else's house you behave as I've taught you to do at home.'

'Do I?' Aimee said, bemused.

'Yes! You do!' Paula exclaimed. 'You know that.'

'I didn't at me mum's,' Aimee said. 'When I went with me mum to get her Big H, I did as I liked. No one bothered there.'

I thought that just about summed it up! Aimee's social visiting prior to coming into care had consisted of accompanying her mother to drug dens and crack houses, where the rules of decent social interaction clearly wouldn't have applied. Although I'd taken Aimee with me a few times when I'd popped into friends' houses, we hadn't stayed for long and not for a meal. I realized that while Aimee's behaviour was progressing well at home she clearly needed to be socialized more. I made a mental note that when she broke up from school for Christmas and we had more time, we'd visit as many friends as possible, preferably friends who fostered and who wouldn't be fazed if Aimee's behaviour was bad.

As I drove I now went through the dos and don'ts of visiting. 'Always say please and thank you,' I said. 'Don't go rummaging in people's cupboards and drawers unless you are asked to. Don't stand on the coffee table, jump on their sofa or beds, or make gagging noises at the meal table.' Obvious to any child from a normal home, but not to a child like Aimee, who had existed in a feral 'dog eat dog' world for most of her life.

'We'll see Nana and Grandpa again soon,' I said, finishing my lecture. 'So you'll be able to show them how well you can behave.'

'I had a nana,' Aimee said. 'But she was horrid.'

Paula, who was sitting in the passenger seat and still annoyed with Aimee, was unable to conceptualize a nana who was 'horrid'. 'What do you mean "horrid"?' she asked. 'You mean you got told off because of your behaviour?'

'No. Really really horrid,' Aimee said. 'When I was naughty she hit me with a broom and locked me in the shed.' After the way Aimee had behaved this afternoon I had a degree of sympathy with the woman, although I obviously didn't condone the cruelty.

'Was this nana your mother's mother, or your father's mother?' I asked, aware I'd have to log this new abuse in my fostering notes and tell the social worker, so I needed to get the facts right.

'What?' Aimee asked, confused.

'You can have two nanas,' Paula explained. 'One is your mum's mother and the other is your dad's mother.'

'Don't know,' Aimee said. 'I just called her Nana or witch – because of her broomstick. I used to stay with her sometimes, when me mum had had enough of me. Then one day Mum came back early and found me and Grandpa in the shed. There was a big argument and I didn't have to go and stay with them any more, which was good.'

I glanced at Aimee in the rear-view mirror, not sure if this was just a family argument that had led to estrangement or something more sinister. 'Why was your mother angry?' I asked.

'Because I was in the shed with Grandpa!' Aimee said, her voice rising as if I should have understood.

'Why should that make her angry?' I asked. Aimee didn't answer.

'What was happening in the shed to make your mother angry?' It was a question I would never have thought of asking when I first started fostering but experience had taught me that such a question could unlock more disclosures of abuse.

'Nothing!' Aimee said too quickly.

'So why did your mother stop you from visiting?'

'Because Grandpa …' Aimee began. Then stopped. 'Don't know. Can't remember.'

'All right. But if you do remember one day I hope you will be able to tell me.'

'Maybe,' Aimee said thoughtfully.

'And Aimee,' I added before I let the subject go, 'I don't know what your grandparents were like, I've never met them, but ours are lovely, kind and caring people. They would never hurt anyone, and if they knew you'd been hurt they would be very sad.' It needed to be said because Aimee's experience had shown her otherwise.

'OK,' Aimee said. 'Thanks for telling me. I'll try and be good next time I see them. But don't expect an angel.'

'We won't,' Paula said.

When we got home Aimee, having eaten no dinner, was hungry, so I made her a sandwich, while reminding her that the next time we visited Nana and Grandpa she'd eat what Nana cooked for us. Aimee agreed she would at least try the food. I wondered how much of Aimee's negative behaviour at my parents' had been a result of the experience she'd had with her own grandparents – if indeed they were her grandparents. Some abused children are taught to call their abusers Nan, Grandpa, Aunty or Uncle, to cover the fact the child is spending a lot of time with an unrelated adult, which could arouse suspicion. With each new disclosure Aimee made I was coming to the conclusion that anything was possible.

Going for Gold

After Aimee had eaten it was time to phone her mother, for although the Guardian had said she'd see if she could reduce or stop phone contact I still had to make the phone calls until I was officially told to stop by the social services.

As it turned out, I called a halt to the phone contact very quickly, for as soon as Susan spoke it became clear she was under the influence of something – drink or drugs I didn't know. The phone was on speaker as usual, so Aimee and I both heard her slurred speech as her words ran together and she appeared to be confused. 'Is that my youngest child,' she drawled. 'Or my eldest? Or maybe it's the devil's child!'

'What the fuck are you on, Mum?' Aimee said, clearly recognizing the signs of substance misuse, as I did.

'It's the devil's child!' Susan returned and laughed hideously.

'Susan, it's Cathy,' I said, leaning towards the mic on the phone. 'Are you able to talk to Aimee properly?'

'Who the fuck are you?' she demanded.

'I'm Aimee's carer. Aimee is in foster care.'

'In hell, more like!' she said, laughing again.

'Susan, I'm stopping this call,' I said. 'I'll explain why to the social worker. Would you like to say goodbye to Aimee?'

There was silence on the other end of the phone, although the line was still open.

'Say goodbye to your mother,' I said to Aimee.

'Bye, Mum. See you tomorrow,' Aimee said, subdued.

There was still no response from Susan, so I said 'Goodbye, Susan,' and cut the call.

'Sorry,' I said, turning to Aimee. 'But I can't let you talk to your mother while she's like that. Do you understand why I ended the call?'

Aimee nodded, and then said quietly, 'I hope Mum is OK.'

'I am sure she will be,' I said, silently annoyed that Susan had treated Aimee so badly on the phone and Aimee was now worrying about her mother.

Aimee remained quiet and subdued as she had a bath and got ready for bed. I asked her a few times if she was all right and she nodded unconvincingly. Eventually, as she was about to climb into bed, she said: 'I'm really worried about my Mum. When she's like that I have to put her on her side to stop her choking. She's sick and it goes down her throat. I'm not there to help her. Can you go to the flat and help her?'

Clearly I couldn't, and I was appalled that a child of eight had been put in that position, although I appreciated why Aimee was worried. And the fact that Susan had suddenly gone quiet on the end of the phone raised my own concerns.

'I'll tell you what I'll do,' I said, as Aimee stood by her bed, looking at me anxiously. 'You get into bed and look at a book, and I'll phone your mum and make sure she's all right. How about that?'

'Thank you, Cathy,' Aimee said very sweetly, and my heart clenched. The poor child had had so much responsibility.

I settled Aimee in bed with a book and then went round the landing and into my bedroom. I picked up the phone from my bedside cabinet and keyed in the numbers to Susan's mobile, which I now knew by heart. Her phone rang a number of times and then went through to her voicemail, which heightened my concerns for her well-being. Was she lying on the floor, unconscious and choking in her own vomit? For, despite all the problems she'd caused me and her dreadful neglect of Aimee, I didn't wish the woman harm. I didn't think there was any point in leaving a message on her voicemail, so I cut the call and re-dialled. Again there were a few rings and then the call was directed through to her voicemail. I decided to try once more and if she didn't answer, I would phone our local police station.

Going for Gold

I'd explain who I was and the position regarding Susan, and ask if an officer in the area could check Susan's flat and make sure she was all right. In the past I'd always found the police very helpful in respect of children in care.

However, phoning the police wasn't necessary, for on the third try Susan answered. 'Yes? Who is it?' she asked groggily. I breathed a sigh of relief.

'It's Cathy Glass, Aimee's carer,' I said. 'I just wanted to make sure you were all right. Aimee was worried you might be sick.'

'Who?' Susan asked, clearly disorientated. 'Who's sick?'

'No one. I was just checking you were OK.' As Susan was clearly conscious and not choking, but still impossible to hold a conversation with, I said, 'I'll tell Aimee you are all right. Do you have someone with you?' For if she did I thought I could reassure Aimee on that point too.

'What the fuck has it got to do with you who I see?' Susan snapped.

'Goodnight,' I said, and replaced the receiver.

As I left my bedroom I heard the scamper of feet along the landing, so I guessed Aimee had been out of bed and listening. 'Your mum's fine,' I said, going into her bedroom, where Aimee sat innocently in bed.

'Thank you, Cathy. I'm never taking drugs or drinking beer. You don't drink, do you?'

'Only the occasional glass of wine with a meal,' I said.

'But you never get drunk, do you?'

'No,' I said.

'It's frightening for kids to see their parents off their heads with drink or drugs. That's why I'm in care, isn't it?' Aimee may have been a long way behind in her learning but in some respects she was the smartest kid I knew – having learned lessons from life.

'Yes, that's one of the reasons you're in care,' I said. 'Parents can't look after their children properly if they take a lot of drugs or drink heavily.'

Satisfied and reassured her mother was all right, Aimee snuggled down in bed, and then suddenly sat bolt upright again. 'Hug!' she said, stretching out her arms.

I smiled and sat on the edge of the bed. Taking my cue from Aimee, I hugged her for as long as she wanted, and then as she snuggled into bed I lightly kissed her forehead. Although Aimee was slowly putting her trust in me I knew there was still a huge area of her life before she came into care which was a closely guarded secret and would probably remain so for a long time to come.

Now I no longer had to see Susan at contact, my life had become a good deal easier. Being on the receiving end of her anger and derogatory comments three times a week had been getting me down quite badly. But instead of seeing Susan I now saw Hatchet, who was tied up outside the family centre at the end of each contact. Perhaps he was there to scare me, as Aimee had said, but I found Hatchet far less threatening than Susan.

We were now heading through December at an alarming rate and I was busy planning and shopping for Christmas. Aimee wanted to buy her mother a present and I took her shopping. After the first time I'd taken Aimee shopping – when she'd first come into care – when she'd thought it was all right to steal if the item was a gift, I kept a watchful eye on her. But Aimee had learnt that stealing, like much of her other behaviour, was no longer acceptable. We had a pleasant couple of hours' shopping and eventually Aimee chose a silver necklace as a present for her mother. I gave her the money and then stood by and let her pay the cashier. She looked so proud as she returned, clutching the little bag, the change and the receipt.

'I'll wrap it in Christmas paper and I'll put a bow on it,' Aimee said, joyfully. 'That will make Mum happy. She's never had a Christmas present before.'

As well as December passing at an alarming rate we were going through social workers at a similarly worrying pace. Kristen had been the social worker responsible for bringing Aimee into care, and then as was normal practice the case had been passed to the children in care team, where Beth, an agency social worker, had taken over. Beth had gone very quiet and hadn't been in contact with Jill or me as we would have expected, given that there was a lot going on with Aimee's case at present. Then, purely by chance, Jill found out that Beth had left the local authority the week before and a new (agency and therefore temporary) social worker had taken over. She was in post long enough to phone me and introduce herself as Dolores before she was replaced by Tony, who came and went within the week. By the middle of December we were awaiting the arrival of social worker number five. 'Five social workers in six weeks!' Jill quipped. 'Perhaps they're going for gold.' Meaning the social services might be trying to set a record, but it was no record to be proud of.

A week before Christmas someone at the social services realized that Aimee's child in care (CIC) review – a legal requirement – was now more than two weeks overdue. A CIC review is a meeting for all those involved with a child in care, to share information and to make plans for the child to ensure that all the child's needs are being met. Beth had commented that Aimee's review needed to be arranged but hadn't done so before leaving, and with all the changes of social worker it had subsequently been overlooked. The team manager had picked up the omission and a CIC review was quickly convened for 11.30 the following morning, which was also the last day of the school term. It was to be held at the council offices. With so little notice,

Another Forgotten Child

Jill and the Guardian couldn't attend, as they had prior appointments; the school couldn't spare anyone on the last day of term, and with no permanent social worker appointed an agency social worker was despatched to stand in at the last minute. It soon became clear that I was the only person present who knew Aimee and therefore had any idea what they were talking about.

Chapter Twenty-Two
Perfect Christmas

There were three of us at the CIC review: the temporary agency social worker, myself and the independent reviewing officer, who chaired and minuted the meeting. Normally at a review, in addition to the social worker, the foster carer, the carer's support social worker and the reviewing officer, one can expect to see the Guardian, the school nurse, the child protection police officer, a representative from the school, the manager from the family centre, a psychologist if one has been appointed, possibly the child's parents and anyone else immediately connected with the child. I assumed the poor attendance was due to the meeting having been arranged at the last minute. It would have made sense to postpone the review until after Christmas so that others could attend, but I knew that hadn't happened because to delay further an already overdue meeting would have looked bad for the social services when they were inspected.

The chairperson, having introduced himself as Philip Case, made a note of the names of those present in a large black-covered book; then, looking at the agency social worker, said: 'So can we expect anyone else to arrive?'

'I don't know,' she said. 'I was only told to attend this review half an hour ago.'

Philip Case looked at me with the same question.

'I know the Guardian and my support social worker have prior engagements,' I said. 'But I don't know about anyone else.' I wouldn't know who had been invited to a child's review or who was attending unless the social worker told me.

'Let's begin, then,' Philip said, making a note of the time. We formally introduced ourselves and after that the rest of the review was farcical. A review usually takes over an hour, with everyone present giving their reports on the child and then discussing any changes that need to be made to help the child. Now I was the only person present who knew Aimee or had the least idea of her family's troubled history, so I gave an update on Aimee's progress, answered a couple of questions Philip had about Aimee's learning and self-care skills, and the meeting might as well have been closed.

'What stage are we at in the care proceedings?' Philip asked the social worker referring to the legal timescale.

'I'm sorry, I don't know,' she replied.

'Aimee is in care under an Interim Care Order,' I said. 'I don't know if the date has been set for the final court hearing.'

'Do you know the date for the final court hearing?' Philip asked the social worker.

'No, I don't,' she said.

'Is the case being contested?' he asked her, meaning were Aimee's parents fighting to have Aimee returned.

'I don't know,' the social worker said.

'Do you know what the long-term care plan is for Aimee?' he asked her, with a slight frown, presumably anticipating her reply.

'I'm sorry, I don't know,' she said. 'I am not at all familiar with the case.' She wouldn't be, I thought, having been assigned the case half an hour before, and I wondered if as an agency social worker this type of situation happened a lot to her.

'I understand Aimee won't be returned home,' I said, stepping in and stating what I knew. 'The Guardian and the social worker who placed Aimee were adamant that there was no chance of her returning home.'

'No, quite so, given the history,' Philip said. 'It's a wonder the child wasn't brought into care sooner.' As the independent reviewing officer he would have received a referral with the basic information about the case. 'Do you know if there are any relatives who might be able to look after Aimee long term?' he asked me. This is usually considered to be the next best option if a child cannot be looked after by their own parents, although the question would normally have been asked of the social worker.

'As far as I know there is no one,' I said.

'So the care plan will presumably be adoption or a long-term foster placement?' he said, more thinking aloud than asking the question.

'I think so,' I said, and the social worker agreed.

'Well, unless there is anything else, I may as well wind up and close the meeting,' he said. 'I'll set the date for the next review, which will hopefully be better attended.' Then to the social worker: 'Will you be staying in post as Aimee's social worker?'

'I don't know,' she said. Which was understandable, as agency social workers are usually on temporary short-term contracts, which often only last a few weeks.

I made a note in my diary of Aimee's next CIC review, scheduled for three months' time; then Philip wished us both a merry Christmas and we said goodbye. All the meeting had accomplished was to allow a box to be ticked on a social service's spreadsheet: 'CIC 1st review ✓'. I knew there were other meetings that were overdue – for example, the child's Personal Education Plan (PEP) to discuss Aimee's progress at school –

and which should have taken place within twenty days of Aimee coming into care. But without a permanent social worker this meeting and similar ones had been overlooked. I couldn't organize them, as they had to be actioned by the child's social worker.

Apart from which, I had other things on my mind beside overdue meetings, for I knew that by the time I arrived home, Adrian should be there, having returned home from university for Christmas. I was looking forward to seeing him, but I also wanted to talk to him about Aimee before I collected her from school.

As soon as I pulled into our road I saw Adrian's car (financed by his student work), parked on the driveway. Pleased he'd made good time and hadn't been stuck in traffic, I let myself in the front door and found him in the hall, surrounded by his bags and admiring the Christmas decorations, having only just arrived.

'Hi, Mum!' he said with a huge grin. He immediately came over and hugged me, slightly lifting me off the floor as he did.

'I'm sure you've grown again!' I said.

'No, Mum, you're shrinking,' he joked, and set me down.

'Great to see you,' I said, giving him another hug. 'Come into the kitchen and tell me all your news while I make us some lunch.'

'Yes, I'll leave the unpacking. I'm starving.'

So while Adrian filled the kettle and made us coffee and I made us some lunch we talked, catching up on all the news. He was in his last year at university and was thinking that when his course ended he would take a year out to go travelling before applying for a permanent job, which I thought was a good idea. He hadn't taken a gap year before going to university, so once he'd finished his degree seemed a good time. We took our lunch to the table and continued chatting there. Adrian mentioned he'd spoken to his father on the phone earlier in the week and would arrange to see him, with Paula, over the Christmas holiday, which was what had happened in the past.

Once we'd finished catching up on our news and had finished eating I decided I couldn't put off any longer what I needed to say about Aimee. I didn't want to upset Adrian but I knew I had to make him aware of Susan's allegations; for while I'd been told the matter wouldn't be taken any further, I wanted to make sure there was no chance of similar allegations being made over Christmas, when we would all be together for two weeks. Adrian always played with the children we fostered, treating them like younger siblings, but sadly that wouldn't be possible with Aimee.

'Adrian, you're going to have to be very careful when you are around Aimee,' I began, going straight to the point. 'Her mother has made a number of allegations by twisting things Aimee told her and it's caused quite a lot of trouble.'

'Like what?' Adrian said, immediately concerned.

'All sorts of things. Some are really silly, like I'm making her have a bath and eat vegetables, and I limit her sweets and television, but others are more serious. You remember when you and your friends stopped by on the way back from the Lakes?'

'Yes,' he said, frowning.

'Aimee told her mother that I'd let "big boys" kiss her here. Not a kiss on the cheek but a full opened-mouth kiss on the lips.'

'You're joking!' Adrian exclaimed, looking horrified, as I knew he would.

'Don't worry. It's been dealt with, but I want you to be careful when you are around Aimee, for your own protection. You know the sort of thing: keep some distance between you; don't be left alone in a room with her; and don't go into her bedroom even to reach something down for her – call me.'

Adrian nodded. We'd had to take similar precautions with some of the other children we'd fostered. 'But she's only eight,' he said with a sigh. 'Why's she been saying things like that?'

'She's been sexually abused,' I said. There was no point in avoiding the subject; Adrian needed to be aware. 'We don't know the full extent of the abuse, and Aimee's not saying much at present. But what she has said is bad enough. She has a sexual awareness well beyond her years.'

'Like Jodie?' he said.

'I don't think she's been as badly abused as Jodie,' I said. 'And she doesn't have the same psychological problems Jodie had, but there are similarities.'

Adrian gave a heartfelt sigh and pushed his chair slightly away from the table. 'I wish you'd tell me when there's a problem, Mum,' he said. 'You insist on dealing with all these things alone. When I'm away I worry about what's going on here.'

'Don't!' I said forcefully. 'I've told you before we're fine. I'd phone you if I needed help.'

'I'd like to think you would,' Adrian said pointedly. 'But I'm not convinced.'

I met his gaze. It was true I still tried to protect my children, even though they were grown up. Since their father had left us many years before I'd purposely been careful not to heap too much responsibility on to Adrian, as the eldest child and only male. Now as I looked at him across the table, my heart swelled with pride as I recognized, not for the first time, what a fine young man he'd grown into – responsible, kind, caring and wanting to help me.

'All right,' I said, with a smile. 'I'll try to confide in you more. Now let's forget all about that. Christmas is coming and we're going to have a great time.'

'Sounds good to me,' he said.

* * *

Perfect Christmas

Our Christmas was just as Lucy had promised Aimee it would be. We all went to church on Christmas Eve for a lovely candle-lit carol service, where we saw many of our old and dear friends. We returned home and with mounting excitement Paula helped Aimee arrange a mince pie and carrot on a plate, which they left in the porch for Father Christmas and his reindeer. Then the 'children' hung pillowcases on the front door, ready for Father Christmas's visit that night. Aimee was hugely overexcited, which was how it should be for a child of eight: not a care in the world and just looking forward to Christmas. She took a long while to go to sleep and of course was awake early on Christmas morning.

'Cathy! Come quick! Father Christmas has been!' she called out at 6.00 a.m.

Grabbing my camera from where I'd left it ready on top of the chest of drawers, I went round to her bedroom. She was sitting in bed and staring in amazement at the pillowcase by her bed, now overflowing with presents.

'Come on, start unwrapping them,' I encouraged, for it seemed Aimee was so overawed she might simply look at them.

Gradually, one at a time, she carefully took the presents from the pillowcase and unwrapped them as I took photographs. 'How did Father Christmas know I wanted that?' she exclaimed time and time again.

'It's all part of the magic of Christmas,' I said. And the look on Aimee's face made all the hard work and planning that goes into Christmas completely worthwhile.

Adrian, Paula and Lucy woke later and unwrapped their Father Christmas presents, and then we all had breakfast together. My parents and my brother and his family arrived mid-morning to join us for Christmas Day, and we settled with drinks and mince pies in the sitting room, where we exchanged more presents. Aimee was a bit hyperactive but it didn't matter, for so too were my niece and nephew, Fiona and Ewan, and the adults were pretty loud too! I saw that Adrian, in line with our discussion, was keeping some distance between him and Aimee, so that if, for example, she sat on the same sofa as him he made sure someone else was sitting between them. It was a pity that this and similar measures were necessary, but given what Aimee had previously told her mother, any physical contact could be turned into an allegation: 'I sat on the sofa next to Adrian.' Accompanied by one of Aimee's giggles and a flutter of her eyelashes, such an accusation could easily lead to more trouble-making from Susan. I also had to keep an eye on Aimee when she was around my brother and my father to make sure they weren't compromised either.

The dining table looked lovely with its festive tablecloth, matching napkins and holly centrepiece. I set out the food and we helped ourselves: a choice of soup or prawn cocktail for start-ers, and then turkey with all the trimmings for the main course. We decided to have a break from eating after the main course and before the Christmas pudding, as we were all full, added to which Aimee, Ewan and Fiona had grown restless sitting at the table. We all trooped into the sitting room, where Paula and Lucy organized some games to win prizes from the tree. Aimee behaved well and joined in all the games nicely.

Shortly after six o'clock I quietly told Aimee that we needed to leave the room to phone her mother. She pulled a face but came with me down the hall, where I used the phone on the hall table to make the call, but Susan didn't answer. I tried three times, as I'd been told to do, but each time an automated message said *It has not been possible to connect the call*. Aimee wasn't worried; indeed she was more interested in returning to the sitting room to play more games.

It was nearly midnight when my parents and my brother and his family began to leave, thanking us for the lovely time they'd had. We always have a nice Christmas, and each Christmas seems even better than the last. I was especially pleased that we'd been able to give Aimee a really good Christmas – one that she'd remember. That night as her head lay on the pillow and I kissed her goodnight she said: 'I'm so happy. Our Christmas was just like the ones you see on television. Perfect.'

Chapter Twenty-Three

A New Year

Aimee had seen her mother on the Friday before Christmas, when they'd exchanged gifts, and they'd spoken to each other on the phone on Saturday (Christmas Eve); then we'd tried to phone on Sunday (Christmas Day), but Susan hadn't answered. Monday, Boxing Day, was a bank holiday and there'd been no contact, as the family centre had been closed. It was now Tuesday and Aimee and I were sitting on the sofa with the phone between us, ready to make the scheduled call to her mother. Aimee would see her mother again as usual on Wednesday. I pressed 'hands-free' to put the phone on speaker and keyed in the numbers, wondering what sort of Christmas Susan had had, and if she would complain we hadn't phoned on Sunday, although we'd tried.

Her mobile was answered almost immediately, but not by Susan. A male voice said, 'Hello.' Which made Aimee jump.

I thought I must have misdialled and was about to apologize and cut the call when Aimee, recognizing the voice, said a subdued, 'Hello.'

'Do you know him?' I asked her quietly. She nodded.

'Hello, Aimee, how are you?' the man asked with a London East End accent.

'All right,' she said quietly. I noticed she had gone quite pale.

'Who is he?' I whispered to her.

A New Year

She shrugged, either not knowing his name or not wanting to tell me.

'What have you been doing with yourself?' he asked familiarly. 'It's a long time since I saw you.'

'I've been doing Christmas,' Aimee said.

The man laughed. I didn't know who he was or how he fitted into Aimee's life, but there was something in his tone I didn't like. I couldn't simply cut him off because I didn't like the sound of his voice, but I was supposed to be monitoring the call. 'I'm sorry to interrupt,' I said. 'I'm Aimee's foster carer. Can I ask who you are, please?'

'You can ask, but I ain't telling you,' he said with another throaty laugh.

It went quiet at the other end of the phone and the next voice we heard was Susan's. 'Aimee, it's Mum here,' she said.

'Hello, Mum,' Aimee said, clearly relieved to hear her mother's voice. 'Where are you?'

'At JJ's.'

'What! I've told you not to go there,' Aimee fumed, jutting her face towards the phone, and taking responsibility for her mother. 'What do you want to go there for?'

Susan gave a small laugh. 'I came here over Christmas to have a good time. I can do that if I want.'

'You're stupid!' Aimee said.

No one had mentioned JJ before, but clearly he was well known to Susan and Aimee.

'When are you going home?' Aimee demanded of her mother, very worried that her mother was at JJ's.

'After the New Year, I guess,' she said. 'I'll be at contact.'

'When's New Year?' Aimee asked me with a frown.

'Next weekend,' I said.

'You're stupid,' Aimee said again to her mother. 'You'll never get me back if you keep going to JJ's!'

Susan went quiet and then said in a small voice, 'I won't be getting you back anyway. So it doesn't really matter where I go or what I do.' Aimee looked as though she was about to cry.

The reason foster carers are asked to monitor phone calls is to safeguard the child and intervene if the content of the call is inappropriate or upsetting for the child. I now decided it was time to step in. 'Susan, I think it might be best to change the subject. Don't you?'

'I agree,' she said easily, and without the angry outburst I'd anticipated. 'Aimee, did you have a lovely Christmas at Cathy's?' she asked. 'I bet you did.' Which was a nice thing to say. Aimee began telling her mother all about Christmas, and Susan 'oohed' and 'aahed' in appreciation and seemed genuinely pleased Aimee had had a nice time. My thoughts went back to what the Guardian had told me about the abuse Susan had suffered that had led to drugs and resulted in all her children being taken into care, and again I felt sorry for her.

Because Aimee and her mother hadn't spoken or seen each other for a few days they had a lot to talk about and their call ran on, but it didn't matter as long as it stayed positive. Aimee told her mother about the presents she'd received – from Father Christmas and my family; the games we'd all played on Christmas Day; my family; what she'd eaten – 'lots of chocolate, oh yes and some turkey'; and that she wanted another Christmas very soon. She and her mother were on the phone for over half an hour and I noticed that Susan didn't once mention her Christmas and Aimee didn't ask her. I guess the fact that she'd spent it at JJ's probably said it all.

Once they'd finished and had said goodbye and hung up I asked Aimee if the man who'd answered her mother's phone and she'd spoken to was JJ.

'No,' Aimee replied. 'He's one of Mum's friends. Can't remember his name. He goes to JJ's house.'

A New Year

'Who is JJ?' I asked.

'Another of Mum's friends,' Aimee said.

'Do you know where he lives?'

'Sort of. It's in an old house on the other side of town. Mum gets Big H there sometimes when the other guys get busted. It's like the other houses we went to. Lots of people sleep there and we did a few times. It's smelly and dark and there's thick smoke that makes you feel sick. Horrible.' She shivered. Aimee was clearly talking about one of the drug dens and crack houses that had supplied her mother with drugs and that she'd mentioned before. That Aimee has stayed in those houses and had breathed in that smoke was shocking.

'I can understand why you are worried about your mum staying at JJ's,' I said. 'But she is an adult and as an adult she makes her own decisions. Some of those decisions will be wrong, but that is not for you to worry about.' I'd said similar things before, for Aimee, like other children I'd fostered, assumed responsibility for her mother, which was inappropriate and would make her anxious.

Aimee couldn't tell me any more about JJ, his house or the man who'd answered the phone, so while she went off to play I wrote up the main points from the call in my fostering log. There wasn't enough information as to where JJ lived to alert the police so that they could raid the house and close down the drug den, but the reference to JJ might be useful in future if more evidence came to light. And of course it was another indication of the dreadful life Aimee had led before coming in care, all of which I would pass on to her new social worker when we had one.

Aimee saw her mother at contact the following day and then again on Friday. As usual I took her into the centre at the start of contact and then waited in the car at the end of contact for the supervisor to bring her out to me. Aimee was grumpy and unsettled after each contact and it wasn't obvious why. The contact supervisor hadn't given me any feedback and when I asked her if contact had gone well she said 'Yes' and hurried back to the centre, presumably wanting to see Susan off the premises so she could go home. When I asked Aimee if she'd had a nice time with her mother she shrugged and said, 'Suppose so.' Seeing her mother must have stirred up many painful memoires and must have been difficult for her and Susan. Given that Aimee definitely wouldn't be returned to live with her mother I again wondered if seeing her mother three times a week plus telephone contact was in her or her mother's best interest. But contact had been set by the judge in accordance with family law, and until the law is changed nothing can be done for cases like Aimee's.

Saturday was New Year's Eve and I explained its significance to Aimee. Lucy and Paula had been invited to friends' parties and were sleeping at their friends' houses, so I didn't have to worry about getting them home. Adrian was going out with a few of his mates to a nightclub in town which was holding a ticketed event, and they'd booked a cab at an extortionate fee to drop them off at their respective houses afterwards.

That left Aimee and me to see in the New Year together, and Aimee was soon caught up in the excitement. We cooked popcorn, made some chocolate crispy cakes, opened a bottle of fizzy drink and then settled on the sofa with our drinks and nibbles. We played with some of the games she'd had for Christmas and then watched a children's film on television, but by eleven o'clock Aimee was fast asleep with her head resting on my shoulder, and I was starting to doze too. Then suddenly my eyes shot open as a loud cheer rose from the television, together with a male voice starting the countdown to midnight.

A New Year

'Come on, wake up, Aimee,' I said, gently shaking her shoulder. 'It's nearly midnight. Soon it will be a new year.'

Aimee lifted her head from my shoulder and stared, bleary-eyed, at the screen as the revellers in central London continued the countdown. Big Ben began to strike midnight and the crowd shouted, whooped and jumped for joy; fireworks began exploding into the night sky, both on the television and outside.

'Happy New Year,' I said to Aimee and gave her a big hug.

'Happy New Year,' she returned sleepily, her eyes already starting to close.

Switching off the television, I then helped one very tired child off the sofa and upstairs. We stopped off in the bathroom for her to go to the toilet and have a quick wash and brush her teeth; then I helped her into bed. As soon as her head touched the pillow her eyes closed again. 'Hug,' she said dreamily without opening her eyes. I gave her a goodnight hug and kissed her forehead.

'Night, love,' I whispered, but there was no reply, Aimee was fast asleep.

I gave her forehead another kiss and then crept from the room. Would she be with us this time next year? I dearly hoped so, and every year.

Adrian was returning to university on Wednesday, and Paula and I helped him load the car and then kissed him goodbye in the hall. Lucy was at work – he'd said goodbye to her that morning – and at my suggestion he'd already said goodbye to Aimee. I'd then settled her at the table in the kitchen with paints and paper while we helped Adrian load the car and say goodbye, thereby avoiding any chance of her wanting to kiss Adrian goodbye and inviting another allegation from Susan. It was sad that I had to take this and similar precautions but they were necessary for Adrian's protection, as he understood. As we waved goodbye I felt pretty confident that nothing had happened over Christmas and the New Year that if Aimee told her mother could be misinterpreted by her and result in another allegation. But it was impossible to be 100 per cent certain.

The following day Paula returned to the sixth form to continue studying for her A-level exams, and Aimee's school returned for the spring term. It was a wrench getting back in the routine after the lovely Christmas break, made worse by the grey skies, short days and long winter nights. But once we were in the routine the weeks flew by and it was only when we reached the end of January that I realized a whole month had passed without any contact from the social services, presumably because there was no social worker assigned to Aimee's case. Jill had phoned me for regular updates and had also visited – one of her six-weekly supervisory visits, which all support social workers should make.

During the month Aimee also had her second dental appointment to complete her treatment. The dentist still looked a bit wary when he saw her, remembering the first time when she'd bitten him, but she was good and kept her mouth open for what was an unpleasant but necessary procedure. When he'd finished he told Aimee that as long as she brushed her teeth thoroughly and didn't eat too many sweet foods she shouldn't need any more fillings, which I repeated to Aimee outside the surgery, and later at bedtime.

Aimee continued to make progress at school in January. I saw her TA, Heather, in the playground at the end of school and she kept me informed. Aimee also made another new friend, who lived closer to us than some of her other friends, and we invited her to tea. Contact at the family centre continued, with no feedback from the supervisor, and the phone calls to Susan were problematic – as to whether she answered or not. There were no complaints from Susan (through the duty

A New Year

social worker) and while Susan didn't speak to me on the phone, neither did she go out of her way to criticize me or make nasty remarks as she had done previously. I thought that perhaps she was finally losing her anger and accepting that her child was in care. I'd seen parents of other children I'd fostered adjust and then work with the social services and the carer. Not that it would change the outcome for Aimee – Susan wouldn't be allowed to keep Aimee, as there was too much history of drug addiction, abuse and neglect – but at least it could make life more pleasant for all those involved, especially Aimee, who would gradually become less anxious about her mother's welfare.

Then at the beginning of February there was a sudden burst of activity. A team manager from the social services phoned and, having apologized that Aimee had been left without a social worker for so long, said a new permanent social worker was being appointed and would be in place the following week. Then the day after, Eva, the Guardian, phoned and said she'd like to visit me at the end of the week. I was looking forward to seeing her again, as I hoped by now she'd have read the files and have the answer to the question everyone was asking: why had Aimee been left to suffer at home for so long?

Chapter Twenty-Four

Jason

As soon as we'd settled with coffee in the sitting room Eva looked at me gravely and took a moment before speaking. I'd formed the impression from when I'd met her before that she was very conscientious in her role as a Guardian Ad Litem. This was confirmed by what she now said.

'As a society I believe we have a collective responsibility to protect our children and keep them safe, but we have failed miserably with Aimee. She was left unprotected to suffer when all the warning signs were there. Not only did her parents let her down but so too has the social care system; we are individually and collectively to blame. Just before Christmas I was given access to the social services' files, and I took them home and read them over Christmas and the New Year. Six very thick files – one for each of Susan's children. I was shocked and deeply saddened by what I read. There will be an inquiry into what has gone wrong; lessons need to be learned.'

Eva paused to sip her coffee and I waited, tense with anticipation yet almost dreading what I was about to hear.

'Aimee was on the "at risk" register at birth,' Eva continued, setting her cup slowly in the saucer. 'Having read the files, it is my opinion Aimee should have been removed at birth. Nothing had changed in Susan's life since her older children were taken into care, and it's not clear why the decision to remove

Jason

Aimee wasn't taken when she was born. Susan was still using drugs and her flat was filthy. The social worker at the time noted that Susan appeared agitated and confused. Susan claimed she was receiving help from a woman she referred to as Nana Jane. There is no indication who this woman was, and no one seems to have met her. But it is possible that Susan's claim she was receiving this support persuaded the social services that Susan could care for Aimee with this woman's help. Also at that time, Susan said Aimee's father was helping her to parent Aimee, although my research shows he was in prison for most of that period.' Eva sighed and paused to take a breath.

'Aimee was kept on the "at risk" register and monitored for two years,' Eva said, looking directly at me. 'Then for reasons I don't understand she was taken off the register, as she was considered to be no longer at risk. Susan then disappeared with Aimee and they went "under the radar" for the next year. There is no indication of where they were living, on what or with whom, but I can guess it was pretty dreadful. They briefly reappeared when Aimee was three, when Susan took her to hospital with a cut to her leg, claiming Aimee had fallen off a swing. She needed four stitches. The doctor had concerns about Aimee's general condition and alerted the social services. Susan didn't return to the hospital to have the stitches removed, and mother and daughter disappeared again for another six months. Then they reappeared in a neighbouring county, where Susan put Aimee into nursery. Concerns were immediately raised by the head teacher of the nursery: Aimee always arrived late, was grubby, hungry, and appeared to be developmentally delayed. When the staff tried to talk to Susan about their concerns she became very agitated and aggressive.'

I nodded, aware just how intimidating Susan could be when angry.

Another Forgotten Child

'The school alerted the social services and after a case conference Aimee was put on the "at risk" register again, and there was some talk about her being brought into care. But Susan disappeared with Aimee before any further action could be taken. What steps were made to trace her and Aimee isn't clear. There were a number of social workers involved and the notes are inconclusive. A few months later when Aimee was four Susan reappeared in the area she now lives in and registered Aimee at the nursery at Hayward Primary School – her present school.

'When you say "disappeared", what exactly do you mean?' I asked. 'I thought there was a central register to stop this type of thing happening, and that all the agencies – health, education and so on – worked together?'

Eva gave a small cynical smile. 'That was the government's plan, but we're a long way from that yet. And remember, this was eight years ago. Many families who came to the notice of the social services kept moving to avoid detection. It took time for the social services to catch up – it still does sometimes – and by then the family had moved again.'

I shook my head in disbelief: that with all the modern communication systems and databases it was still possible for families at risk to simply disappear. 'But Aimee's school raised concerns right from the beginning,' I said. 'When I met Lynn Burrows, when Aimee first came to me, Lynn told me she'd been phoning the social services ever since Aimee joined the school – four years ago.'

'That's right,' Eva said. 'Aimee was still on the "at risk" register and was being monitored. But Susan is very good at telling professionals what they want to hear. She's had a lot of practice with her older children. And possibly the case was given to an inexperienced social worker who wanted to see the best in people, or a social worker with a huge caseload. Whatever the case, the outcome was that Aimee was taken off the "at risk" register two years later when she was six.'

'To continue living in squalor, sleeping at crack houses and being abused!' I said scathingly.

Eva nodded solemnly. 'Although the social services clearly didn't know all that at the time,' she said, offering a small defence. 'Fortunately, Lynn Burrows kept raising concerns. The records show Aimee's attendance at school was very poor and when she did appear she was filthy with head lice, sores around her mouth and bruises on her arms and legs. Lynn also reported that Susan was impossible to deal with and was often angry and verbally abusive. In fact all the concerns that had been raised before. Aimee was put back on the "at risk" register and then one day Aimee told Lynn that her father had hit her and showed her fresh bruises. A social worker made an unannounced visit to the flat and found it, quote, "unfit for human habitation". It was filthy, there were no carpets, curtains or bed for Aimee, no food, heating or lighting, and dog excrement on the floor. An unnamed male was sitting on the sofa smoking an illegal substance and watching an adult movie while Aimee sat next to him. An emergency child protection case conference was convened, but even then it took three months to bring Aimee into care.'

'Why?' I gasped in amazement. 'Why did it take so long?'

'In court, through her barrister and solicitor, Susan told the judge what he wanted to hear: that she needed help and promised to cooperate and work with the social services. Susan vowed to do all that was necessary to keep Aimee, including attending a drug rehabilitation programme. I understand it was a very emotional plea and it clearly worked, for the judge agreed to give Susan one last chance. One chance too many, in my view. The rest you know. Despite all the help that was put in, nothing changed and Aimee was finally removed and came to you.'

It was heavy stuff and we were both silent for a moment. Then Eva added: 'I wish I could say it was the only case like this I've come across but it's not – not by a long way. It happens too often: lots of changes in social worker, with no one person responsible for any length of time, and a catalogue of errors and oversights that leave a vulnerable young child to suffer.'

I knew Eva was right. I'd looked after children before who'd 'fallen through the net' of social care; some of them I'd fostered years before. I wondered how long it would be before the system was finally improved. In an ideal world no child would need to be removed from his or her parents, but this isn't an ideal world. There are vulnerable children who need an effective social care system to protect them and there probably always will be.

'How many social workers were involved in Aimee's case?' I asked, out of interest. 'She's had five since coming to me,' I added.

'I don't know exactly,' Eva said. 'It's difficult to tell from the records. I'd guess twelve or more before she came to you and that's just for Aimee. There were many other social workers involved with the older children, but decisions appear to have been made sooner for them. I had a look through their files and it was obvious Susan had never been able to look after any of her children. The evidence was so clear that by the time Aimee was born the decision to bring her into care and have her adopted should have been made within months, not eight years. As far as I can see from the files, and having spoken to the social services, the older children are doing well. And isn't it lovely that Jason has applied to look after Aimee permanently?'

'Permanently? Jason?' I queried, completely thrown. 'I'm sorry, I don't understand.'

'You don't know?' Eva asked.

'No.' I shook my head.

'Oh dear. How insensitive of me! I expect the information hasn't got through to you yet because of the lack of a social worker. Jason is the eldest of Aimee's half-siblings. He's twenty-seven and married with one child. He and his family live in Norfolk, and last week he put himself forward to look after Aimee permanently. Once the new social worker is in place they'll look into his suitability. Sorry, I didn't realize you hadn't been told.'

'I see,' I said, trying to recover from the shock of what I'd just heard. 'No, I'd no idea. The last I'd heard was when you asked me if I'd be prepared to look after Aimee long-term.'

'And you kindly agreed,' Eva said with a small reassuring smile. 'And that is still an option for Aimee. Jason and his family will be assessed once a new social worker is in place. Nothing is certain yet.'

'I see,' I said again. 'Thank goodness I haven't discussed Aimee staying with Adrian, Paula and Lucy. I haven't had a chance – with Christmas and everything – but I'll wait now until we know more. I don't want to build up their hopes and then have them dashed. Paula and Lucy especially have grown close to Aimee.'

Eva looked at me kindly. 'It must be very difficult for you to keep having to say goodbye to the children you look after. I'm sure I couldn't do it.'

'It is difficult,' I said. 'It's hard even when you know the child is going to a kind and loving home. Some of the children keep in contact, which is nice, and sometimes you don't hear from them for years and then they suddenly phone or arrive on your doorstep, which is fantastic.'

Eva smiled kindly again. 'Well, as I said, nothing is settled yet and there's a lot to take into account. Apart from assessing Jason and his family to see if they can successfully parent Aimee and offer her a suitable home, I will want to know if Jason is in contact with Susan. And if he is, how often he sees her. I'm now of the opinion that in order for Aimee to have the best chance in life the less she sees of her mother the better. Sad though it is, I will be recommending contact between Aimee and her mother to be no more than twice a year; otherwise Susan's influence will prevail and she'll try to disrupt Aimee's life just as she did with the other half-siblings.'

I knew Eva was right. Aimee deserved a fresh start, away from her mother's influence, and then hopefully she wouldn't repeat the same mistakes her mother had made. Eva then asked me for an update on Aimee, which I gave, and after that she confirmed that a new permanent social worker should be in place the following week. She said she'd tried to see Susan but she wasn't returning her calls, which would do nothing for her case in court.

'Do you think Susan has given up the fight for Aimee?' I asked. 'Does she know Jason has applied to have her?'

'She knows and she's opposed to Jason looking after Aimee.'

'Why? I'd have thought she'd find it reassuring to know her son was looking after her daughter.'

'Susan says because Jason was adopted he's not family, and therefore has no right to look after her. I know it doesn't make sense, but a lot of what Susan says doesn't make sense. Her solicitor told me that some days she's barely functioning and can't put a sentence together.'

'And all those years she was looking after Aimee!' I said. 'It's a wonder Aimee isn't more disturbed.'

Eva nodded. 'It doesn't bear thinking about. Let's hope that with therapy Aimee can put the past behind her and move on with her life.'

I agreed. Eva thanked me for all I was doing for Aimee and said that the school had commented on how happy Aimee was, and what excellent progress she was making in her learning.

She promised to keep me updated. We said goodbye and I saw her out.

Eva had left me with a lot to think about, not least of which was what Aimee would say if she knew her half-brother, whom she'd never met, had applied to look after her permanently. I wouldn't be telling Aimee yet – not until Jason and his family had been assessed, approved, and the court had made its decision; only then would the social worker or I explain to Aimee what was going to happen. At her age such decisions are made for the child, while an older child is usually part of the decision-making process. However, there was nothing to stop me from preparing Aimee for the possibility that she might not be staying with us forever; indeed it was important I did. For while I hadn't actually told Aimee I'd agree to her staying and becoming a permanent member of our family, she was so settled that there was a feeling on all our parts – an assumption – that she would be staying and this was her permanent home. I also thought I needed to start preparing Lucy and Paula for all eventualities.

The opportunity to do this presented itself that evening when Aimee was in bed and three of us were in the sitting room waiting for a television programme to start.

'The Guardian visited today,' I said. 'There is a possibility that Aimee might go and live with one of her half-brothers. Don't say anything to her yet, as nothing is decided, but I thought you should know.'

'If she doesn't go to him, then she'll stay with us,' Paula said matter-of-factly. 'I'd like her to.'

'Yes, that would be my hope too,' I said, reassured by the firmness of Paula's offer. 'What do you think, Lucy?'

'As long as Aimee's happy, that's all that counts,' she said.

And that was that. I'd tell them more when I knew more.

Then at the weekend Aimee was looking through some of my photograph albums, which included many pictures of the children I'd fostered. She began pointing to the children and asking me who they were and where they were now. This was a golden opportunity to say what I needed to, so I joined her on the sofa and we continued looking through the album together.

'That's Donna,' I said. 'She stayed with us for over a year and then went to live with a forever family, not far from here. And that little girl is Alice. Her mummy loved her but she couldn't look after her, so she went to live with her gran.'

'Why couldn't she look after her?' Aimee asked, pausing from looking at the page to look at me.

'Unfortunately she had problems with drugs, a bit like your mummy,' I said, while omitting to mention that Alice's mother had recovered from drug addiction, so that her daughter had been returned to her, an opportunity Susan had wasted.

'And that smart young man is Tayo,' I said, as Aimee pointed to his photograph. 'He stayed with me for nearly a year and then went to live in a different country with his gran. And that's Reece. He lives with his aunt and uncle on a farm.'

'So all these kids lived here, and when the judge made his decision they went to live with a forever family?' Aimee said. We'd already talked about the judge and forever families, so Aimee had an understanding of these terms.

'Yes, that's right,' I said. 'And they're all very happy.'

'Did the kids have to go?' Aimee now asked, closing this album and opening the next.

'Yes, and they wanted to,' I said. 'The judge is very wise and knows what's best for children, and what will make them happy.'

'I see,' Aimee said, turning another page. 'I guess the judge will say I can't go back to live with my mum?'

Jason

'I think that will be his decision, yes,' I said gently. 'Your mother loves you but she can't look after you, can she?'

Aimee shook her head. 'No. I had to look after my mum. She didn't look after me, and it was very hard.'

'I know. That was too much responsibility for a child. It can make you sad and very worried. Parents need to look after their children, not the other way round.' I'd said similar things before, but Aimee's life for eight years had been exactly that, and it did no harm to confirm from time to time what should have been.

Aimee came to the end of the album and, having had enough of looking at photographs, slipped from the sofa and went off to play. The notion that children left me to live happily with forever families had been seeded in Aimee's mind, so that if the judge decided to send her to live with Jason it wouldn't come as such a shock. I always try to prepare the children I foster for all eventualities, and if Aimee stayed with us, well, no harm had been done. I'd no idea of the timescale or when the final court hearing would be, but once the permanent social worker was in place the following week I hoped it would all become clearer. Such uncertainty is not only unsettling for the child, who doesn't know where they will be living in the future, but also for the foster carer and their family too. I couldn't, for example, plan ahead and book a summer holiday, as I didn't know if Aimee would be with us.

Chapter Twenty-Five
A Winner Now

It was the end of the following week before the new social worker phoned and when he did it was clear he'd been very busy. Introducing himself as Norman, he told me he'd arranged two meetings for the following week, which he hoped I would be able to attend: the long-overdue PEP (personal education plan) and a permanency planning meeting. I reached for my diary and, confirming I could attend, wrote in the dates, times and venues for the meetings.

'I also need to visit Aimee,' Norman said. 'Can I come on Tuesday of the week after? After school – say four fifteen?'

'Yes, that's fine,' I said, and turning the page in my diary made another note.

Norman had a warm but authoritative voice with a slight trace of a north of England accent. I guessed he was an experienced social worker from the way he'd quickly grasped Aimee's case and prioritized what needed doing. He asked how Aimee was and I gave him an update. Then he asked if I had any issues that needed addressing.

'Nothing new,' I said, 'although telephone contact between Aimee and her mother remains problematic and unsatisfactory. Aimee gets annoyed if her mother doesn't answer and when she does they don't seem to have much to say to each other. I'm wondering if Susan finds the phone contact difficult too. I mentioned this to the Guardian and she was going to look into it.'

'I haven't heard anything from Eva. I'll phone Susan and see if she will agree to a reduction in phone contact,' Norman said.

'Have you spoken to Susan?' I asked, mindful that past experience suggested Susan wasn't agreeable to much.

'Not yet. I haven't had a chance. But I'll do so now and get back to you.'

I was impressed by Norman's efficiency, and relieved that at last we had a permanent social worker. I was even more impressed (and relieved) when an hour later Norman phoned again and said that Susan had agreed phone contact was difficult and suggested it stop completely.

'Susan said it was a worry for her,' Norman continued. 'Aimee was often angry with her at contact if she hadn't answered her phone the night before.'

'Has Susan mellowed?' I asked, for it seemed that not long ago she wouldn't have agreed to anything.

'My manager thinks so,' Norman said. 'Certainly Susan was fine with me on the phone and thanked me for calling.'

So again I wondered if Susan was coming to terms with the possibility that Aimee wouldn't be returned to live with her, which although sad – it's sad that any parents should lose their child – would be better for them both in the long term.

That afternoon when I collected Aimee from school to take her to contact I told her that she had a new social worker and he was called Norman. I said I'd spoken to him on the phone and that he would be visiting us the week after next, and that he sounded very pleasant and was easy to talk to.

'Oh, goodie, a man,' Aimee said flirtatiously, batting her eyelids.

'He's an adult male and he's your social worker,' I said firmly. 'There's no need to be silly about it.' For while Aimee was improving in her attitude towards men and boys, she still needed correcting sometimes. In this matter as with others I was teaching her how to behave appropriately, which children of responsible parents learn naturally from the good example of their parents.

When we arrived at the family centre the contact supervisor said that Susan hadn't arrived yet, which was very unusual. I couldn't remember a time when Susan hadn't been in the contact room, ready and waiting for Aimee. I waited with Aimee in reception, aware that Susan would have to pass me on the way in, and I wondered what her attitude towards me would be. I hadn't seen her for over two months – since the new arrangements for contact had begun – and I hoped that now, if she wasn't so angry, we'd be able to establish a working relationship, which would be much better for Aimee.

We waited fifteen minutes and then the contact supervisor came out of the office and said that Susan had just phoned to say she wouldn't be able to make contact tonight; no reason had been given, but she sent her apologies. Aimee was annoyed and a little upset. I reassured her that she would see her mother on Friday, and we returned home, where she watched some television while I made dinner. I waited until after dinner to tell Aimee that there would be no more phone contact, for I was aware that this news coming straight after her mother missing contact at the family centre could seem like a rejection. So after I'd helped Aimee with her homework I said that it had been decided phone contact was difficult for both her and her mother and it would stop. Aimee accepted this with no fuss, so I guessed that in her heart of hearts she knew the phone calls to her mother hadn't been good.

However, I was very concerned when we arrived for the next contact – on Friday – and Susan wasn't there again.

'We've tried to phone her mobile but it's switched off,' the contact supervisor said insensitively in front of Aimee.

'Perhaps Mum's ill!' Aimee said, very worried and her eyes watering.

'I'm sure she's not,' I said. 'We'd have been told.' I put my arm around her and reassured her as best I could as we stood in reception and waited.

Five minutes later I heard the phone ring through the open door of the office, but I couldn't hear the conversation. Presently the contact supervisor appeared again. Aimee and I both looked at her expectantly. I hoped that if she had bad news she wouldn't blurt it out in front of Aimee.

'That was Aimee's social worker on the phone,' the supervisor said. 'Susan's not coming tonight.'

'Why?' I asked. Aimee snuggled closer to my side.

'He said he'll phone you shortly and explain.'

There was little I could do but comfort Aimee, and we left hand in hand to return to the car. Outside I eased up the collar on her coat as a biting easterly wind cut into us. I knew Aimee was feeling rejected and I also knew she would be very anxious about her mother. 'I'm sure your mum is all right,' I said. 'Your social worker is phoning soon and I'll tell you what he says.'

Aimee gave a small nod and I opened the rear door of the car and saw her in. Having checked her seatbelt was secure I closed her door and went round the back of the car to get into the driver's seat. However, just as I was about to open the driver's door my phone began to ring. Quickly taking it from my pocket I saw an unknown mobile number appear on the display.

'Hello?' I answered tentatively.

'It's Norman,' Aimee's social worker said. 'Can you talk?'

'Yes.'

'Aimee can't hear you?'

'No, she's in the car. I'm just outside it.'

'I understand Susan didn't go to contact tonight?'

'No. Nor the last time.'

'So I've been told. Susan's solicitor phoned about an hour ago and said Susan had decided to stop all contact with Aimee.'

'Oh no. Why?' I asked in amazement.

'She had a meeting with her solicitor and as a result of that Susan's made the decision to stop seeing Aimee.'

'Whatever did the solicitor say?' I asked.

'Apparently he gave her an honest appraisal of her case and said that the chances of Aimee being returned to her were minimal, if not non-existent. He advised her not to contest the case, as there would be no chance of her winning.' It was another aspect of the adversarial nature of childcare proceedings that there was a 'winner' and a 'loser'.

'And Susan agreed? Just like that?' I asked, incredulous and concerned.

'With some conditions,' Norman said. 'Also Susan is now saying she will agree to Aimee going to live with Jason as long as she can have regular contact – every two months, as she has with one of her older children. Her solicitor advised her that if it was an uncontested hearing, and Aimee went to live with Jason, then she was more likely to get regular contact.'

Norman stopped and there was a small silence. I shivered inside my coat as the wind nipped me. 'I see,' I said. 'And are you going to agree to that level of contact?' I asked, worried.

'If it means we have Susan's cooperation and we can avoid a protracted court case, then very likely yes. We have to think what is best for Aimee and it will mean we can get her settled at Jason's quickly. It will of course be supervised contact.'

'And what about Susan's influence on Aimee?' I asked, still concerned. 'I thought it was a worry that with regular contact she could undermine and manipulate the situation, as she has done with some of her older children.'

'Contact will need to be carefully monitored,' Norman said. 'I'll be speaking to my manager in the morning but sometimes we have to accept a compromise.' Which I knew to be true. In this case it would be a payoff between Susan's cooperation with regular contact and a protected legal battle that would leave Aimee in the care system and in limbo for a year, and the social services with a costly bill. 'In the meantime,' Norman continued, 'could you explain what's happening to Aimee?'

'I'll try but it won't be easy. It would have been better for Aimee if contact could have been gradually reduced.'

'I know, but Susan has told her solicitor that she doesn't want to see Aimee again until after the move to Jason. Perhaps it's her way of dealing with it, so we have to respect that.'

'Yes,' I said, not convinced. This was going to be difficult for Aimee. Often, as parents, we have to sacrifice what we would like in favour of what is in our child's best interest. But of course Susan had never been able to do that.

'To be honest I'm not sure what to tell Aimee,' I said. 'I mean, it's not definite yet that Aimee will go to live with Jason, is it? He hasn't been assessed.'

'Well, actually he has,' Norman said, and he sounded as though he was smiling. 'Good fortune. I found out this morning that he and his wife have recently been assessed as foster carers, which should help the timescale enormously.'

'What a coincidence!' I said.

'Yes. It appears Jason was so grateful for the foster care he received before he was adopted that he wanted to give something back and help others. I'll tell you more when I see you at the permanency planning meeting next week. For now mention Jason to Aimee but explain nothing is definite yet. I'll have to meet Jason and his family before anything is finalized.'

'I'll think of something to say,' I said.

'Thank you.'

I said goodbye to Norman, returned my phone to my pocket and steeled myself before getting into the car.

'Well? What did he say?' Aimee asked, guessing it had been her social worker on the phone.

I turned in my seat to look at her; the interior light in the car was still on and her little face looked pale and anxious. 'Your mother is well, love. She is not ill, but she's had to make some difficult decisions.'

'She doesn't want to see me any more, does she?' Aimee blurted, tears immediately springing to her eyes.

I reached over and took her hand. 'She does, but it won't be quite so often. And there is good news as well. Aimee, it's cold and dark, so let's go home first and then I'll tell you what Norman has told me. I'd rather take time and explain it to you. Is that all right?'

Aimee gave a small nod and I passed her a tissue so she could wipe her eyes. 'The main thing is your mother is not ill,' I said again, by way of reassurance.

Aimee sniffed. 'It's those drugs,' she said. 'She should never have had kids if she couldn't look after them.'

'I know, love,' I said sadly. I couldn't disagree.

Once I was sure Aimee was all right I turned in my seat to face the front, started the engine and drove home.

When we arrived home the house was empty; we were earlier than usual, so Paula hadn't arrived home from sixth form yet, and Lucy was still at work. I helped Aimee unbutton her coat and hang it on the coat stand; then we went through to the sitting room, where we sat side by side on the sofa. I began by reassuring Aimee that her mother wasn't ill, and then I told her what I knew about Jason and his family. Aimee had heard her mother mention him a few times but had no details. I said that as a young child he'd been in foster care and had then been adopted. I said he was married and had one child, and he and his wife had asked if they could look after Aimee permanently and be her new forever family. I emphasized that Jason and his family were very nice people who had a lovely home, for I understood that when Jason had been mentioned by Susan what she'd said had been negative. I also emphasized that before anything was definite her social worker would meet Jason and his family to make sure their home was the best place for Aimee to live.

Aimee sat quietly, taking all this in, and then when I'd finished asked, 'So Jason is my brother?'

'Yes. Your half-brother really.'

'What's a half-brother?'

I purposely hadn't gone into this too deeply, as all Aimee's brothers and sisters had different fathers. 'He has a different father to you,' I said.

'And when Jason was little he had a new mummy and daddy?' Aimee sensibly asked.

'Yes, that's right. He was adopted.'

'Does he still see my mum?'

'I don't think so.'

'But I will?'

'Yes. But there's going to be a break for now, which was why your mother wasn't at contact. It's been decided it would be better if you and your mum stopped seeing each other until everything is sorted out. Then when all the decisions have been made you will see each other again.' By saying 'it has been decided' rather than 'your mother decided' I hoped to lessen Aimee's feelings of rejection.

However, Aimee exclaimed: 'A break! Mum's always having breaks from me! When I was at home she left me with anyone who would have me.' Which I knew to be true from the original referral and what Kristen, the first social worker, had told me.

'Your mum had a lot of problems,' I said. 'But try not to be angry and blame her.' It doesn't do children any good to be angry with their parents, because if they are they can grow into angry adults.

'And Jason doesn't do what Mum does and get drunk and smoke or take drugs?'

'No. Absolutely not,' I said firmly. 'He's been assessed as a foster carer, as I have, so he won't do any of those things – for sure.'

'Good,' Aimee said. 'Pity Mum wasn't a foster carer.'

She fell silent and I slipped my arm around her and drew her to me. Aimee no longer resisted when I hugged her; indeed she often came to me during the day for a hug, and always wanted a hug and kiss goodnight. As I held her and felt her body relax against mine, I thought how far she'd come from the angry feral child, filthy and crawling with head lice, to the girl who sat beside me now and was just like my daughter.

'If you do go to live with Jason we're all going to miss you,' I said quietly, allowing my head to rest on hers.

'I'm going to miss you too,' Aimee said. 'Will you guys come and visit me?'

'I hope so. We'd like to.' Although I knew it would be up to Jason and his family if there was any contact and how much.

'And what if I don't go to Jason?' Aimee now asked quietly. 'Who's going to have me then?'

'I hope you will stay with us,' I said. 'We'd like you to.'

Aimee gave my hand a little squeeze before she said, 'I'm lucky. Two families want me now as their daughter. Before no one did.'

I felt a lump rise to my throat. 'That just shows what a lovely person you are,' I said. 'But Aimee, it wasn't that your mum didn't want you, she couldn't look after you.'

'So you keep telling me. But, Cathy, if my mum had wanted me badly enough, she would have changed. She would have stopped taking drugs, cleaned the house, cleaned me and taken me to school. That's what she should have done if she wanted me bad enough.' Aimee raised her head and looked at me sadly, wide eyes imploring.

What could I say? She was right, of course. I'd worked with parents before who'd turned their lives around, so desperate were they to get their children back. Susan had been given the same chances but had been unable to make the necessary changes to keep her children.

Aimee sighed and gave a little shrug. 'Oh, well, I guess that's life,' she said. 'You win some and lose some. But I'm a winner now, aren't I, Cathy?'

'You certainly are, love.'

When Paula arrived home from sixth form Aimee leapt from the sofa and greeted her with: 'Guess what? I've got half a brother and he's going to be my dad.' Little wonder Paula looked confused!

I came out from the kitchen, where I'd been making dinner, and quickly explained to Paula who Jason was and the possibility that Aimee might be going to live with him and his family. I told Paula I'd tell her as soon as I knew more and Paula told Aimee she was happy for her. However, when Lucy arrived home an hour later and Aimee rushed into the hall to greet her, she cried: 'I'm going to live with my brother and he's sexy!'

'Aimee!' I cried, immediately going into the hall. 'That's not how you talk about your brother or any family member. You know that. I've told you before that little girls don't call men sexy. It's not nice. Do you understand?'

Aimee nodded. 'Sorry,' she said, subdued, and I felt awful for telling her off. But Aimee's words were a reality check – a harsh reminder that she still had a way to go. Jason would need to be told the details of Aimee's background so that he could help her deal with the abuse she'd suffered and also put in place measures to protect himself and his family, just as I'd had to. With the high level of contact that was being planned, if Susan decided not to cooperate any longer she could easily twist what Aimee told her, just as she had done with us. If the social services didn't make Jason fully aware of Aimee's background then I would. It would be unfair not to tell him and leave him wide open to the possibility of allegations of abuse.

Chapter Twenty-Six

Progress

Most people working in social care will agree that decisions often take far too long to be made, and the court system for children in care is laboriously slow, but Aimee's case now speeded up like a runaway train. On Tuesday morning I attended the long-overdue PEP (personal education plan) meeting, which was held at Aimee's school. The PEP meeting is relatively small, short and informal, but it is a statutory requirement for all children in care. The aim of the meeting is to draw up a working document that the school can use in order to help the child reach his or her full potential. As well as containing basic information about the child, it identifies the child's strengths and weaknesses; outlines any extra support the child might need; and sets targets for the child to achieve during the term.

On Tuesday morning I waited in reception at the school for Norman to arrive. I hadn't met him before, but when a lone male came through the door I thought it might be him. This was confirmed when he told the school secretary he was Aimee's social worker and here for her PEP meeting.

'Hi, I'm Cathy Glass,' I said, introducing myself when he'd finished at reception. Norman looked at me blankly. 'Aimee's foster carer,' I clarified.

'Oh, yes of course. Sorry, Cathy. I've had so many new cases and faces to learn that the names escape me sometimes. Pleased to meet you.'

We shook hands. I guessed Norman was in his late thirties; he was short – not a lot taller than me – but broad-shouldered. There was an authority in his manner that I'd already noted in his voice when I'd spoken to him on the phone. 'How is Aimee doing?' he asked.

'Very well,' I said. 'I had a chat with her about Jason and she has an understanding of the situation.'

'Thank you. I'll be seeing her next week.'

Lynn Burrows, the designated teacher, appeared in reception; she smiled and said hello to me, and introduced herself to Norman. We then went with her up a flight of stairs to her office, where the meeting was to take place. There would just be the three of us.

Once we were seated around the table Lynn began by giving the results of some tests Aimee had taken, which showed her to be working at about the level of a four-year-old. Norman made notes on the PEP form as Lynn spoke. She said Aimee had missed so much school in the early years – when the building blocks of learning should have been put in place – that it would take some time for her to catch up with her peer group. At present she was four years behind. Lynn said that Heather, the teaching assistant, was helping Aimee, going back to the very basics and teaching her phonetic sounds, vowel and consonant blends, number sequencing, elementary adding and subtracting, etc., all of which Aimee would have done in year one had she been in school.

'Aimee's making steady progress,' Lynn confirmed. 'But she can become frustrated if she doesn't understand something.'

It appeared from what Lynn said that there were no big issues in respect of Aimee's learning, such as dyslexia or learning difficulties; Aimee just had a lot of catching up to do from having missed so much early schooling. When Lynn had finished I thanked her for all she and the staff were doing for Aimee and confirmed I would obviously continue to give Aimee all the help I could at home, and that I was in daily touch with her TA, Heather.

Lynn thanked me for all I was doing at home to help Aimee and then, looking at Norman, frowned and said, 'Aimee has told Heather that she may be moving to live with her brother. Is that right?'

'It's a possibility,' Norman said, and briefly explained the situation. 'I'll know more in a couple of weeks.'

'And if she doesn't go to live with Jason?' Lynn asked.

'I hope she'll stay with me,' I said.

'Good.' Lynn smiled, and looked relieved. 'The poor kid needs stability after everything she's been through. She's a different child since she's been with you, Cathy. We'll miss her if she does go. You'll miss her too, won't you?'

'Very much,' I said.

Norman noted Aimee's schedule of learning for the next term, which Lynn showed him, and then finished the meeting by saying he'd enter the PEP on the computer system and would send us both a printed copy in the post. We said goodbye and I left ahead of Norman, who'd asked Lynn if he could use the staff toilet. The meeting was pretty much as I'd imagined and was really to confirm Aimee was progressing well and set learning targets for her.

Outside I began down the path that ran alongside the playground and led to the road. It was morning break and the children were in the playground. As I walked I glanced through the gaps in the shrubbery but couldn't see Aimee among the scores of running, shouting, excited children. I continued down the path, towards the main road, and as I did Hatchet suddenly appeared at the end of the path on a lead, followed by Susan. She was looking straight ahead as they crossed the path and therefore didn't see me.

As the path met the pavement I turned right. Susan was just ahead of me, peering through a gap in the hedge that ran along this side of the playground, presumably looking for Aimee. Hatchet was crouched beside her, straining to do his business on the pavement.

I went up to her. 'Hello, Susan,' I said.

She jumped and, turning, looked at me guiltily. 'You scared me,' she said, pinching out a half-smoked cigarette between her thumb and forefinger. 'What are you doing here?'

I could have asked her the same question, although we both knew why she was here. 'I've been to a meeting in the school,' I said. 'To make sure Aimee is learning as she should.'

Susan nodded and then shivered. She looked dreadful. It was cold and she only had on a thin grubby jacket, T-shirt, jeans and what looked like plimsolls on her feet. Her face was more gaunt and paler than the last time I'd seen her, three months previously, almost grey, and very heavily lined. She still didn't have any false teeth and there was a large open cold sore on her lip. I didn't know if she was shivering from the cold, lack of nutrition or drug withdrawal.

'Susan, if you'd like to know how Aimee is doing at school and generally, why don't you ask Norman to set up a meeting?' I suggested, trying to establish a working relationship. 'Then I can tell you all about Aimee's progress. We haven't seen each other for a while.'

'Oh yeah, OK,' Susan said, agitated and clearly eager to get away. 'I'll remember that. See ya, then.' Turning, she headed back along the pavement, leaving Hatchet's large poop in the centre of the path. I'd tried to talk to her but she hadn't wanted to know. I looked at the steaming pile of dog's mess and considered calling after her and asking if she was going to clear it up, but thought better of it. I wondered if her coming to the school was a regular occurrence; clearly Lynn Burrows wasn't aware, or she would have mentioned it.

I didn't tell Aimee I'd seen her mother outside school, but that evening after dinner when she was helping me to clear the table I asked casually, 'Do you often see your mum at playtime?'

Aimee looked at me with the same guilty expression her mother had. 'Sometimes,' she said.

'Does she talk to you?'

'Until the playground supervisor sees her and then she goes.'

'OK. I just wondered.' And we continued with the dishes.

I didn't say anything more to Aimee on this matter; it was no good telling her not to go to the hedge when her mother was there. It was her mother's responsibility, and incumbent on her not to initiate unsupervised contact. I'd have to make a note in my log that I'd seen Susan outside the school and of what Aimee had told me; I'd also have to inform the social worker and the school. For while a mother wanting to catch a glimpse of her daughter might seem innocent enough, who knew what Susan was telling Aimee before the playground supervisor spotted her? Susan could, for example, be telling Aimee not to talk about certain things – warning her off disclosing more abuse, perhaps. I'd looked after children who'd been threatened into silence by their parents at snatched impromptu meetings and even at supervised contact when the supervisor hadn't been vigilant. Also it was confusing for Aimee to be told she wouldn't be seeing her mother at the family centre and then see her outside school. A child in care has enough to cope with without such additional anxieties.

* * *

On Wednesday Jill visited me for one of her six-weekly supervisory meetings, when I updated her on Aimee's progress at
home and school, including details of the PEP. Jill then checked
and signed my log notes, after which we discussed the agency's
forthcoming training programme, to which I contributed. Jill
was happy that Aimee's placement was going as planned and
she passed me two copies of the report she'd written of her last
supervisory visit. I read the top copy, signed and dated them
both, and then handed one copy back to Jill. This would go
on the agency's file and the other copy I'd keep for my records.
Jill then asked me if I wanted her to attend the permanency
planning meeting, which was due to take place on Thursday. I
said I didn't think there was any need, as it would be straightforward. Lastly we arranged a date for Jill's next visit – in
six weeks' time. 'Assuming Aimee is still with you, of course,'
Jill said.

'Oh, she will be,' I said. 'She can't possibly be moved that
quickly. Can she?'

'It's possible, but not likely,' Jill said.

The permanency planning meeting was held on Thursday at
2.00 p.m. at the council offices. I arrived ten minutes early, as I
do for all meetings, although goodness knows why, for I couldn't
ever remember a meeting at the social services starting on time.
Norman hadn't previously notified me of which room the meeting would be held in, so having signed in at reception, I used my
mobile to phone him, assuming he was somewhere in the building. He wasn't. He was outside in the smoking area having a fag
and said he'd be with me as soon as he'd finished. Presently
Norman arrived and said we needed to find Stacey. I didn't
know who Stacey was or why we needed to find her, but
Norman explained.

'Stacey's leading and chairing the permanency planning

meeting,' he said. 'She's from the family finding team. But I don't know which room we're using.'

'That makes two of us,' I said with a smile.

I fell into step beside him as we left reception and began up the stairs to the first floor. Stacey wasn't where Norman thought she would be, so we hunted around until we found her – on the phone in an office that wasn't her own. We respectfully waited outside the office door until she'd finished. When she came out she apologized for keeping us waiting and said we just had to collect Laura, who she said was a trainee social worker and wanted to sit in on our meeting. Five minutes later we found Laura in the main office, and then Stacey wondered out loud which room we should use for the meeting, as none of the interview rooms had been booked and most of them appeared to be in use. I knew better than to ask why no room had been booked, and tagged along, aware the meeting should have started over twenty minutes previously.

As luck would have it, one of the rooms was suddenly vacated and we quickly went in before anyone else could, and the four of us arranged ourselves around the table. Stacey switched on her laptop and we waited expectantly. She apologized that it was taking some time for her to log in, as there were problems with the new wireless networking system. We waited some more while she stared at the screen, clicked the mouse and told us she was trying to find the folder she needed to open for the meeting. 'Oh for good old-fashioned pen and paper,' she said with a sigh.

Norman and I agreed, while Laura, the trainee, smiled politely.

Eventually we got started, thirty-five minutes late. We introduced ourselves, and I said I needed to leave in forty minutes to collect Aimee from school.

'OK, we'll speed up,' Stacey said. 'As this is the first permanency planning meeting for Aimee, I'll need to enter her details first.' She then asked Norman for Aimee's full name, date of birth, ages of siblings, when she came into care and what type of care order had been granted, all of which I thought could and should have been entered before the meeting had begun to save time. But I'm used to having these thoughts in meetings at the social services and rarely voice them.

Once Norman had given Stacey the information she needed and she'd typed it into her laptop, she asked for an update on the court proceedings. Norman explained that the care plan had been to apply for a full care order so that Aimee could be adopted, but as Susan was now cooperating and a member of the extended family (Jason) had offered Aimee a permanent home, there probably wouldn't be any need to apply for a full care order. Stacey typed this into her laptop and then asked Norman a number of questions regarding the legal position, which again I'd have thought she should have been made aware of before the meeting.

'So you won't really be needing family finding, then?' Stacey asked Norman.

'No, I suppose not, because if Aimee doesn't go to Jason then she'll stay with Cathy. So we won't have to look for a permanent family.'

'But if Aimee is going to move, then we'll need to meet again to plan the introductions and timescale of the move,' Stacey pointed out.

'Yes,' Norman confirmed. 'I'll phone you when I know for definite what is happening.'

Stacey typed this into her laptop and with ten minutes left before I had to leave to collect Aimee from school she asked me to give an update on Aimee, which I did, emphasizing how well she was doing.

Stacey entered this into her laptop. Then I said, 'Sorry, I really need to be going now.'

Progress

'That's fine,' Stacey said easily. 'I think we've just about finished.' She looked at Norman for confirmation.

'Yes,' Norman agreed. 'I've got another meeting soon anyway.'

Stacey thanked me for coming, closed her laptop and then closed the meeting. I said a hurried goodbye and left, wondering what Laura, the new trainee and doubtless an enthusiastic social worker, had made of the meeting. It was hardly the best example of efficiency, and I knew from experience it certainly wasn't a 'one-off' in this respect. Like many meetings in social care, it would have flagged up on their computer system as due – another box to tick – while in effect the exchange of information could have easily taken place in a phone call and saved all those present a lot of time.

Although the meeting hadn't progressed Aimee's case, the care plan continued to chug along at quite a speed. Later that day Norman phoned me to ask if he could change the date of his planned visit the following week from Tuesday to Thursday, as Tuesday was the only day Jason and his wife were free to see him. 'I don't want to leave seeing them until the following week,' he said. 'I want to get things moving.'

'Thursday is fine with me,' I said, always the accommodating foster carer. 'We'll be home from school by four o'clock.'

'I'll come at five past four, then,' Norman said. 'And I should have a lot to tell you and Aimee.'

True to his word, Norman arrived at five past four and he stayed for over two hours, talking to Aimee and me about Jason and his family and the plans for Aimee to go to them.

After he'd gone Aimee and I were exhausted and Aimee had gone very quiet. I knew instinctively something was wrong.

Chapter Twenty-Seven
A Chance Meeting

'**A**re you all right, love?' I asked.

Aimee didn't answer. We were sitting side by side on the sofa and I had my arm around her shoulder. She was snuggled into my side and in her hand, resting on her lap, was the photograph Norman had given to her of Jason and his family. It was a nice photograph, taken in the garden of their home last summer, showing Jason, his wife Jenny, their three-year-old daughter Emily, and a pet rabbit. But whereas Aimee had excitedly admired the photograph when Norman had first given it to her, it now lay face down in her lap.

'There's a lot to think about and take in, isn't there?' I said gently.

Aimee gave a small nod. 'Yes.'

'What are you thinking about now?' I asked softly. 'I'm thinking Jason and his family sound very nice people.'

'That's what Norman said, so I guess I have to believe him.'

'He wouldn't have said that if he wasn't sure,' I said. 'He wants what's best for you. We all do.'

Aimee fell silent and then asked, 'And you'll stay with me when I first meet them?'

'Definitely. You remember Norman explained that Jason, Jenny and Emily will come here to meet us first? Then we'll go to their house for a short visit. Then we'll see each other more and more over two weeks, until everyone feels relaxed and happy with each other.' Although Norman had explained this to Aimee it was a lot for her to remember and understand. 'Don't worry,' I reassured her. 'I've seen children to their permanent families many times before and it always works out fine.'

'But what if they don't like me when they meet me?' Aimee blurted, raising her head to look at me. 'They might change their minds and say they don't want me.'

'No, they won't,' I said firmly. 'Norman will have made sure they're sincere in wanting to look after you. And of course they'll like you. I'm sure of it.' For while I knew that occasionally couples who'd been approved to look after a child permanently did change their minds after meeting the child, which was devastating for the child, I was certain it wouldn't happen here. Jason and his wife were already foster carers and would therefore have a realistic and sincere expectation of what it was like to look after a child who wasn't their own. Added to which they were family.

Aimee clearly had many worries about meeting Jason and eventually going to live with him, and I knew her questions and comments would continue until she met him and his family. I'd found in the past that once the child had met their forever family and seen just how nice they were, they felt reassured and most of their worries vanished. The timetable of the introduction would be drawn up at the next permanency planning meeting, when I would get the chance to meet Jason and Jenny. In the meantime I'd have to answer Aimee's questions and reassure her as best I could, basing my answers on what Norman had told us. I thought it was just as well that Susan had decided to stop the supervised contact: it would be less upsetting for Aimee. The way social care law is written at present, children can see their natural parents right up to the day before they meet their forever family, which is very confusing and upsetting for the child, who has to say goodbye to one set of parents and then hello to the new with no time to adjust.

While I waited to hear when the next permanency planning meeting would be, life continued in its present routine. Without contact Aimee had time to watch television and play games after dinner, when she'd done her homework, which made for a far more relaxing evening. However, each day when I took Aimee to school or collected her in the afternoon I always kept a watchful eye out for Susan. Although I'd informed Norman and the school that Susan had been seeing Aimee at playtime, and I assumed Norman had spoken to Susan about this, I knew from experience that at times like this – when a parent was about to lose a child for good – emotion ran high. Susan had nothing to lose by making trouble or accosting me, and she knew I would be at school at 9 a.m. and 3.30 p.m. However, when Susan found me it wasn't outside school but in a deserted cul-de-sac on the edge of town.

It was the first day of March, a cold but bright day when the sun was thawing the snow of the week before and turning it to slush. I'd parked my car in a quiet cul-de-sac at the far end of the town to avoid the congestion of the multi-storey car park in the shopping centre. Having got out of the car, I stepped over the slush piled in the kerb, stood on the pavement and pointed the fob at the car. As the locks clicked into place I heard a voice say, 'Cathy.'

I turned and, squinting into the sunlight, saw Susan walking towards me. I glanced up and down the road but there was no one in sight. I had to pass her to go up to the high road, for behind me was a dead end. Hatchet wasn't with her, thank goodness, but that was little consolation.

'Hello, Susan,' I said evenly, trying to hide my anxiety. 'This is a surprise.'

A Chance Meeting

'I saw you drive past. I'm here to see me therapist,' she volunteered, coming to stand directly in front of me.

'Well, I hope it all goes OK,' I said, and went to step past her. She placed a restraining hand on my arm.

'Can I speak to you?' she said. 'I've got half an hour before my appointment.'

I assumed it was to complain, at the very least, or to vent her anger and frustration. 'I'm sorry, I'm in rather a hurry,' I said, gently releasing my arm. 'Why don't you arrange a meeting with Norman as I suggested, and we can all have a chat then?'

'It's not about Aimee,' Susan blurted loudly. 'It's about me. I want you to know I'm not as bad as you think I am.'

'I don't think you're bad,' I said quickly, surprised that Susan cared what I thought of her. 'I've never told Aimee that either – just the opposite, in fact. I've always told her you love her but unfortunately you can't look after her.'

'Yes, I know,' Susan said, lowering her voice. 'Aimee told me and I'm grateful for that. Thank you.'

I thought I must have misheard. Susan thanking me? That couldn't be right. Not the woman who'd issued so many threats, complaints and allegations that Adrian and his friends had come under suspicion and I'd nearly resigned.

Foster carers often have to make snap decisions about whether they are being told the truth, but it's usually when the child they are fostering is trying to bend the rules on what they are allowed to do. Now I had to make a snap decision as to whether Susan was sincere in her wish to talk to me or if it was a ploy. For all I knew, her gangster friends might be waiting around the corner to teach me a lesson; anything was possible in the twilight underground drug-fuelled world she inhabited.

'Can we sit in your car and talk?' Susan now suggested. 'It's cold.' She had her arms folded across her chest and was shivering. She was wearing the same thin jacket she'd been wearing the last time I'd seen her, outside the school, with T-shirt, threadbare jeans, and plimsolls that were sopping wet. I looked at her. I wasn't going to risk sitting in my car with her in this deserted road.

'Shall we go for a coffee?' I asked after a moment. 'There's a place on the high road.'

'Wouldn't mind,' she said, shivering again. 'But I haven't got any money.'

'I'll pay,' I said. 'Come on.' I stepped past her and began up the road to the busier high road. Susan followed a step or two behind me, treading in the centre of the path to avoid the slush piled on either side. I still wasn't convinced she only wanted to confide but I'd be safer in the high street. I'd had parents of other children I'd fostered wanting to share some of their life experiences with me, but in those cases I'd established a good working relationship with them, so that confiding seemed to come naturally and I wasn't worried. That wasn't so with Susan, but I had a few minutes to spare and the poor woman looked as though she needed a hot drink, so I could hear what she wanted to tell me.

We stood side by side and waited to cross the main road; then Susan followed me into the coffee shop and up to the counter. The girl behind the counter was busy serving a couple in front of us and as we waited I saw Susan eyeing the selection of savouries and cakes displayed beneath the glass-topped counter.

'Do you want something to eat?' I asked.

She shrugged.

'Say if you do and I'll pay.'

'Can I have a sausage roll, please, and one of those cakes with the pink icing on top?' She was like a child asking for a treat and I felt her humiliation.

'Have whatever you want,' I replied gently. 'They do a very

good English breakfast here. My son used to have it when we'd been shopping.' I felt I needed to try to persuade her to eat, as she was so thin and ill-looking.

'Oh, go on, then,' she said, with a small nervous laugh. 'Treat me to a full English breakfast.' I thought a decent meal was probably a treat for her. I saw the girl behind the counter looking at Susan as she served the couple. Susan looked so wasted that she attracted stares; she wasn't the type of customer normally found in a nice coffee lounge.

When the assistant had finished serving the couple in front of us we moved along the counter and I ordered the breakfast – egg, bacon, sausage, hash brown, beans, tomatoes and mushrooms – and two mugs of coffee, and then paid. Placing the mugs of coffee on a tray, with the cutlery Susan would need for her breakfast, I carried the tray to a corner table. The breakfast would be cooked fresh and brought to our table when it was ready. I saw the occupants on the other tables glance up and look at Susan as we passed.

Once seated either side of the table, we sipped our coffee. Susan cupped her hands around her mug, drawing its warmth. Gradually her fingers lost their mauve appearance as they began to thaw out.

'You could do with some gloves in this weather,' I remarked, as one would tell a child.

Susan nodded but didn't say anything. Although we were now in this public place and I felt safer, I was still uncertain what exactly she wanted of me.

'Aimee's making good progress at school,' I tried presently. 'She's a lot of catching up to do, but I help her with her reading and maths each evening.'

Susan nodded again and then set down her mug. 'Aimee listens to you,' she said. 'She never would to me. I tried to help her but she used to push me away.'

'I have to be firm sometimes,' I said. 'Aimee knows she doesn't watch television until she has done her homework.'

Susan shrugged. 'That's the difference between you and me. You know how to look after kids. I never did. I'm not a bad person, I just can't look after kids properly. I told the social [services] to take Aimee off me when she was born. But all they did was put her on the ["at risk"] register and send me to parenting classes.'

I stared at Susan in utter amazement. 'You asked the social services to take Aimee into care when she was born?' I said. 'But I thought you'd been battling to keep her?'

'Yeah. Recently I have, 'cos I grew to love her. But when she was a baby it would have been easier to let her go. I've told a few social workers over the years to take her. I couldn't look after her. But they kept giving me help. I knew it wasn't going to do any good. I knew where it would lead – same as me older kids. You can't teach an old dog new tricks.' Susan gave a small nervous laugh and her hand instinctively went to her mouth to cover her missing teeth. 'They should have taken Aimee when she was born like I told them. Before I loved her and she loved me.'

I shook my head in dismay. I could picture only too well the scenario Susan had just described: the succession of social workers following correct social work practice and trying to keep the family together, even though all the odds were stacked against it succeeding. The Guardian had mentioned the years of support and monitoring, not only for Aimee but for the older children. Eva had also told me that Susan had been badly abused throughout her own childhood and had then run away and got into drugs, although Susan wouldn't necessarily know I knew.

'It can't have been easy for you,' I said.

'No, it bloody wasn't. Not for me or me kids. I did try, a few times, to get off the drugs, but once they get into your brain they screw you up for life – well, they did for me. I'm not going to live to see Aimee become an adult, so it's best she goes to Jason. But I want to see her regularly while I can. I love her.'

'I know you do,' I said gently. 'I've told Aimee that.'

'Thanks,' Susan said quietly and took another sip from her coffee. I wasn't sure if her reference to not living to see Aimee become an adult was a result of a diagnosed medical condition or if she meant that the drugs would eventually kill her, as they did so many. It didn't seem appropriate to ask. 'I blame my step-father for screwing up my life,' Susan said. 'And me mum. She knew what was going on. I told her enough times. But she called me a liar and chose him over me.'

'I'm sorry,' I said, at a loss to know what to say.

'Yeah, well,' Susan said dismissively. 'Shit happens, doesn't it? And it happened to me.'

The breakfast arrived and as it was set down on the table in front of her Susan's face lost its pinched expression and lit up. Seizing the sauce bottle with child-like enthusiasm, she squirted swirls of tomato ketchup all over the food. It was sad and peculiarly touching.

'Aimee likes tomato sauce too,' I offered.

'Tell me about it!' Susan said, setting down the sauce bottle and picking up her knife and fork. 'I couldn't nick enough of the stuff to keep up with her. Whoops – shouldn't have told you that,' she said with smile.

I returned her smile and thought that if stealing tomato sauce had been Susan's only wrongdoing her life would have been very different. She ate ravenously, as though she hadn't eaten in ages, and very possibly she hadn't, for a drug habit is expensive and I knew that buying them took precedence over all other needs for an addict, even food. I sipped my coffee as Susan ate and very soon her plate was clear. She set down the knife and fork and drained the last of her coffee.

'Thanks,' she said. 'That was nice.'

'You're welcome,' I said. 'Do you want another coffee or anything else?' She looked warmer now and had some colour in her cheeks.

'No thanks. I've got to go to the therapist soon.'

While I felt sorry for Susan, and it was now clear she meant me no harm, I was also mindful of the anguish and upset she'd caused my family, as she had done the carers of her older children.

'When Aimee goes to Jason I hope you won't make things up to upset them,' I said, looking her straight in the eyes.

'I don't make things up!' she said defensively.

'You did with me. You were always complaining about the way I looked after Aimee, or rather didn't look after her, and all that stuff about my son and his friends kissing her. You must have known that wasn't true.'

'Yeah, well, I was angry,' she said, looking very slightly guilty. 'I wanted to get at you. You did such a good job looking after Aimee it seemed to show up what a crap parent I'd been. It was like rubbing my nose in it. Every time I saw Aimee at contact she would come in and tell me about her nice bedroom and all the things you did for her. Then when she started telling you she'd been abused by my friends I was angry and wanted to get back at you.'

'But I didn't make things up,' I said. 'I was just doing my job and reporting the abuse Aimee had disclosed to me. I believe she's telling the truth – some of your friends did abuse her.'

Susan looked away. 'I know,' she said, her voice dropping. 'I tried to protect her as much as I could, and if I found anyone touching her I went for them. But most of the time I hadn't got a clue what was going on. I was completely off my head with drugs. That's the trouble with drugs – they put you in cuckoo land. I couldn't protect Aimee or myself. She saw things no kid should see. I know that. Like I said, they should have taken her off me when she was born. It would have been kinder. It's too late for me but I hope Aimee can be saved.'

I looked at Susan's downcast face, ravaged by years of drug abuse and old beyond her years, and my heart went out to her. 'It's never too late to change,' I said. 'Aimee will be fine with Jason and you can change too.'

'Yeah,' Susan said dismissively. And I could see from her expression she knew otherwise. 'Anyway, I need to go and see me therapist now,' she said, scraping back her chair. 'Thanks for breakfast, and for listening. Oh yeah, and thanks for looking after Aimee.'

I smiled weakly. 'There's no need to thank me,' I said. 'She's a nice kid. She'll be fine. If I don't see you again, good luck, and look after yourself.'

'I'll try,' she said without conviction.

'Susan, one last thing. Why did you tell the social services that Aimee killed the kittens when it was Craig?'

'He told me to.'

'And you always do what he tells you? Even when it's wrong?'

'I have to. He's my supplier.'

Standing, she turned and headed towards the door, and I watched her go out into the cold again. If ever anyone needed a fresh start and looking after it was that poor woman.

Chapter Twenty-Eight
Peter Rabbit

Two weeks later Aimee stood at the window in the front room, looking out. 'Is it eleven thirty yet?' she asked, for the umpteenth time that morning.

'Nearly. They'll be here soon,' I replied. 'Any time now.'

'I wish they'd hurry up. I've been waiting for ages!'

I smiled. Aimee was watching out for the first sign of Jason and his family. It was Wednesday and she'd been allowed time off school to meet and get to know her forever family.

Jason and his wife's application to look after Aimee had been approved, and the day before I'd attended a permanency planning meeting, where I'd met Jason and Jenny for the first time. I'd immediately taken to them: they were a warm, open couple in their late twenties, easy to talk to and sincere in their commitment to Aimee. Jason and Jenny had met while at university and had been married for five years. The permanency planning meeting had run smoothly, unlike the last one. All those present – Norman, Stacey, Jason, Jenny and me – agreed that the sooner Aimee could be settled with Jason and Jenny, and therefore able to get on with her life, the better it would be for her. Stacey had drawn up a timetable for the introduction, which involved Aimee seeing Jason and Jenny nearly every day for two weeks, and culminated in her moving in. Two weeks may not seem long for a child to bond with his or her new parents but I knew from experience it was long enough; any longer and the child feels in limbo and dispossessed. I'd returned home from the meeting with an album of photographs from Jason and Jenny, which showed them and their three-year-old daughter, Emily, in their home and garden. Aimee and I had looked at the album many times during the evening so that Aimee could familiarize herself with her new family before they met. Now she was excitedly looking forward to their arrival.

'Cathy, there's a car pulling up,' Aimee cried a minute later. 'Come and see. I think it's them.'

I joined Aimee at the window and looked at the car Aimee pointed to. Then I saw the profile of Jenny sitting in the passenger seat and a small child in the rear. 'Yes, that's them,' I said. 'Come on, let's go and welcome them.'

I began across the room but Aimee held back, her previous excitement now replaced by nervous apprehension as the moment of their meeting finally arrived. 'Come on,' I encouraged, returning to offer her my hand. 'Jason and Jenny will be as nervous as you are, if not more so. You don't have to say anything unless you want to.'

Aimee gave a small shy smile and slipped her hand into mine. I gave it a reassuring squeeze. 'Good girl.'

We went to the front door but as I opened it Aimee held back again. 'I'll wait here,' she said.

'OK, love. Whatever you feel comfortable with.'

I went down the front path and out on to the pavement. 'Hello. Good to see you again,' I said, going to greet them.

Jenny was reaching into the rear of the car to release her daughter's seatbelt. She straightened and gave me a hug while Jason came round from the driver's side and, smiling warmly, shook my hand. 'Good to see you, Cathy.' Jason had Susan's nose but that was where any similarity ended.

'Hello, love,' I said to Emily as she scrambled out of the car and stood next to her mother on the pavement. 'You must be Emily. I'm Cathy. How are you?'

'I'm very well, thank you,' she said sweetly. She was an engaging child who had her mother's thick brown hair and petite features.

I could see Jenny and Jason looking past me and into the house for any sign of Aimee – the reason they were here. 'Aimee's gone a little shy,' I said. 'It's understandable. It's a big day for her.'

'Oh, yes, absolutely,' Jenny said. 'We'll just stay for the hour, as arranged, and then see her again tomorrow when you come to us.' As foster carers they knew the importance of keeping to the timetable of introduction, which was carefully designed to allow the child to get to know and bond with his or her new family without feeling overwhelmed. Emily would also need time to adjust to having a new sister, and Jenny and Jason had been preparing her for the changes just as I had been preparing Aimee.

I led the way down the front path and into the hall, where Adrian appeared from upstairs and on his way out. 'This is my son, Adrian,' I said, introducing him to Jason and Jenny. 'He's home from university for Easter and is about to go out.' They shook hands.

'Where's Aimee?' I asked Adrian before he left, for she was nowhere to be seen.

'Hiding in the sitting room,' Adrian said. 'She wants you all to go and find her. I think she's playing hide and seek. See you later. Nice to meet you,' he called to Jenny and Jason as he let himself out.

'And you,' they returned.

With a knowing smile at Jason and Jenny I led the way down the hall, and as we entered the sitting room I said in a voice loud enough for Aimee to hear: 'I wonder where Aimee can be? I hope we can find her soon. I know how much you are looking forward to meeting her.'

'I hope so too,' Jason said, joining in the game.

'And Emily's looking forward to playing with Aimee,' Jenny added.

The mention of Emily wanting to play was enough for Aimee to lose her reservations and spring out from her hiding place behind the armchair. 'Here I am!' she cried.

'Great!' I said.

'Hello, good to meet you,' Jenny said easily. 'I'm Jenny and this is Emily.'

'Hello,' Emily said, and Aimee smiled at her.

'And I'm Jason,' Jason said, smiling. 'Good to meet you, Aimee.'

Aimee looked at them from across the room, surveying them up and down, and I thought what a poignant moment it was as she met her forever family for the first time. Jason and Jenny knew better than to rush over and smother Aimee in hugs and kisses, which I could tell from their expressions they'd have liked to. They knew from their foster care training and also probably from good sense that Aimee would need time to adjust, and that they had to let her come to them when she was ready.

'Coffee?' I asked.

'Yes please,' Jason and Jenny said gratefully.

'What about Emily? Would you like a drink?'

Emily nodded.

'Water, please,' Jenny said.

'Can we play now?' Emily asked Aimee.

'Yes,' Aimee said. 'Here are some of my toys. I got them ready for you.' Aimee took Emily's hand and led her the few steps to the boxes of toys we'd brought into the sitting room that morning. The girls squatted on the floor and began playing while Jason and Jenny settled on the sofa.

'Lucy and Paula are at work and school,' I said in case they wondered where they were.

'And you've got the day off from school to meet us.' Jenny said to Aimee. She nodded.

I went into the kitchen to make the drinks and arrange some savoury snacks on a plate. From the kitchen I could hear Aimee talking to Emily about the toys they were playing with and asking her what she liked to play. Then, a minute later, I heard Aimee ask her: 'Have Jason and Jenny always been your mummy and daddy?' Although I'd talked a lot to Aimee about Jason, Jenny and Emily it must have been confusing for her.

Clearly Emily, aged three, must have found Aimee's question equally confusing and didn't know what to say. There was a small silence and then Jenny replied, 'Yes. Emily is our daughter and soon you will be our daughter too.' Her comment was just right: it would reassure Aimee and make her feel included. Then Jenny added, 'We are also foster parents, like Cathy, but we won't be fostering for a while. So it will just be you, Emily, Jason and me.' For it had been agreed at the planning meeting that Jason and Jenny should wait at least a year before fostering so they could concentrate on Aimee and Emily, which is normal practice when a child is placed permanently.

I returned from the sitting room with a tray of drinks and savouries and set it on the coffee table. I chatted with Jason and Jenny as we ate the nibbles and drank our coffee, and the girls played. I noticed Aimee was talking to and playing with Emily to the exclusion of Jenny and Jason, but that was only to be expected. Aimee would feel more confident to begin by interacting with another child, and it was important she established a good relationship with Emily – who was to be her sister – as much as it was with Jason and Jenny, her new parents.

The time flew by and as the end of the hour approached I said to Aimee, 'Jason, Jenny and Emily will have to go soon. We'll see them tomorrow, but is there anything you'd like to ask them before they go?'

Aimee paused from playing and shook her head.

'Well, if you think of anything,' Jenny said, 'you can ask us tomorrow or you can ask Cathy to ask us.' Which was sensitive of Jenny, who recognized that Aimee might not yet feel comfortable asking them a direct question.

Aimee continued playing and then after a moment she looked up again. 'I've got a question,' she said. 'Will I see your rabbit tomorrow?'

'Yes,' Jason said, smiling. 'Definitely. He's called Peter. Do you know Peter Rabbit in the Beatrix Potter books?'

Aimee's face lit up. 'That's one of my favourite stories,' she said.

'Mine too,' Jason said. 'I've still got all the books from when I was a child. I read them to Emily and I'll read them to you too.'

Aimee beamed. 'I like Peter Rabbit and Jemima Puddle Duck too,' she said. Her initial reserve had gone and I was pleased she was now talking naturally and appropriately to Jason. Jason and Jenny had been made aware of Aimee's history of abuse and as foster carers they knew the importance of practising safer caring – to keep everyone safe. While Jason would develop a loving relationship with Aimee, he would also have to make sure he didn't put himself in a position that could be misinterpreted by Aimee; so if, for example, they went swimming Jason would change in a separate cubicle to Aimee. It was sad he would need to be on his guard but it was essential, especially in the early months when they were still getting to know and trust each other. Jenny and Jason appreciated such measures were necessary, as Aimee's experiences were very different from their own daughter's or those of any child from a responsible and loving family.

When Jason and Aimee had finished their discussion of Beatrix Potter books, Jenny said it was time to go. We confirmed the arrangements for the following day, when Aimee and I would visit them, and they prepared to leave.

'It went very well,' I said quietly to Jason and Jenny, as Aimee helped Emily on with her shoes.

'Yes, better than I expected,' Jenny said, and Jason agreed.

Aimee and I saw them out and waved goodbye. As we closed the front door I said to Aimee: 'Well? What do you think?'

'Hmmm,' she said, and placed her fingers to her chin as though deep in thought. Then: 'I think they are nice. Just like you!' And she rushed into my arms and gave me the biggest hug ever.

Chapter Twenty-Nine
The Visit

The following day at 11.30 a.m. I drew up outside the neat semi-detached house where Jason, Jenny and Emily lived, and which I recognized from the photographs. Aimee was peering out of her side window. 'That's it! Number twelve,' she cried, also recognizing the house from the photographs, and reading the number from the gate. 'Twelve Acorn Street.'

'Yes, that's right,' I said. Now Aimee could read she read everything in sight, and she'd read the street sign as we'd come into the road.

I cut the engine and climbed out of the car and then opened Aimee's door. As I did so the front door to number twelve burst open and Jason, Jenny and Emily spilled out.

'Hi! How are you both?' they called, coming down the garden path.

As I'd thought might happen Aimee fell silent, again overcome by shyness and apprehension – that was until she saw that Emily was holding a lead and on the end of the lead was a rabbit!

'Look! There's Peter Rabbit,' Aimee cried, now leaping from the car and running up the path. 'Their rabbit's on a lead!' There couldn't have been a better icebreaker. Aimee rushed to Emily's side and, squatting down, began petting him.

I followed her up the path and hugged Jason and Jenny. Emily was busy showing Aimee how to stroke Peter – 'From his ears down to his tail,' she said.

'I know,' Aimee said. 'My mum's got a dog but he bites.'

'Peter doesn't bite,' Emily said a little defensively. 'But he does lots of poo-poos.' As if to prove the point Peter took a couple of hops along the path and left a trail of pellets in his wake. Emily giggled.

'Yuck,' said Aimee, screwing up her nose.

'Don't worry,' Emily said. 'Mum will clear it up.'

'She will,' Jenny said with a laugh. 'She usually does! I'll get the dustpan and brush later.'

'Let's go inside,' Jason said. 'It's freezing out here.'

'Does Peter come into the house?' Aimee asked.

'He's allowed in for a little while,' Emily explained. 'But we all have to watch him to make sure he doesn't nibble through the wires.'

'As he did once!' Jenny put in. 'It was the television cable, so there was no television until it was repaired.

'Does he do poos in the house?' Aimee now asked, which had crossed my mind too.

'No,' Emily said.

'He's house-trained,' Jason explained, and I was as impressed as Aimee. A house-trained rabbit on a lead wasn't something I'd come across before!

In the hall Jason took our coats and hung them on the hall stand, and we went through to the lounge-cum-dining room, which ran the depth of the house. It was a light and spacious room with a sofa, armchair and child's beanbag at one end, and a dining table and chairs at the other. In an alcove by the fireplace were bookshelves containing DVDs, CDs, books, games and puzzles. To the side of the shelves were large brightly coloured toy boxes overflowing with Emily's toys. It was a child-friendly house with a relaxed and inviting family atmosphere.

'Can I hold the lead now?' Aimee asked Emily.

The Visit

I saw Emily hesitate, and then Jenny said, 'It's nice to share, Emily.'

A little reluctantly Emily passed the lead to Aimee. 'That's a good girl,' Jenny said. Clearly Emily would be getting used to sharing with Aimee just as Aimee would have to learn to share with Emily. For until now Emily had been an only child and, with all her older half-siblings in care, effectively so too had Aimee.

Peter Rabbit flopped on the carpet and then stretched out his back legs just like a small dog, and both girls knelt beside him and stroked and petted him. I was as fascinated as Aimee was by the rabbit, who seemed to think he was a dog, but to Emily he was simply a much loved pet. Jenny made us drinks and then suggested we have a look around the house. One of the reasons for this first short visit was so that Aimee could familiarize herself with her new home before she stayed for longer, over-night, and eventually moved in. Jason said it was time for Peter to go back into his hutch, and the girls gave him a last stroke before Jason took the lead and led Peter out of the room.

'I want a rabbit,' Aimee said.

'So do I,' I said, laughing. 'He's lovely.'

'You can both share Peter with me,' Emily said, which was very sweet.

'Thank you, love,' I said.

Jenny began the tour of the house in the kitchen, which was at the end of the hall and looked out over the back garden. From the window we could see Jason lifting Peter into his hutch. 'On a warm day Peter stays in the garden,' Jenny explained. 'But when it's cold, like today, he comes into the house for a while – for some exercise – and then goes back to his hutch, where it's nice and warm.'

'Does he poo in his hutch?' Aimee asked.

'Yes, but only in one corner. He's very clean.'

From the kitchen window we could also see a swing and some climbing apparatus, similar to the ones we had at home. 'It will be lovely to play out there in the summer,' I said to Aimee, and she nodded.

We left the kitchen and followed Jenny upstairs, where she first showed us the bedroom where she and Jason slept. I was pleased Aimee just looked and didn't make a silly comment about sex, as she had when I'd first shown her my bedroom. Moving to the next door that led off the landing Emily proudly said, 'This is my bedroom. You can come in if you like.'

'Yes please,' I said.

We followed Emily into her room. It was a lovely room, beautifully furnished with Cinderella wallpaper and similarly themed accessories. A goldfish bowl stood on a small table in one corner with one goldfish in it.

'Is that fish yours?' Aimee asked Emily, clearly impressed and a little envious.

'Yes, he's called Chips,' Emily said. 'Dad gave him his name. I won him at the fair.'

'So we had to rush out and buy a bowl, weed and fish food,' Jenny added.

'Will I be able to have a goldfish in a bowl in my bedroom?' Aimee asked Jenny.

I was about to rescue Jenny and say that one goldfish was enough when Jenny said, 'I don't see why not if you'd really like one, but we'll be sharing the rabbit. The hutch isn't big enough for two.' Clearly Jenny had anticipated Aimee's next question and didn't need any help from me.

'Thank you,' Aimee said, very excited. 'I'd like a goldfish of my own, I really would.'

We left Emily's room and followed Jenny across the landing, where she showed us the bathroom and then a smallish bedroom, unused at present, with a built-in wardrobe, bed and chest of drawers.

'And this,' Jenny said, pausing outside the last door leading off the landing, 'will be Aimee's bedroom. I hope you like it.' Looking at me she crossed her fingers and then opened the door. Aimee went in first and I saw the look on her face before I saw the reason for it.

I stepped in and gasped in amazement. The room had been freshly decorated in pink with the theme of the Disney Princesses, which were Aimee's favourite. It was incredible, a work of art, and Aimee stared, open-mouthed and speechless. Images of the three beautiful princesses were on the wallpaper, duvet cover, curtains and bedside rug. A pink cushion with the same images was on her bed, and beneath the window were three large new toy boxes with a Princess sticker on each.

'How wonderful!' I exclaimed. 'You have been busy! However did you know it was Aimee's favourite?' Aimee was still standing in the centre of the room, saying nothing and completely overawed.

'You mentioned it at the permanency planning meeting when you were talking about Aimee's likes and dislikes,' Jenny said. 'You probably don't remember.' I shook my head. 'Well, Jason and I remembered and on the way home we stopped off and bought the wallpaper. Jason decorated the room the next day, and then last weekend we bought all the accessories. Do you like it, Aimee?'

'You've got princesses and I've got Cinderella,' Emily said.

Aimee, still overwhelmed, managed a small nod, but it was obvious she liked it. Although her bedroom at home with me was comfortable I had to keep the colours neutral to accommodate the different tastes and ages of the children I fostered, boys and girls. This room was beyond Aimee's wildest dreams and I could tell from her expression she was as touched as I was by the thoughtfulness and hard work that had gone into making her room so perfect.

'You're a very lucky girl,' I said to Aimee. 'Say thank you to Jenny.'

'Thank you,' Aimee said. 'It's lovely. I can't believe I'm so lucky.'

'You're very welcome,' Jenny said.

Emily and Aimee wanted to stay upstairs and play in Aimee's bedroom, which Jenny said was fine. So Jenny and I went downstairs to the lounge, where Jason was, having returned from putting Peter Rabbit into his hutch and also clearing up the rabbit droppings on the front path. 'Thanks, love,' Jenny said. She then told Jason that Aimee's bedroom was a great success and he was pleased and relieved. I thanked them both for all their hard work and thoughtfulness.

Jason then took out their copy of the timetable of the introduction and move, and suggested we ran through it to confirm times, for although the days had been decided at the permanency planning meeting some of the times had been left for us to arrange. The following day Jenny, Jason and Emily were due to come to my house again, but this time it would be for three hours and they would take Aimee out while I stayed at home. This was to start getting Aimee used to being with her new family, without me present. It would include a light lunch out.

'Shall we arrive at eleven thirty?' Jason suggested.

'Yes, that's fine with me,' I said. 'There are plenty of eating places on the high street. I'll give you directions.'

'Thanks.'

The day after I would bring Aimee to their house again and leave her for three hours so that she could begin getting used to her new home without me being there. Then it would be the weekend and we would all have a break from seeing each other, to give everyone involved time to reflect and consolidate the changes that were happening. Then on Monday I was to bring Aimee to Jenny and Jason's again and leave her for the whole day. It wasn't worth me making the two-hour drive home, so I planned to go shopping locally or, if it was a nice day, visit the coast, which was only a couple of miles away. 'I'll aim to arrive at ten o'clock,' I said.

'Yes, that's fine with us,' Jenny confirmed.

We were then timetabled to have Tuesday off. On Wednesday, if everything was going to plan, I would bring Aimee and she would stay the night. If that went well she would stay again on Thursday night, and if everything was still going well she'd move in on Saturday. This type of introduction is typical for most children in care who go to live with a forever family and it is vital for everyone involved. Not only does it prepare the child, but also members of the child's forever family and the foster family that the child is leaving. The schedule takes a lot of time and energy and is emotionally draining, and takes over the lives of those involved. Aimee was having time off school and Jason had booked time off work; fortunately his employers had been understanding and accommodating when he'd explained why.

Today's hour's visit soon passed and when I called upstairs to Aimee and said it was time to go, she called back that she didn't want to leave. This was a good sign; however, what wasn't so good was the face she pulled and the way she stamped her foot when I went up to her room and told her again it was time to leave. Jenny had followed me up and stood behind me at Aimee's bedroom door, and saw Aimee scowl and stamp her foot. 'Not going yet,' Aimee said, her face set, and her chin jutting out just as it used to when she'd first come to me.

'That face isn't going to impress Jenny or Emily,' I said, trying to make light of it.

'Don't care,' Aimee said rudely.

'You'll come here again the day after tomorrow,' Jenny said. 'And tomorrow we're going to take you out for some lunch.'

But Aimee was having none of it. Her scowl deepened and I could see she was determined to have her own way. She was still sitting on the floor and she pointedly turned her back on me and carried on playing with the toys she and Emily had brought into her room. Emily, clearly worried by Aimee's abrupt change in behaviour, stood up and went to stand beside her mother.

Jason and Jenny knew that Aimee's behaviour had been 'challenging' with her mother and when she'd first come into care, but at the permanency planning meeting I'd reassured them that with routine and firm boundaries Aimee had responded very quickly. They also knew that during the introduction and just after the move Aimee might become unsettled and revert to some of her previous bad behaviour. I thought it was just as well she was doing it now rather than suddenly after the move, which could have caught them unprepared.

'Aimee, I think you need some quiet time,' I said evenly, 'so you can think about the right decision you need to make.' This was one of the strategies I used with her at home if she resisted what I'd asked her to do, although recently it hadn't been necessary. 'We'll go downstairs and you can come down when you've thought about what I've asked you to do, and have come to the right decision,' I said. Turning, I left the room and then followed Jenny and Emily downstairs.

'Aimee will be down soon,' I said to Emily as we entered the lounge, for she still looked worried. 'She's had such a good time playing with you, she doesn't want to leave.' Which was true, but Aimee knew she needed to do as the adult looking after her said.

'Emily understands that it's going to be a bit strange for us all to begin with,' Jenny said as Emily sat on her father's lap.

The Visit

I smiled and sat on the sofa with a stoical expression, hoping that Aimee would appear soon and not let me down. At home a few minutes' quiet time usually did the trick, but of course we weren't at home now and Aimee might be thinking she could do what she pleased here with Jason and Jenny. Jason began reading Emily a story while Jenny made light conversation with me, but I think we were all listening out for any movement upstairs. I didn't think Aimee would let me down, but of course she was testing the boundaries here in front of Jenny and Jason so I couldn't be sure. I was beginning to consider an alternative strategy when a couple of minutes later, to my relief, we heard footsteps on the stairs, and then Aimee appeared at the lounge door.

'I'm ready to go now,' she said a little sheepishly.

'Good decision.' I smiled. 'Well done. Now let's say goodbye nicely, and we'll see everyone again tomorrow.'

That evening Adrian, Lucy and Paula were in for dinner all at the same time – an increasingly rare occurrence in our house now they were all older. It was like old times as we sat around the table talking, eating, laughing and sharing our news, although Aimee did most of the talking: about Jenny, Jason, Emily, her new home and bedroom, and Peter the house-trained rabbit who went for a walk on a lead.

Adrian, Lucy and Paula were pleased that Aimee was so enthusiastic and excited about her new home and family, but there was also an underlying sadness. The enthusiasm Aimee was showing for her new home was a sign of the attachment she was forming to her new family, and the start of her detachment from ours. Although no one said anything, we were acutely aware that we'd have to start getting used to the idea that Aimee was going, and quite soon. Adrian, always one to internalize his feelings, looked particularly pensive and thoughtful as Aimee chatted. I'm sure he would have liked a closer relationship with her, as he'd had with other children we'd fostered, had things been different. I'd never told Adrian all the details of the allegations Susan had made against him and his friends, so he was unaware of how close he'd come to being the subject of a police investigation. I shuddered every time I thought of what could have happened if the social services hadn't seen Susan's complaint for the nasty troublemaking it was. Lives are ruined by unfounded malicious allegations, as ours and his friends could so easily have been.

That evening after dinner Adrian and Lucy went out with their respective friends while Paula stayed in to revise for her A-levels, which began in four weeks' time. Once I'd seen Aimee into bed I took Paula up a cup of tea, as I usually did when she was studying. As I opened her bedroom door I saw she looked sad and deep in thought.

'Try not to worry about your exams,' I said. 'You'll do your best, and that's all you can do.' Paula had set her sights high on passing with good grades and I was worried she was overdoing it.

'It's not so much that,' she said quietly, sitting back in her chair at the small table where she worked.

'What is it then, love?'

She gave a small shrug as I placed the mug of tea on the table beside her.

'You can tell your old mum, can't you?'

She smiled but it was a sad smile. 'I keep thinking back to the evening you told me Aimee was coming to live with us. Do you remember what I said?' I shook my head. 'I was horrible. I said I didn't want her to come and live with us. I hope she didn't realize I didn't want her.'

'Of course not. And you weren't horrible,' I said, surprised and concerned that Paula remembered this and was now worrying about it. 'You were cautious because you had exams coming, and I hope I understood that. You've been great helping me look after Aimee. You all have.' I kissed the top of her head.

'I haven't spent a lot of time with her because of my exams,' Paula said. 'Aimee knows that, doesn't she? It's not that I've been avoiding her.'

'Of course she knows that. Please don't worry.'

'I'm sad she's going,' Paula said quietly. 'I was hoping she might stay.'

'I know, love. We all felt the same. Hopefully Jason and Jenny will keep in touch, and we'll see Aimee after she's moved.'

'I do hope so,' Paula said.

Chapter Thirty
An Incredible Family

'I will still see you guys when I'm gone, won't I?' Aimee said, giving me another hug.

'Yes,' I said. 'Jenny and Jason have promised to keep in touch. They'll phone to arrange for us to visit when they feel you have settled in.'

'Good,' Aimee said, kissing my cheek. 'I'm going to miss you all.'

It was Friday evening and the end of the two-week introduction period, which had gone very well. Aimee would be leaving us in the morning to go and live with her forever family. We'd had a little farewell party earlier in the evening when my parents, some friends of mine who fostered and three of Aimee's friends from school had come for supper and to say goodbye. It had been a happy-sad occasion, for while everyone was obviously pleased Aimee was going to have a loving family of her own we were clearly all going to miss her.

Now I was settling Aimee into bed and saying goodnight, for what would be the last time. I was trying to keep a firm lid on my emotions so that I wouldn't upset Aimee.

'Will you bring Adrian, Lucy and Paula when you come and visit me?' Aimee now asked.

'Yes, of course I will, love.'

'When will you visit?' she asked again.

'In a month or so when Jenny and Jason feel the time is right,' I confirmed. While Aimee was looking forward to going to live with Jenny, Jason and Emily she was also struggling with leaving, just as we were. I knew that once she was on her way in the morning she'd be fine. 'Come on, off to sleep then,' I said. 'You've a busy day tomorrow.'

Aimee continued to sit upright in bed and found more questions to ask. 'Are they all coming?'

'Yes, as far as I know.'

'What time are they coming?' she asked, although I'd already told her.

'Ten thirty,' I said again. 'As long as the traffic is OK.'

'So I will be home with them for lunch.'

'Yes, you will,' I said. During the two-week introduction Aimee had slowly gone from referring to Jenny and Jason's house as my 'new home' to just 'home', which was positive. 'Now, off to sleep. Then you'll be bright and fresh in the morning.'

Aimee finally laid her head on her pillow, but then she sat bolt upright again. 'We mustn't forget to pack Kerry,' she said, referring to the soft toy cat she was cuddling.

'No, we won't,' I said. 'I know we've got to pack Kerry, the pyjamas you're wearing and your washbag. Don't you worry, I'll remember.' I'd already packed all Aimee's other belongings, and the suitcases, bags and boxes were stacked in the hall. 'Now snuggle down and try and get some sleep,' I said again.

'OK,' Aimee said. 'But first I need to tell you something.' And I thought she was going to tell me that she was going to miss us all, as she had been saying on and off all evening. But she didn't. Instead she said, 'Cathy, you know when I told you about Craig, and Mum's friends who did bad things to me?'

'Yes?' I said, taken aback and puzzled that she was suddenly thinking of this now.

'Well, I'm sorry, but I didn't tell you the truth.'

I stared at her and my heart sank as a cold chill ran down my spine. 'What do you mean?' I asked, hardly daring to hear her reply. For if Aimee was now telling me she'd made up the allegations of abuse, then innocent men had been accused, and she was a plausible and convincing liar who could never be trusted. The police, social services, Jenny and Jason would need to be informed and I'd been completely taken in.

Aimee lowered her eyes from mine and clutched Kerry tightly to her chest. I sat on the bed beside her and felt my pulse beating loudly in my chest. 'Well?' I asked. 'Tell me what you mean.' Unpalatable though it was, I needed to know so that I could inform all those involved.

'Well,' she said, still not looking at me. 'You know I told you I couldn't remember the names of the other men who hurt me?' I nodded. 'Or why I was so scared I wet myself? And you said when I did remember I should tell you.'

'Yes?'

'Well, I did remember, a long time ago, but I didn't tell you. I told you I didn't know, which wasn't true. It was a lie. I always remembered the men's faces and some of their names, and I know where some of them live. I can remember the things they did to me, and I know why I was so scared I wet myself. I'm sorry I didn't tell you the truth, Cathy. I do remember.'

Relief that she hadn't made up the allegations flooded through me before a chill of a different nature began to settle on me. 'Why didn't you tell me?' I asked.

Aimee shrugged.

'Can you tell me now? So those men can be arrested.'

Aimee shook her head and, finally raising her eyes to mine, said, 'I can't tell you because if they find out I told they'll be angry and come looking for me and Mum. You don't understand because you live in a nice house and have nice friends, but the people Mum knows are horrible. They carry knives and hurt people if they tell on them. I don't want Mum hurt and I don't want to be hurt, so I'm not telling you.'

'Oh, love, I do understand,' I said, putting my arms around her and drawing her to me. 'I understand you are scared and that you want to protect your mother. But if you don't tell me and those men aren't put in prison, they'll be free to hurt other people. Also, it often helps if we can share our hurts. Are you sure you can't tell me?'

'I'm sure,' she said quietly.

'All right. Perhaps when you are at Jenny and Jason's you'll be able to tell them? They live a long way from here.'

'But Mum will still live here and they'll come looking for her,' Aimee said, which was true. I held her close.

'I understand,' I said again. 'Maybe in years to come you'll feel differently. It's never too late to tell the police if an adult has hurt you. And in the meantime, do you remember I explained that once you're settled with Jenny and Jason you'll be seeing a play therapist?' The social services had decided that Aimee would benefit from play therapy to help her come to terms with everything that had happened to her and this would start after the move.

Aimee gave a small nod. 'To paint pictures and make models,' she said, resting her head on my shoulder.

'That's right. Some children find they can tell the play therapist things they have been keeping to themselves – worries they hadn't been able to tell other people. Maybe you will.'

'Maybe,' she said quietly, in her quaint way. 'But I'm glad you know I haven't been telling the truth. You've been so nice to me. I felt bad about telling you lies.'

'Oh darling, they weren't really lies,' I said, hugging her. 'You're just not ready to talk about what happened yet and I understand that.'

'Do you?' she said, kissing my cheek. 'Good. You understand lots of things. I'm going to miss you.'

'I'm going to miss you too, love.' And I felt my eyes start to fill.

The following morning, and unusually for a Saturday, all members of my family were up, washed and dressed and in the sitting room just after 10.00. Everyone wanted to see Aimee off and we were now waiting for the arrival of Jenny, Jason and Emily. We'd just given Aimee her leaving present – a musical jewellery box – and a farewell card. I was helping her read the words in the card, for although her reading was improving she still had a limited sight vocabulary. I'd read the printed verse in the card and was now reading the personal messages we'd written. *You're a good kid. Look after yourself. All best wishes, Adrian.*

'That's nice,' Aimee said. 'Thank you, Adrian.'

'You're welcome,' he said, slightly embarrassed.

'This is from Lucy,' I said, pointing to the message she'd written: *Keep smiling that cheeky grin. I'll be thinking of you. Love and kisses, Lucy.*

'Ahhh, that's nice,' Aimee said, and Lucy smiled.

'And here Paula has written: *Take care little sis. I'll miss you. Loads of love, Paula.* With more kisses.'

Aimee now smiled at Paula. 'Thank you, big sis.'

'And this is mine,' I said, pointing to the words I'd written. 'I've put *I'm very proud of you, Aimee. You've achieved so much. I'll be thinking of you. Take care. All my love, Cathy.* And there's a line of kisses.'

Aimee smiled and studied the card for a while longer and then slid it carefully into its envelope. 'Can you put my card and present in my case so I don't forget them?' she said quietly.

'Of course, love,' I said. Standing, I carried the present and card to the hall, where I zipped them carefully into one of the holdalls, and then returned to the sitting room. It was very quiet.

After a busy week, the gaiety of our little party the previous evening and then having been occupied this morning with cooking breakfast and packing the last of Aimee's belongings, none of us had had much time to dwell on Aimee going, but now we were grouped in the sitting room waiting for the doorbell to ring, the atmosphere was bleak.

'It's great everyone is able to be here to see Aimee off,' I said, trying to lighten the mood.

Lucy managed a small 'Yes', while Paula stared pensively at Aimee and Adrian concentrated on the floor.

'Shall we play a game of cards?' I suggested. 'We've got time.' But it was like suggesting we dance the hokey-cokey at a funeral. They looked at me and no one moved. 'Cluedo? Snakes and Ladders?' I tried. Same response.

Then the doorbell suddenly rang, making us jump. 'Perhaps they've arrived early,' I said, hopefully, leaping from the sofa. It wasn't that I wanted to get rid of Aimee – far from it – but now the day had come when she was definitely going she needed to be on her way for everyone's sake.

Aimee came with me down the hall to answer the door, while Adrian, Lucy and Paula peered expectantly from the sitting room. I opened the front door and was relieved and pleased to see Jenny, Jason and Emily stepping into the porch.

'Welcome,' I said, opening the door wider. 'Good journey?'

'Yes, we're early,' Jason said. 'Is that all right?'

'Absolutely.'

Aimee was pleased to see them too and gave each of them a big hug in turn and then took hold of Emily's hand. 'I want you to meet the big boy and girls,' she said in her quaint old-fashioned way. She led Emily down the hall to the sitting room. My children hadn't met Aimee's new family yet.

'That's some cases you've got there,' Jason said, meaning there were rather a lot.

'Yes. A bit different from when Aimee arrived,' I said. For they knew Aimee had arrived in what she stood up in.

'How is she now the big day has come?' Jenny asked, lowering her voice so she couldn't be overheard and unbuttoning her jacket. 'We've been nervous, so goodness knows how Aimee must be feeling. We were all up at six o'clock!'

'I know the feeling,' I said. 'But she seems to be doing all right. It's the rest of us. Come through and meet my family.'

I led the way down the hall and into the sitting room, where I introduced Jenny and Jason to Lucy and Paula and they said hi to Adrian. I then offered Jason and Jenny coffee.

'We stopped off for one on the way,' Jason said. 'Thanks anyway.'

'We thought it best to keep the goodbye short,' Jenny added, which I fully appreciated. Prolonged and emotional goodbyes are upsetting and not in anyone's best interest. 'We'll use the bathroom and then go, if that's OK with you?'

'Yes, of course.'

I showed them to the bathroom and then when they returned to the sitting room there was an awkward silence before Jason said, 'Well, Aimee, we'd best be on our way, then.'

'I'll give you a hand loading the car,' Adrian said, and we all traipsed into the hall.

Lucy and Paula helped Aimee into her coat and shoes and then stayed in the hall with her and Emily, while Adrian, Jenny, Jason and I loaded the car. It was a fine spring day outside, clear and fresh with birds fluttering in the hedgerow, nest-building. It took a number of trips in and out before the hall was empty. Their car was large – a people carrier – which was just as well. The boot was full and we'd stacked a couple of bags on the rear seat. Returning to the hall for the last time I checked around for any stray bags but it was clear. 'If I do find anything, I'll send it on,' I reassured Aimee.

Everyone fell quiet again and there was another awkward silence. Then Emily left Paula and Lucy, and went over and took her father's hand, while Aimee looked at us in turns, uncertain. Adrian broke the silence and, stepping forward, offered his hand to Aimee to shake. 'Bye then, little un,' he said, ruffling her hair. 'Take care.'

'I'm not little,' Aimee said, flattening her hair. We laughed and the tension eased, for standing beside Adrian, who was over six feet, she was indeed a 'little un'.

Having said goodbye, Adrian stepped back and Lucy went forward. 'Bye rascal,' she said, hugging Aimee. 'Be a good girl. You're very lucky to have such a nice family. Remember that.' Jason and Jenny looked emotional and I swallowed hard.

Then it was Paula's turn. She hugged Aimee and said, 'Bye, little sis. I'm sorry if I didn't play with you as much as you would have liked, but I had to study for my exams.' I felt choked up.

'That's OK,' Aimee said easily. 'I understand. I hope you pass your exams.'

They kissed goodbye, which just left me. 'Big hug,' I said, spreading my arms wide to receive her. Aimee buried her head in my chest and I felt her arms tighten around my waist.

'I'm going to miss you,' she said, her voice trembling.

'I'm going to miss you too,' I said. 'But I know you're going to do just fine with Jenny, Jason and Emily. We'll wave you off at the door and then visit when you are settled.' I gently released her arms and passed her to Jenny. Aimee wasn't crying but she was close to it.

'We'll phone,' Jenny said.

I smiled. 'Thank you.'

Adrian, Paula, Lucy and I followed them out of the front door and then stood on the drive as they got into their car. Jason settled Emily into her seat in the rear while Jenny did the same with Aimee.

'Goodbye,' we all called before the rear doors closed.

'Goodbye!' Aimee and Emily returned, waving. Aimee was smiling now but it was a brave smile and I could see her bottom lip trembling, as indeed was mine.

Jenny climbed into the passenger seat and Jason the driver's seat, and they called goodbye again before they closed their doors. The windows lowered and there were more shouts of 'Bye' as the car engine started and they slowly pulled away, Jason and Jenny in the front smiling and waving, and their two children smiling and waving from the rear. They were like many other families on their way home, but this was no ordinary family: it was a very special family formed from the ashes of abuse and despair. It was a family that had risen to live again – Jason adopted and given a fresh start in life, and then twenty years later doing the same for his younger half-sister. No, this was no ordinary family; it was an incredible family born of love, hope, courage and the determination to put the past behind them and create a better, brighter future.

Goodbye, Aimee, and good luck.

Epilogue

When my children were young and a child left us I always took them on a little outing to take their minds off our loss. Big as they were now, after Aimee left that Saturday I still thought we needed some diversion, so I suggested we went out for lunch. It was nothing grand, just our local carvery, and then on the spur of the moment we decided to go to the cinema. The film showing was *Brokeback Mountain*, which went on to become a classic. It was a long time since we'd all been to the cinema together and I relished every moment. It also gave Paula a much needed break from studying. When we arrived home there was a message on the answerphone from Jason saying that they'd arrived safely and were busy unpacking.

I didn't hear anything further from Jason or Jenny for two months. I wasn't expecting to, as I was aware Aimee needed time to properly settle in before we visited. Then one evening in July, Jason phoned and after he'd told me all about Aimee and how well she was doing he invited us for Sunday dinner the week after next. Adrian couldn't make it, as he was travelling in Europe for the summer before he started work in September, but Paula, Lucy and I looked forward to seeing Aimee and her family again.

We arrived as arranged at 12.30 p.m., and no sooner had I parked the car outside their house than the front door opened.

With cries of delight Aimee and Emily ran down the path to greet us, followed a little more sedately by Jenny and Jason.

'You've both grown!' I exclaimed to Emily and Aimee, passing the flowers and chocolates we'd brought to Jenny and then hugging the girls.

'They have,' Jenny said. 'Thanks for these. It's so good to see you all again.'

We kissed and shook hands, and then once inside Emily and Aimee whisked the 'big girls', as they called Paula and Lucy, upstairs to show them their bedrooms. I followed Jenny and Jason into the kitchen, where from the window Peter Rabbit could be seen hopping around the enclosed garden in the sun. Jason filled the kettle for coffee while Jenny checked on the roast cooking in the oven. I admired the delicious smell, and Jenny said Aimee had told them how much she used to enjoy our Sunday roasts. We took our coffees into the lounge, where Jenny and I sat on the sofa and Jason took the armchair. The dining table at the far end of the room was already laid with a white tablecloth, neatly folded napkins and a little flower centrepiece. I was touched they'd gone to so much trouble. We talked while the dinner cooked and Jenny and Jason told me how Aimee had been doing, both at home and at school. She'd made friends and had also joined an after-school club as well as starting ballet lessons.

'And Emily and Aimee are getting along all right with each other?' I asked, mindful they had both previously been only children.

'Just like sisters,' Jenny said, with a laugh. 'One day they're best of friends, playing happily for hours, and the next they're squabbling. All perfectly normal. I know, I had three sisters!'

'We had one setback,' Jason admitted, a moment later, glancing at his wife. 'For me more than Aimee.'

Epilogue

I looked at him, concerned, and Jenny threw me a pointed look.

'Aimee saw her mother last month,' Jason explained. 'Contact has been set at four times a year – supervised at our contact centre.' I nodded. 'I took Aimee, and I met Susan, for the first time in twenty years. I didn't have to go,' he added quickly. 'Jenny could have taken Aimee, but I felt it was something I needed to do. I won't be going again. It really unsettled me.'

Jason fell silent and I could see just how difficult meeting his birth mother after all those years had been. I could understand why.

'Jason said Susan looked dreadful – ill,' Jenny added. 'In fact he was so concerned that because of Susan's history of drug abuse, we asked for Aimee to be tested for HIV, so we could get the necessary treatment if necessary. Fortunately the test result was negative.'

'Good,' I said. 'That's a relief.' They knew that when Aimee had been with me the paediatrician had raised the same concerns.

'There was nothing on Aimee's medical records to say she'd been tested as a baby,' Jenny added. 'So we went ahead with the test and we're pleased we did.' Jenny then said that although Aimee hadn't disclosed any further details of her abusers, she did sometimes mention her mother and the life she'd led with her, which they both found upsetting to hear.

'Aimee's on the list to receive play therapy,' Jason said. 'But the list is long and Aimee isn't considered a priority, so she won't be seen for a few months yet.'

'But generally she's doing all right,' Jenny confirmed.

Presently Aimee came downstairs and wanted to show me her bedroom. So while Jenny and Jason went into the kitchen to put the finishing touches to dinner I went upstairs. With her possessions now occupying every shelf, drawer and toy box, and her posters on the walls, the room looked very homely, and as though it had been hers for years rather than a few months. Aimee also proudly pointed out the goldfish in a bowl on top of the chest of drawers. 'I've called the fish Cathy,' she said. I wasn't sure if I should be pleased or offended.

'You're a lucky girl,' I said.

'I know,' Aimee said quietly. 'I just wish my mum could have been as lucky when she was a child.'

'Yes, I know, love,' I said thoughtfully.

The following month we heard that Paula had passed her A-level examinations with the grades she wanted and then in October, Adrian was awarded his degree. The girls and I visited Aimee again two weeks before Christmas and we swapped presents. Peter Rabbit came into the house for a visit, as it was winter, and then returned to his hutch. Their house looked beautiful, decorated for Christmas, and I thought back to the previous Christmas when Aimee had been with us. It had, in effect, been her first proper Christmas, which she'd described as 'just like the ones you see on television'. I realized how far she'd come in a year; to look at her now – so happy and settled in her family – you would never have imagined the shocking life she'd led before coming into care.

Before we left I asked Jason and Jenny if they were thinking of fostering now Aimee was settled.

'Not yet,' Jenny said with a twinkle in her eye. 'We've just had some good news.' I could guess what it was. 'Last week,' Jenny said, slipping her hand into her husband's, 'I had my pregnancy confirmed. We're expecting a baby next year in June.'

'Congratulations,' I said. 'How wonderful! I'm so happy for you all.'

* * *

Epilogue

But while Aimee's story has a happy ending, not all children are as lucky. It is a sad fact that many children like Aimee are overlooked, forgotten almost, and left at home to suffer. Aimee's story is not a 'one-off'; she is not a lone example of a child slipping through the social care safety net, but one of millions of children worldwide who are not rescued when their parents fail. Time and time again I come across parents who are given second chances well beyond what is reasonable or in the best interest of the child, when it's obvious – sometimes even to the parents – that they won't ever be able to look after their child. While no one wants to see a family split, sometimes it is essential, for not only does intervention give a child a fresh start but it can and does save lives.

Cathy Glass

One remarkable woman, more
than **100** foster children cared for.

Learn more about the many
lives Cathy has touched.

Another Forgotten Child

Eight-year-old Aimee was on the child protection register at birth

Cathy is determined to give her the happy home she deserves.

A Baby's Cry

A newborn, only hours old, taken into care

Cathy protects tiny Harrison from the potentially fatal secrets that surround his existence.

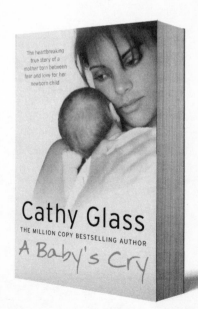

The Night the Angels Came

A little boy on the brink of bereavement

Cathy and her family make sure Michael is never alone.

Mummy Told Me Not to Tell

A troubled boy sworn to secrecy

After his dark past has been revealed, Cathy helps Reece to rebuild his life.

I Miss Mummy

Four-year-old Alice doesn't understand why she's in care

Cathy fights for her to have the happy home she deserves.

The Saddest Girl in the World

A haunted child who refuses to speak

Do Donna's scars run too deep for Cathy to help?

Cut

Dawn is desperate
to be loved

Abused and abandoned,
this vulnerable child pushes
Cathy and her family to
their limits.

Hidden

The boy with no past

Can Cathy help Tayo to
feel like he belongs again?

Damaged

A forgotten child

Cathy is Jodie's last hope.
For the first time, this abused
young girl has found someone
she can trust.

Inspired by true stories...

Run,
Mummy, Run

The gripping story of a
woman caught in a horrific
cycle of abuse, and the
desperate measures she
must take to escape.

Cathy Glass
THE MILLION COPY BESTSELLING AUTHOR
Run, Mummy, Run
A novel inspired by a true story

My Dad's a Policeman

The dramatic short story about a young boy's desperate bid to keep his family together.

The Girl in the Mirror

Trying to piece together her past, Mandy uncovers a dreadful family secret that has been blanked from her memory for years.

Sharing her expertise...

Happy Kids

A clear and concise guide to raising confident, well-behaved and happy children.

Happy Adults

A practical guide to achieving lasting happiness, contentment and success. The essential manual for getting the best out of life.

Happy Mealtimes For Kids

A guide to healthy eating with simple recipes that children love.

Be amazed
Be moved
Be inspired

———

Discover more about Cathy Glass
visit www.cathyglass.co.uk